LACANIAN PSYCHOANALYSIS WITH BABIES, CHILDREN, AND ADOLESCENTS

LACANIAN PSYCHOANALYSIS WITH BABIES, CHILDREN, AND ADOLESCENTS

Further Notes on the Child

Edited by

Carol Owens and Stephanie Farrelly Quinn

Routledge
Taylor & Francis Group
LONDON AND NEW YORK

First published 2017 by Karnac Books Ltd.

Published 2019 by Routledge
2 Park Square, Milton Park, Abingdon, Oxon OX14 4RN
52 Vanderbilt Avenue, New York, NY 10017

First issued in hardback 2019

Routledge is an imprint of the Taylor & Francis Group, an informa business

British Library Cataloguing in Publication Data

A C.I.P. for this book is available from the British Library

ISBN 13: 978-0-367-10405-4 (hbk)
ISBN 13: 978-1-78220-449-7 (pbk)

Typeset by V Publishing Solutions Pvt Ltd., Chennai, India

To my sons,
Carol Owens

To all the other sons (and daughters),
Stephanie Farrelly Quinn

CONTENTS

ACKNOWLEDGEMENTS

We want to begin by jointly thanking our contributors for responding so vividly to our invitations to participate in this project. Reading each essay has been a captivating experience, as we encountered every one as a precious instance of each psychoanalyst's desire. We duly recognise the labour involved in bringing each essay from its first draft to its final version and thank each contributor from the bottom of our hearts for their time, their work, and their part, in helping to bring to life an idea that sparked from a Masters thesis: that we could assemble in one collection contemporary clinical experiences and approaches to working with children from Lacanian psychoanalysts around the globe. We thank Ian Parker for his encouragement and friendly advice about the project. We thank Brian O' Connor for his invaluable advice and most kind support. We thank Olga Cox Cameron for bringing the precious gift of Françoise Dolto's voice to this book. We thank Constance Govindin and Rod Tweedy at Karnac for their enthusiastic interest in our book, and for their helpful support throughout the process.

Carol wishes to acknowledge an ongoing debt to Rex Stainton Rogers who first taught her the compelling enjoyment of working collegiately which has inspired all of her joint and collaborative projects. She also wishes to give a special thanks to Carles for his loving support, and to her incredible, beautiful, loving sons, Tomàs and Oscar.

Stephanie would like to express her gratitude to everyone who believed that this project was possible and to her family and in particular her husband John for his patience and understanding.

Finally, we gratefully acknowledge the permissions granted to include various elements in the book:

The L Schema and Graph of Desire in Chapter Three are included here by the kind permission of W. W. Norton & Co., Inc.

The material from the Seminars on Child Psychoanalysis (I & II) from Chapter Four (previously published as *Seminars on Child Psychoanalysis*, by Françoise Dolto, translated by Olga Cox, in *The Journal of the Irish Forum for Psychoanalytic Psychotherapy*, Vol. 5, numbers 1 and 2, Spring/Autumn 1995), is included here with the kind permission of the Irish Forum for Psychoanalytic Psychotherapy.

The lyrics from the song "Higgs Boson Blues" by Nick Cave in Chapter Ten are included here by kind permission of Mute Song Ltd.

Page 40 from *The Standard Edition of the Complete Psychological Works of Sigmund Freud, Volume X* (1909), Two Case Histories: "Little Hans" and the "Rat Man", translated and edited by James Strachey, published by Hogarth Press, is reproduced on the book cover by kind permission of the Random House Group Ltd.

The painting of the giraffe is by Oscar Pujol Owens (when he was a very small boy), who also gives us his kind permission to use it on the cover of our book.

ABOUT THE EDITORS AND CONTRIBUTORS

Editors

Dr Carol Owens is a psychoanalyst and clinical supervisor in private practice in North Dublin. She has lectured on psychoanalysis at Trinity College Dublin, Dublin City University, and Independent Colleges, Dublin. A registered practitioner member of the Association for Psychoanalysis and Psychotherapy in Ireland and member of the Irish Council for Psychotherapy, she is also the founder and convenor of the Dublin Lacan Study Group. She edited *The Letter: Lacanian Perspectives on Psychoanalysis* from 2003–2006, and the *Annual Review of Critical Psychology* on Jacques Lacan in 2009. She has published articles and book chapters on the theory and practice of Lacanian psychoanalysis, and on encounters between Lacanian theory and critical psychology, critical management theory, film and TV, philosophy, and queer theories. She co-organises the annual Irish Psychoanalytic Film Festival.

Stephanie Farrelly Quinn is a psychoanalytic psychotherapist in private practice in Co.Louth. She is currently a course coordinator and tutor on the Early Childhood Care and Education programme in Coláiste Dhúlaigh CDETB. Upon completion of her MA in psychoanalytic psychotherapy in 2014 she was awarded the Independent Colleges Dublin President's Award in recognition of her academic achievements, clinical expertise, and Master's thesis "Further Notes on the Child: A Freudo—Lacanian analysis of contemporary approaches to the clinic of the child". She is a member of the editorial board of Lacunae, international journal for Freudian and Lacanian psychoanalysis. She is a member of the Association for Psychoanalytic and Psychotherapy in Ireland (APPI) and member of the Irish Council for Psychotherapy.

Contributors

Bice Benvenuto is a psychoanalyst practising in London, a founder member of CFAR and of the Maison Verte-UK, Director of the Dolto Association in Rome. She is a visiting Professor at the New School of Social Research (NY) and at Florida Atlantic University and has lectured extensively in UK and internationally. She is co-author of *The Works of Jacques Lacan: An Introduction* (FAB) and the author of *Concerning the Rites of Psychoanalysis* (Polity/Blackwell), among several books and articles on psychoanalysis and literature.

Dr Kate Briggs is a practising psychoanalyst, and a lecturer in the School of Counselling at the Australian College of Applied Psychology, Melbourne, Australia. She has worked as a clinical specialist and consulted widely in the field of social welfare. She has published on psychoanalytic theory and practice in international journals and her essays on contemporary art have appeared in catalogues and books such as *Radical Revisionism: An Anthology of Writings on Australian Art*. She is a member of the Lacan Circle of Melbourne and is deputy convenor of the Australian College of Counselling and Psychotherapy Educators.

Dr Kaye Cederman practises psychoanalysis and psychotherapy with children and adolescents in New Zealand. She is a registered practitioner member of the Association for Psychoanalysis and Psychotherapy, Ireland, and the Child and Adolescent Therapists' Association, Centre for Lacanian Analysis, cartel of the Lacanian School, New Zealand. She is a research Fellow at Trinity College Dublin, taught Gender & Women's Studies, and Early Childhood Pedagogy at the University of Limerick. She is an Editor of the *Journal of New Zealand Research in Early Childhood Education*. She is published in critical-cultural, feminist theory, philosophy, and early childhood pedagogy. Recent seminars include: "Noting the Child in Aotearoa New Zealand", "Lacan and the hyper-civilised child", "So What? A critique of current child mental health services".

Dr Olga Cox Cameron is a psychoanalyst in private practice in Dublin for the past twenty-eight years. She lectured in Psychoanalytic Theory and also in Psychoanalysis and Literature at St Vincent's University Hospital and Trinity College from 1991 to 2013 and has published numerous articles on these topics in national and international journals. She is the founder of the annual Irish Psychoanalysis and Film Festival, now in its eighth year, held this year at the Irish Museum of Modern Art with a focus on psychoanalysis and documentary.

Françoise Dolto (1908–1988) was a French psychoanalyst, pioneer in the field of child psychoanalysis, and advocate for children's rights. Together with Jacques Lacan, she was one of the founding members of the Société Française de Psychanalyse (SFP) the French psychoanalytic professional body formed in 1953, in a split from the main body of French psychoanalysts, the Société Parisienne de Psychanalyse (SPP). She became widely known in France through her radio program in the mid-seventies addressing herself to issues around child rearing, education, and child psychology. In 1979 she founded the Maison Verte a nurturing centre for the social education of infants to age three or four years, a place where a child and her/his parents/caregivers were welcomed to spend time—speaking and/or playing—in the company of the Maison Verte team, of whom one member was a psychoanalyst. The success of the Maison Verte has led to the setting up of new centres in other countries since then. During that time she continued to work in her psychoanalytic practice in the Etienne Marcel centre and with children placed with the social services. Author of many books in the field of Psychoanalysis with children and adolescents, only three however have been translated into the English language. *Le Cas Dominique* was translated as *Dominique: Analysis of an Adolescent* and published in 1974 in the US, and 1974 in the UK, and *When Parents Separate* was published in the US in 1995. Her doctoral thesis has been translated into English as Psychoanalysis and Paediatrics. *Key Psychoanalytical Concepts with Sixteen Clinical Observations of Children* and was published by Karnac in 2013. Further biographical material on the life of Dolto can be found in *Theory and Practice in Child Psychoanalysis: An Introduction to the Work* *of Françoise Dolto*, edited by Guy Hall, Francoise Hivernel, and Siân Morgan, published by Karnac in 2009.

Hilda Fernandez received an MA in Clinical Psychology from the Universidad Nacional Autónoma de México (UNAM), an MA in Spanish Literature from the University of British Columbia (UBC) and she has more than twenty years of Lacanian training. She practises psychoanalysis and psychoanalytic therapy in Vancouver, Canada, registered with the BC Association of Clinical Counsellors. She co-founded the Lacan Salon in 2007, served as its president from June 2014 to January 2017 and currently she acts as its clinical director. She is engaged in a PhD Program in the Department of Geography at Simon Fraser University (SFU), where she is conducting research on discursive spaces of trauma in the mental health institution and the impact on the provision of services. She has published articles on psychotherapy and psychoanalysis and is passionate about the transmission of psychoanalysis and community building. She is involved in the academic community as an associate with the SFU Institute for the Humanities.

Joanna Fortune is a Psychoanalytic Psychotherapist specialising in child and adolescent psychotherapy. She is a registered practitioner member of the Association for Psychoanalysis and Psychotherapy in Ireland (APPI); an accredited member of the Irish Forum for Psychoanalytic Psychotherapy (IFPP), the Irish Council of Psychotherapy (ICP), and the Theraplay Therapeutic Institute (TTI); and an approved supervisor with Play Therapy International (PTI). Joanna provides specialist clinical work in the area of Child Attachment. Joanna spent twelve years working in the NGO sector in Ireland before founding Solamh Parent Child Relationship Clinic in 2010. As a clinician, well-established training consultant and guest speaker in her field, Joanna is a regular contributor in the media. She has been a panellist at psychoanalytic events in Ireland and has published articles on a variety of topics. More information is available at: www.solamh.com.

Dr Kristen Hennessy, PhD, is a psychologist in private practice in rural Pennsylvania where she specialises in the treatment of children and adolescents "in the system". Dr Hennessy's recent presentations include Lacanian clinical work with children and adolescents with histories of abuse, psychoanalysis and intellectual disability, traumatised masculinities, and the intersections of psychoanalysis and qualitative research. In addition to her work in the United States, Dr Hennessy has experience developing and running psychoanalytically informed seminars for orphanage caregivers in Nakuru, Kenya.

Cristina R. Laurita received a PhD in Clinical Psychology from Duquesne University. She was also awarded a fellowship through the Psychoanalytic Center of Philadelphia. She maintains a private practice in Princeton, New Jersey, where she works with children, adolescents, and adults from within a Lacanian psychoanalytic orientation. Her publications have appeared in *Journal of Lacanian Studies, International Journal for Critical Psychology, Janus Head, Umbr(a),* and *Lacan and Addiction: An Anthology.*

Elizabeth Monahan is trained in the Freudian-Lacanian tradition and has been working as a psychoanalyst in private practice in Dublin for over ten years. Formerly a director of the Association for Psychoanalysis & Psychotherapy in Ireland (APPI), and currently a committee member of the Affiliated Psychoanalytic Workgroups (APW), Elizabeth has presented papers internationally, lectured in Ireland on various psychoanalytic subjects at graduate and post-graduate levels, and is a member of the Dublin Lacan Study Group.

Ona Nierenberg, PhD, is a psychoanalyst in private practice in New York and a Senior Psychologist at Bellevue Hospital Center, where she was Director of HIV Psychological Services for thirteen years. She is also a Clinical Instructor in the Department of Psychiatry at New York University Langone Medical Center, a member of Après-Coup Psychoanalytic Association, an Honourary Member of Lacan Toronto, and an Overseas Member of APPI. She has published articles on psychoanalysis, sexuality and the discourse of science, as well as on licensing and the question of lay analysis. Among her current interests are the history of psychoanalysis, psychoanalytic institutionalisation and transmission, and fate and chance.

Michael Gerard Plastow is a psychoanalyst (Analyst of the School, The Freudian School of Melbourne, School of Lacanian Psychoanalysis, and member of l'Association Lacanienne Internationale) practising in Melbourne, Australia. He is also a child and adolescent psychiatrist based at Alfred Child and Youth Mental Health Service. He has co-convened a seminar on "Psychoanalysis and the Child" for the last nine years. He is the author of *What is a Child? Childhood, Psychoanalysis, and Discourse*, published by Karnac, London, 2015. His translation of Lacan's seminar *The Knowledge of the Psychoanalyst* appeared in 2013 as a bilingual edition, in a non-commercial publication of Éditions de l'Association Lacanienne Internationale, Paris. His current projects include a book on the writings of Sabina Spielrein.

Donna Redmond is a psychoanalyst in private practice in Dublin where she specialises in the treatment of adolescents. She was an inaugural member of the APPI Child and Adolescent Analysis Group, supervised by analysts of the Espace Analytique in Paris. Donna has worked for over fifteen years in the Irish Public Health Service providing psychological interventions to children, adolescents and adults. Aside from her private practice, she provides consultations within the Irish national counselling agency with adult survivors of abuse and in an educational setting working with disadvantaged children. She is a member of The Irish School for Lacanian Psychoanalysis and an associate member of Analyse Freudienne.

Dr Leonardo S. Rodríguez is a psychoanalyst, a founding member of the Australian Centre for Psychoanalysis, an Analyst Member of the School of Psychoanalysis of the Forums of the Lacanian Field, a former Senior Lecturer with the Department of Psychiatry, Monash University and the Coordinator of the Master of Psychoanalysis program, Victoria University. He has published *Psychoanalysis with Children* (London and New York, Free Association Books, 1999) and numerous book chapters and articles on psychoanalytic theory and practice in different languages. Address for correspondence: leonardosrodriguez@bigpond.com.

Dr Annie G. Rogers is Professor of Psychoanalysis and Clinical Psychology at Hampshire College in Amherst, Massachusetts, and Co-Director of its Psychoanalytic Studies Program. She is an Analyst Member of the Lacanian School of San Francisco. Dr Rogers has a psychoanalytic practice in Amherst, Massachusetts. A recipient of a Fulbright Fellowship at Trinity College, Dublin, Ireland; a Radcliffe Fellowship at Harvard University; a Whiting Fellowship at Hampshire College;

and an Erikson Scholar at Austen-Riggs; she is the author of *A Shining Affliction* (Penguin Viking, 1995), *The Unsayable* (Random House, 2006), and *Incandescent Alphabets: Psychosis and the Enigma of Language* (Karnac, 2016).

Dr Stephanie Swales is an Assistant Professor of Psychology at the University of Dallas. She is also a licensed clinical psychologist and maintains a private psychoanalytic practice working with adults and children. Stephanie is undergoing her analytic formation with the Lacanian School of Psychoanalysis based in San Francisco, California. She is the founder and facilitator of the Dallas/Fort Worth Area Lacan Study Group. Her first book, *Perversion: A Lacanian Psychoanalytic Approach to the Subject*, was published by Routledge in 2012.

Catherine Vanier is a psychoanalyst in Paris. She works in the child psychiatric unit at the Delafontaine Hospital in Saint-Denis and is a researcher at the Center for Psychoanalysis, Medicine and Society at the University of Paris VII. She is a member of Espace Analytique Group and the author of numerous books and publications.

Marie Walshe is a psychoanalyst working with adults, children, and couples in Dublin, Ireland. In addition to her private practice, she works in school settings treating acting-out and self-harming behaviours. She was an inaugural member of the APPI Child and Adolescent Analysis Group, supervised by analysts of the Espace Analytique in Paris. She was a Clinical Tutor on the graduate and post-graduate training programmes in psychoanalysis at Independent Colleges, Dublin, from 2008 to 2015. She has been an invited respondent at several psychoanalytically informed seminars in Ireland and has been previously published in *The Letter* (2004, 2006).

Eve Watson, PhD, is a psychoanalytic practitioner in Dublin, Ireland. She also teaches on graduate programmes and directed the MA in Psychoanalytic Psychotherapy at Independent College Dublin (2008–2015). Areas of special interest include sexuality, film studies, cultural and critical theory. She is co-editor of the book *Clinical Encounters: Psychoanalytic Practice and Queer Theory* (Punctum, 2017), and has journal articles in *Lacunae* (2015, 2013, 2012, 2010); *Psychoanalytische Perspectieven* (2015); *(Re)-Turn* (2013); *Open Letter: Negotiating the Bond of Social Poetics*

(2012); *Annual Review of Critical Psychology* (2009); *The Letter*: (2006, 2005, 2004) and in proceedings of the *Paris Ecole de Psychanalyse des Forums du Champ Lacanian* (2011, 2009). A registered practitioner member of the *Association for Psychoanalysis and Psychotherapy in Ireland* (APPI), she has served on various subcommittees as well as the Executive Committee She is the editor of *Lacunae*, the International Journal for Lacanian Psychoanalysis, a peer-reviewed journal published by APPI.

Dr Megan Williams is a Lacanian psychoanalyst practising in Melbourne. She has practised psychoanalysis for more than twenty years, published numerous articles on psychoanalysis, and taught psychoanalysis for ten years at Victoria University in Melbourne. She is an Analyst Member of the Freudian School of Melbourne. She conducts a seminar in Melbourne entitled "The Father in Psychoanalysis".

INTRODUCTION

Further notes on the child …

Carol Owens and Stephanie Farrelly Quinn

> What in sum, is Little Hans? It is the babbling of a five year old child between January 1st and May 2nd, 1908. This is what Little Hans is for the reader who is not prepared. If he is prepared, and it is not hard to be, he knows that these stories have some interest. Why are they interesting? They are interesting, because it is suggested, at least in principle, that there is a relation between this babbling and something that is completely consistent, namely a phobia, with all of the troubles that it brings to the life of a *young subject*, all of the worry it arouses in his entourage, all of the interest it provokes in Professor Freud.
>
> (Lacan, 5th June 1957, our emphasis)

In the long trajectory of his teaching Lacan did not say or write very much exclusively about psychoanalytic practice with children, with "young subjects". What he did say and write about it—even though we should admit that this took place mainly in the margins of his teaching—is regarded however as being of fundamental clinical significance and pertinence by Lacanian psychoanalysts, whether working with children *or* older subjects in analytic treatments. For the most part, the remarks which he made emerged at key points and moments, in the theorising, and critique, of psychoanalytic concepts and themes which he chose to examine in his seminar spanning some thirty years, and in his *Écrits* and other papers. For instance, in his "Presentation on Psychic Causality" (Lacan, 1946) he elaborates on his "Mirror Stage" theory as the means by which he was able to outline the psychological genesis of psychical causality insofar as it is grounded in the operation of identification of the individual with his or her *semblables* (Lacan, 1946, p. 154). Be that as it may, the widely referenced "Mirror Stage" article is a really good example of a piece of Lacan's work which has implications for the psychoanalytic conceptualisation of "the child" even as it is interrogates the notion of ego development, and mobilises the essential Lacanian discovery of the ego in its function as *misrecognition* (Lacan, 1949, p. 76; and see Fortune, Chapter Sixteen in this volume). In fact, there is rich material of clinical relevance for the psychoanalyst working with children from his very early work on the "Family Complexes" (Lacan, 1938), as well as from nearly every one of the early seminars, taking into account that it is during the 1950s, especially in those places where he charts the paternal function and metaphor, the graphs of desire, and attendant commentaries on need and demand, and on "clinical structure", that we find the remarks about the young subject and the child more frequently referenced than in the later seminars (especially after *Seminar X*).

The two notable places where Lacan opines *in particular* about what takes place in the psychoanalysis of a child and about what is represented by the child's symptom are his fourth seminar on the "Object Relation" (Lacan, 1956–1957) and his "Note on the Child" (Lacan, 1969). His seminar on the object relation however also functions as a sustained critique of the notion of the object relation in psychoanalytic theory as well as a thorough-going contribution to the phenomenology of perversion, and an attempt to theorise phobia anew taking for close examination Freud's case history of Little Hans. It is evident that Lacan expects this seminar to have an effect on clinicians from various remarks he makes, but not, however, exclusively upon those working only with children. In the "Direction of the Treatment" paper of 1958 delivered almost a year after the end of his fourth seminar Lacan pronounces, regarding his supervisee Ruth Lebovici's case of transitory sexual perversion, that it is deplorable that the teaching of his fourth seminar couldn't have helped her to get her bearings regarding the so-called phallic mother. Those attending his seminar had, according to him, on the other hand, benefitted from his establishment of the principles that distinguish the phobic object as "an all-purpose signifier to make up for the Other's lack" from "the fundamental fetish in every perversion as an object perceived in the signifier's cut" (Lacan, 1958, p. 510). This extraordinary observation together with the nuanced typology of the object and the lack of object, and the elaborations of the *pèr*(*e*)-mutations of the father and the characteristics of the mother's fantasy in the case of Little Hans, arguably make Lacan's fourth seminar one of his most ground-breaking. What is also remarkable is that the themes he identifies there around the function of the father, and the place of the child in the mother's fantasy, resonate with the remarks he goes on to make in his later brief commentary on the child in 1969.

Again, his "Note on the Child" received gratefully by any practitioner working with children because of his claim there that the child's symptom is found to be in a position of answering to what is symptomatic in the family structure, is also however relevant in the work with the subject regardless of age (see Cederman, Chapter Eighteen in this volume; and Owens, 2016, for example). This claim, that the family structure is both symptomatic and symptom-producing recalls his thesis in the "Family Complexes" article where he had argued that the degradation of the Oedipus complex was coordinated with the rise of the character neuroses, because of the roles that parental objects have in the form of the superego and ego ideal (Lacan, 1938, p. 78). The "degraded form" of the Oedipus complex featured an incomplete repression of desire for the mother, and a narcissistic bastardisation of the father which for Lacan marked the essential aggressive ambivalence immanent in the primordial relationship to one's fellow man. Indeed, in his 1948 paper "Aggressiveness in Psychoanalysis", he argued that the effects of the degradation of superego and ego-ideal functioning together with the promotion and idealisation of the ego lead to a "formidable crack" at the very heart of being, leading to the emergence of self-punishing neuroses, hysterical and hypochondriacal symptoms, obsessional and phobic anxieties, as well as to the social consequences of failure and crime (1948, p. 101). In her chapter here (Chapter Four in the present volume), Bice Benvenuto too reflects on what she calls (following Lacan's comments from 1938 on the consequences of the changes in family structure) the "transformations of family ties, which have deep effects on the psychic development of children". Kristen Hennessy in her essay considers some of the effects of one of the most radical forms of these transformations at work on the child in the foster care system. In his "Note on the Child", Lacan further designates as symptomatic, the "fantasmatic capture" to which the child falls prey if the function of the father is inefficient, becoming instead, the mother's "object", positioned as *objet a* in her fantasy. In her chapter, Megan Williams applies this observation to a case of her own. This observation is clearly commensurate with Lacan's working over of the Little Hans case in 1956 but is conceptualised in 1969 as *objet a*, a concept which was not yet available to his thinking at the time of his fourth seminar.

During Lacan's life-time, and since then, psychoanalysts who have forged, developed, and articulated ways of thinking about, and working with, children and young people which bear the hallmarks of Lacan's teachings do so as "Lacanians" rather than as "child psychoanalysts": the work of Roisin Lefort (1980), Maud Mannoni (1967), Leonardo Rodríguez (1999), Catherine Vanier (2015), and Annie Rogers (2006) are exemplary in this tradition. For the generations of psychoanalysts who work with Lacan's teachings, a persistent and fundamental characteristic of the Lacanian analyst's approach is that the subject who is in question in the psychoanalytic treatment, is first and foremost a subject of language, and in Lacan's later teachings, the *parlêtre* (see Rodríguez, 1999, and Chapter Five in this volume; Plastow, 2015, and Chapter Nine this volume). As Rodríguez puts it in his chapter here: "[S]trictly speaking, we do not treat children in psychoanalysis, but subjects". This approach stands in opposition to the tendency in most psychological therapies to order and install a taxonomy of subject and/or symptom according to which a trained modality specialist is assigned. The categorisation of the symptom as discretely treatable is of course explicit in both psychiatric diagnostics as well as in self-help and non-professional group treatments such as "Recovery" movements and AA and NA (Verhaeghe, 2004). Moreover, the cataloguing of the individual as a "type" who can only be treated by a corresponding "expert" is inherent in psychology as discipline and prevails in the regulatory mechanisms and discourses of Western contemporary psychiatric medicine (see Parker, 2011, 2015; Dunker, 2011). Indeed, the Lacanian approach to the subject opposes the notion also currently prevalent in many child psychoanalytic trainings that the analytic work with children should only be carried out by approved analysts with specific *child* modality training: a notion of course contingent upon discourses of childhood that circulate essentialist and developmental accounts of childhood *per se*, together with a whole set of warrants and pre- and pro-scriptions around the professional practices involving children (*cf.* Stainton Rogers & Stainton Rogers, 1992; Burman, 2008). In this way, the Lacanian approach to the subject may be seen to support a de-essentialised, deconstructed account of "childhood", foregrounding as it does, the speaking subject, immaterial of age.

One of the key points of interest for us in assembling this collection of essays was to bring together accounts of the ways in which the Lacanian analyst practises, and conceives of that practice, with the subject who is a child, in the absence of a theoretical and clinical set of directives from Lacan himself about the work with children. At the same time, we also recognised—as practitioners working with children of various ages ourselves—that the work with children is "different" to the work with adults in certain ways, and we wanted to hear how other Lacanians theorise about, and conceptualise that "difference". Lacanians take for granted that the subject of the psychoanalytic clinic is approached "case by case", and "one-by-one"—preserving the singularity of their symptom and the particularity of their desire. But it behoves us to theorise and explain how the Lacanian treatment is organised around the subject whose agency is subjected to the consent of the Other, especially as this involves working with exigencies that do not perform equally when working with the "adult" subject. Kate Briggs (Chapter Ten in this volume) condenses the essence of this dilemma succinctly. She says: "working with young people has the *particularity* of requiring the agreement and participation of parents and carers in order to arrive at preliminary interviews and support ongoing work" (our emphasis).

Lacan's paper "The Direction of the Treatment and the Principles of its Power" (Lacan, 1957) allowed him to frame psychoanalytic practice in support of his "Return to Freud", previously elaborated in his "Rome Discourse" (Lacan, 1953). The key elements he addressed in this paper—who analyses today, the place of interpretation, the standpoint on transference, how the psychoanalyst acts with her/his being, how to think about desire and its place in the direction of the treatment—functioned as core discussion points in the conversations we had which led to our idea for this volume of essays as well as in a previous project (Farrelly, 2015). In Farrelly (2015), Lacan's remarks in "Note on the Child" are interwoven with clinical applications of these elements from Lacan's "Direction of the Treatment" paper. We developed the idea subsequently that it would be most interesting to put these elements to work once again, in a broader manner, in an attempt to discover, and elaborate upon, the particularities of working psychoanalytically with children from a Lacanian perspective.

Re-examining the questions raised by Lacan in his "Direction of the Treatment" paper means reframing them in terms of their significance for the work with children. We arrived at the following reformulation, which inserts "the child" as an instance of particularity, preserving the tone and emphasis of the original questions crucial to thinking about the direction of any treatment, but "tweaked" in respect of the exigencies of the work with a subject who relies upon the Other's consent:

> Who analyses children today within a Lacanian psychoanalytic frame?
> What is the place of interpretation with children?
> Where do we stand (sit, or play) in the transference with the child and her or his Other(s)?
> How does the analyst working with children act with her or his being?
> How do we take the desire of a child, literally?

As the reader will discover, the contributors to this volume of essays all engage with these questions within the context of a particular aspect of their work with children or young people.

The question of who analyses children today within the framework of Lacanian psychoanalysis is answered in one way or another by every one of our contributors since each author is also a clinician working with children—whether neonates, adolescents, or anywhere in between these two groups. Sometimes the work is situated within the tradition and history of Lacanian psychoanalysis so as to indicate the moment which particularly inspires or influences that practitioner in his or her work (for example, Benvenuto's work on the Casa Verde, and Maison Verte; Rogers, on the later teachings of Lacan).

Interpretation as one of the core interventions in psychoanalytic work is explored in detail in case-work across a range of clinical structures, symptom, and discussions of working with children in systems. Interpretation is also at work in the critical examination of discourse, and of how intersecting and contradictory discourses constitute "the child" and the child's symptom, in the early part of the twenty-first century (see especially the essays in part five).

The question of where the Lacanian child analyst places her or himself in relation to the transference is at the same time a question of managing transference to a manifold Other (particularly in the articulated or mumbled demand). The transference in all of its manifestations is explored in great variety across the collection, from working within institutions (see especially the chapters by Briggs, Hennessy, Plastow, and Vanier), to working within systems (see Benvenuto, and Redmond) to the work in the private clinic, where still, the exigencies of the transference are multi-faceted (see Fernández Alvaraz, Laurita, Walshe, and Swales).

It is both a perpetual question, and at the same time never a question for the Lacanian practitioner working with children and young people, to consider how to act with her or his being, since as the reader will see, one of the touchstones of the Lacanian treatment is the notion that the analyst's being is always involved (see the chapters by Monahan, Rogers, and Vanier for example). But how the analyst's being comes into *play* in the child clinic is unthinkable in the same terms as the work with adults, since the child may reach out to touch or pull the analyst's hair, to enlist her or his help in pulling a trigger on a toy gun, or to cast her or him in the role of "the fool", or "the witch" depending on what is happening in the work (see Briggs, Hennessy, and Swales). How our contributors write about these experiences is particularly valuable since it brings out a rich evocation of the analyst's desire and a rich testimony to the analyst's requirement to make *inventions* as well as interventions in the treatment.

Taking the desire of a child, literally, is the absolute minimum requirement of working with children. The child's desire foments a fantasy and correlates to symptom, jouissance, and *sinthome*. In Lacanian theory, desire is thought with clinical structure. How do we think about structure in the clinical work with children (see especially the chapters by Laurita, Monahan, Rodríguez, and Walshe)? What happens to desire as it encounters the desire of the Other (see Cederman, Fortune, Plastow, Redmond, and Nierenberg and Watson)?

While engaging with the themes which predominate in the direction of the treatment, as outlined above, our contributors also bring to their essays their own particular investments, their own desire as analysts, which mobilises for them a way of working with, and thinking about, the work with children and young people. As such, in order to reflect these trajectories, the collection of essays is presented in five parts.

Part one consists of four pieces on the direction of the treatment with children.

We have chosen to open the book and this section with the piece written by Stephanie Swales which can be read as a prelude for Lacanian practitioners working with children. In her chapter Swales pays close attention to the function of demand as it gets articulated variously at the beginning, and throughout the treatment, *by the child's parents* indicating something of what the child's symptom represents of the parental couple, and then *by the child* as the indication of her or his own investment in the treatment. What Swales "frames" as challenges are the problems of management of the intricacies of this demand at work in the treatment and in the transference. What she refers to as "inventions" are the ways in which the analyst approaches the analytic frame in order to make use of the conceptual repertoire Lacan composed through his teachings (for example: scansion, variable-length sessions) according to the specificity of the work with children and adolescents, but in keeping with the overarching approach of the Lacanian analyst of working with the specificity proper to each case, case-by-case.

Hilda Fernández Alvarez also addresses the function of demand. Taking into account the "at least one adult" who is involved in the treatment with the child (parent, significant other, carer, agency worker, etc.), she explores the exigencies of the transference via the management of demand(s), and how the analyst acts with their being via a consideration of the place of "knowledge" and interventions made "within a space and time". Using clinical vignettes, Fernández Alvarez proposes and explains the utility of certain of Lacan's topological schemas (Moebius, L Schema, Graph of Desire) as spaces upon which the child subject's demand can be mapped.

We are very excited to be able to reproduce extracts here from Françoise Dolto's "Seminars on Child Psychoanalysis" with a preface by Olga Cox Cameron (who translated the first four seminars for the Irish Journal of Psychoanalytic Psychotherapy) for this volume. We chose to extract the elements from the first two seminars in which Dolto very straightforwardly comments upon the position the analyst should take up around the child's demand; the function of the practitioner in drawing out the child's desire; the notion of the child as symptom of the parents; and how to approach the preliminary sessions. As the reader will discover, a number of our contributors quote or otherwise reference Dolto in their pieces: to paraphrase Joni Mitchell from her song "A case of you"—parts of Dolto flow out of these essays on Lacan from time to time. It seemed to us an exceptional opportunity to publish Dolto here in a contemporary collection of accounts of working with children since, as Cox Cameron astutely remarks, she is above all, a clinician, who brings to the psychoanalytic encounter her approach to the child as a "speaking subject". If this is what qualifies the analytic approach as specifically *Lacanian*, then arguably Dolto was one of the first Lacanians. But Dolto was much more than a "Lacanian": and her own inventions and innovations put to work in the creation of the Maison Verte are commented upon by Bice Benvenuto whose chapter we also include in the first part of this book, since it indicates a "new" direction of the treatment.

Bice Benvenuto addresses the decline of the paternal imago and considers how in our time of the "failed patriarch", substitutes for this symbolic function are diffused in social networks (both virtual and "real"). In her piece, she claims that Dolto's invention of the Maison Verte instituted a "polyphonic, convivial dimension in the clinical work with children", and points out common ground and divergences between Dolto, and Lacan and Klein. She goes on to describe her own work in the creation of the Casa Verde in Rome and the Maison Verte–UK in London, and considers the new dimension of transference made possible in that work which she theorises as the "Agora effect". The reader is referred to the excellent collection of essays on the theory and practice of Dolto's work with children by Hall et al (2009) in which Benvenuto's chapter elaborates in greater detail the work in the Casa Verde.

Part two consists of two essays, each of which comment upon the function of "the father" in the psychoanalytic work with children.

The Lacanian formulas about "the father", the paternal function, and the Name-of-the-Father are well-known, especially from his early work (Lacan, 1938; Lacan, 1950, Lacan, 1957–1958, for example). In her chapter, Megan Williams reminds us that Lacan's earlier work transformed the Freudian Oedipus complex into a logic of castration, and the Name-of-the-Father was the signifier able to recognise the subject in the "child-object" of the mother's desire, thereby mobilising the operation of sexuation via the founding of an ego-ideal. Later in his work, Williams points out that Lacan wrote that a subject can do without the Father on condition of having first made use of him, highlighting therefore the necessity of subjective invention. Williams addresses this question in relation to an examination of a clinical case: how a child makes use of a Father, and how from a family constellation and "family guy", a paternal function is engendered. She suggests that it is not the presence or virility of the person of a father which determines the Paternal Function for the child but rather the subjective activity and even his or her invention of a Father.

In her piece, Annie Rogers explores a four-year analysis of a child retrospectively through the "later Lacan". Focusing a child analysis on the Lacan of the "Father of the Name", the Real unconscious and the clinic of Borromean knots—Rogers remarks—allows for a re-setting of the compass of a Lacanian field of psychoanalysis with children. Rogers goes on to examine the precise position of the analyst in that "field", and the invitation to the child to discover a space for the Real in the work of play. Laying out the trajectory of the analysis from a symptom through the primal scene fantasy and a family intervention—indicates how the child makes use of an unspoken family legacy in a leap of his own invention.

Part three examines the concept of the "clinical structure" in the work with children.

Leonardo Rodríguez foregrounds the clinical and ethical principles of "singularity" in clinical work as the decisive guide to his work. In his chapter he comments on cases of each of the three Lacanian clinical structures—neurotic, psychotic, perverse—in order to illustrate the theoretical assumptions in differential diagnosis. Rodríguez claims that despite the changes in the constitution of the family, and other socio-cultural changes such as the increased acceptance of different sexual identities and orientations (in certain parts of the world), the psychopathological organisations of human beings have not changed structurally.

Cristina Laurita considers the theoretical and technical questions at work in the treatment of children who are psychotic. Laurita remarks that while Lacan teaches that psychic structures are fixed, he never took up the question of malleability of structure in childhood. Drawing on her clinical case-work, Laurita addresses this gap in Lacan's theorising, by exploring the idea of whether there might be a "window of time" during which a child's psychical structure might be "transformed".

Elizabeth Monahan and Marie Walshe each look at the exigencies of the clinic of adolescence. Walshe addresses what she calls "the exquisite porous fluidity of the modern adolescent subject" as a transitional stage, attended by a regression which re-visits old psychic wounds.

This is the time of the revision of oedipal ideals, the final emergence of structure, sexuality, and the signifiers of a fantasmatic positioning *vis-à-vis* the Other. Adolescence, according to Walshe, is characterised in our time by the foreclosure of castration: the fragile adolescent subject assailed by the increasing concretisation of language, is offered a death-by-signified, rather than birth-by-signifier.

Elizabeth Monahan presents a case: a "Rapunzel" of our time, whose signifying economy reveals the function of an "unravelling" as a way to negotiate the difficult movement from pre-oedipal to genital stage.

Part four focuses on the "symptom" and "the system".

Lacan remarks in his "Note on the Child" that the child's "symptom" represents the child's truth, the truth of the family couple, and/or the subjectivity of the mother. We were most interested to see how contributors would engage with this notion of the symptom, but also, given that today's "child" more than ever before can live part or all of a "childhood" in care, either in an institutional system, or foster care system, or spend some time participating in a mental health provision system, we wondered how contributors would theorise the child's symptom in and of a system.

We begin this section with the essay by Michael Gerard Plastow. Plastow takes for examination what he calls the "watershed" of the symptom in the difference in approach to the treatment of a child by the psychoanalyst, Sabina Spielrein and the developmental psychologist, Jean Piaget in their work in Geneva of the 1920s. Plastow underscores the differences between the notion of the symptom in psychoanalysis, and that of psychiatry or psychology: the latter reducing the symptom to a deviation from the norms of development, in contrast with Freud's notion of the symptom as something that goes well beyond the description of a behaviour, or a failure to meet developmental norms or milestones. Plastow goes on to examine how the symptom is taken up in psychoanalysis following both Spielrein and Lacan. Plastow's recuperation of Spielrein leads him to claim that Spielrein articulates for psychoanalysis something akin to what Lacan called a *savoir-y-faire*, a knowing what to do with the symptom: a move which opposes the tendency in many of today's psy-practices to remove the symptom.

Kate Briggs also argues that in the dominant discourse of mental health services in our time, symptoms are to be eliminated rather than heard (in the transference) and as such, subjects become deregistered from the particularity of their own unique conditions of existence.

Psychoanalysis therefore has had to redefine its approach to the engagement of the subject and the concept of the Real. She looks to the work of Kohut and Kernberg addressing the question of transference in working with (so-called) borderline and narcissistic disorders as well as in the late work of Lacan, with each one responding to changing presentations in their clinics. Drawing substantively on her work with a young girl in an institutional setting, Briggs argues that it behoves psychoanalysts to communicate what is distinctive about what works in their treatments, in their encounters with care teams in institutional settings.

Taking up Lacan's comment in his "Note on the Child" (Lacan, 1969, p. 1) that "the child's symptom is found to be in a *position* of answering to what is symptomatic in the family structure", Kristen Hennessy remarks that the child who has been removed from the custody of his parents and placed in foster care via a concrete intervention by the law, finds himself then, in a peculiar "position". Moving between clinical vignettes and Lacan's paper, her chapter allows her to explore questions connected to the symptoms of the child in the system: what happens to the symptom in the system? Whose symptom does the child answer? When does the child's symptom become an answer to the system itself?

In the second of his essays on "Contributions to the Psychology of Love", Freud had put forward the idea that there was in some men, a tendency towards the debasement of the "love-object" (Freud, 1912d). In her chapter, Donna Redmond explores the tendency towards debasement in the sphere of female adolescence within an Irish sexual health service for adolescents. Based upon her observations from this clinic, Redmond considers this tendency and reflects on its impact upon female identity and sexuality.

Part five brings together four essays, each of them commenting upon current discursive trends and the practices which become warranted and normalised within and between discourses. As apparatuses of the Symbolic, and "mouthpieces" of the Imaginary, discourses materialise the signifying operations through which the child and the Other(s) are constituted as "speaking beings" and through which, is articulated, "the symptom".

Catherine Vanier describes working with what we can think of as "very new" subjects: these are infants prematurely born and most often resuscitated, beginning lives assisted by new technologies (see also Vanier, 2015). These brand-new subjects are inhabited by scientific and medicalised discourses in which the psychoanalyst has to find her place, both figuratively, and literally in Vanier's case working alongside the medical team in a neo-natal resuscitation unit.

In her chapter, Joanna Fortune considers the impact of new forms of photographing technologies—taken for granted in our time—which she argues impede the Mirror stage, disrupting ego formation, leading to new pathologies in young children. In addition she postulates some techniques for clinical use in order to address this new problem.

Exploring the links between contemporary dominant neo-liberal investments in "equality" and "difference" and the new standard of administering hormone blockers to children who experience an identification with the other sex, is central to Eve Watson and Ona Nierenberg's concerns in their chapter. They draw attention to the rapid ascension to hegemonic status of the "discourse of 'trans'" which is marked by the total medicalisation of transgender identification, a trend which they point out is utterly at odds with psychoanalysis which unpins the subject from anatomical deadlock.

The final chapter in this collection is contributed by Kaye Cederman who explores the intersection of global capitalist-consumer culture and its resonance with the clinic of the psychotic and autistic child. Drawing on Baudrillard and Nietzsche, she asks what sort of being is the child who is inhabited by language in this milieu which mobilises hyper-real simulations of childhood and its counterpart, a deadly circuit of over-stimulated, digitised, (child-) consumers.

In putting this book together, we hoped that we would discover new things about the direction of the treatment with children, that we would encounter new theories about the child's symptom; and it occurred to us that we might, at the end of this work, have "further" *Lacanian* "notes on the child". We hope that the reader will welcome and find useful the accounts which testify to a rich diversity of clinical experience, as well as the theoretical and conceptual innovations that these Lacanian psychoanalysts bring to their work with children, and to this book.

References

Burman, E. (2008). *Deconstructing Developmental Psychology* (2nd edition). London: Routledge.

Dunker, C. (2011). *The Constitution of the Psychoanalytic Clinic: A History of its Structure and Power*. London: Karnac.

Farrelly, S. (2015). *Further Notes on the Child*. Unpublished MA thesis, Independent Colleges Dublin.

Freud, S. (1912d). On the Universal Tendency to Debasement in the Sphere of Love. *S.E., 11:* 179–190. London: Hogarth.

Hall, G., Hivernel, F., Morgan, S. (Eds.) (2009). *Theory and Practice in Child Psychoanalysis. An Introduction to the Works of Françoise Dolto*. London: Karnac.

Lacan, J. (1938). *La Famille: Les complexes familiaux dans la formation de l'individu*. C. Gallagher (Trans.). *Family Complexes in the Formation of the Individual*. Available at: www.lacaninireland.com

Lacan, J. (1946). Presentation on Psychic Causality. In: *Écrits: The first complete edition in English* (pp. 123–160). B. Fink (Trans.). London & New York: Norton & Co., 2006.

Lacan, J. (1948). Aggressiveness in Psychoanalysis. In: *Écrits: The first complete edition in English* (pp. 82–101). B. Fink (Trans.). London & New York: Norton & Co., 2006.

Lacan, J. (1949). The Mirror Stage as Formative of the *I* Function as Revealed in Psychoanalytic Experience. In: *Écrits: The first complete edition in English* (pp. 75–81). B. Fink, (Trans.). London & New York: Norton & Co., 2006.

Lacan, J. (1950). A Theoretical Introduction to the Functions of Psychoanalysis in Criminology. In: *Écrits: The first complete edition in English* (pp. 102–122). B. Fink (Trans.). London & New York: Norton & Co., 2006.

Lacan, J. (1953). The Function and Field of Speech and Language in Psychoanalysis. In: *Écrits: The first complete edition in English* (pp. 197–268). B. Fink (Trans.). London & New York: Norton & Co., 2006.

Lacan, J. (1956–1957). *The Seminar of Jacques Lacan Book IV: the object relation, 1956–1957*. L. V. A. Roche (Trans.). Unpublished. Session of 5th June 1957.

Lacan, J. (1957). The Direction of the Treatment and the Principles of its Power. In: *Écrits: The first complete edition in English* (pp. 489–542). B. Fink (Trans.). London & New York: Norton & Co., 2006.

Lacan, J. (1957–1958). *The Seminar of Jacques Lacan Book V: formations of the unconscious*. C. Gallagher (Trans.). London: Karnac.

Lacan, J. (1969). Note on the Child. R. Grigg (Trans.). *Analysis, 1990, 2*: 7–8.

Lefort, R. (1980). *Birth of the Other*. M. Du Ry, L. Watson, & L. Rodríguez (Trans.). US: University of Illinois Press, 1994.

Manonni, M. (1967). *The Child, his 'Illness', and the Others*. London: Karnac, 1987.

Owens, C. (2016). Not in the Humor: Bulimic Dreams. In: *Lacan, Psychoanalysis, and Comedy* (pp. 113–130). P. Gherovici & M. Steinkoler (Eds.). New York: Cambridge University Press.

Parker, I. (2011). *Lacanian Psychoanalysis: Revolutions in Subjectivity*. London: Routledge.
Parker, I. (2015). *Psychology after Deconstruction*. London: Routledge.
Plastow, M. G. (2015). *What is a Child? Childhood, Psychoanalysis, and Discourse*. London: Karnac.
Rodríguez, L. (1999). *Psychoanalysis with Children*. London & New York: Free Association Books.
Rogers, A. (2006). *The Unsayable*. New York: Random House.
Stainton Rogers, R. & Stainton Rogers, W. (1992). *Stories of Childhood: Shifting Agendas of Child Concern*. Toronto: University of Toronto Press.
Vanier, C. (2015). *Premature Birth: The Baby, the Doctor, and the Psychoanalyst*. London: Karnac.
Verhaeghe, P. (2004). *On Being Normal and Other Disorders: A Manual for Clinical Psychodiagnostics*. S. Jottkandt (Trans.). New York: Other Press.

PART I

DIRECTING THE TREATMENT

CHAPTER ONE

Lacanian psychoanalysis with children: framing challenges and inventions

Stephanie Swales

In our work with adults, we can think about the analytic frame by turning to a host of reference points in the Lacanian and Freudian oeuvre. We read, for example, Freud's papers on technique (Freud, 1911–1915 [1914]), or Lacan's "Variations on the Standard Treatment" and "Direction of the Treatment and Principles of its Power" (Lacan, 1955; 1958). However, with the exception of a few notes here and there, Lacan did not provide us with much direction regarding working with children. We therefore question what modifications should be made to the analytic frame and conception of the treatment when we work with children insofar as they present us with unique challenges. What is more, thoughtful choices must be made in each specific case because whether we are working with children or adults, the conditions for the possibility of analysis are not universal or one-size-fits-all.

The frame must be created in tandem with the creation of the specificity of the psychoanalytic symptom out of the initial demand. The analyst should take the time to listen both to the child and to the parents to see, based on the initial presenting problem, who is demanding what and for what purpose. Toward this end, Lacan said:

> In order to know how to respond to the subject in analysis, the method is to first determine where his ego* is situated—the ego* that Freud himself defined as formed by a verbal nucleus—in other words, to figure out through whom and for whom the subject asks his question. As long as this is not known, we risk misconstruing the desire that must be recognised there and the object to whom this desire is addressed. (1956, p. 250)

In analytic work with children, Lacan said in his "Note on the Child" written to Jenny Aubry that the "child's symptom is a response to what is symptomatic in the family structure ... The symptom can represent the truth of the parental couple" (1969, p. 373). The analyst must therefore learn about the parents as individuals and their relationship with each other, with the child, and with other children in the family. The position of the child in the family history, the desire and narcissism of the parents, and the current family structure is of crucial importance. In working with the child, the analyst attempts to discern the fantasy of each parent, that of the child, and the link between them.

Challenges

It would be a mistake to take on the role of a parent or a teacher even though there is often substantial pressure from such people to side with them. The analyst does not aim to make the child "good" for the parents or for the teacher but instead tries to help the child symbolise what is making him unhappy and to create a different position for him with less suffering. Trying to transform the child into a better student or a well-behaved child is to alienate him further and to side with the *conscious* desires of the parents and teachers, not to listen to the desires of the child, and to ignore the unconscious determinates of the child's symptom within the system. In Lacan's words, in such attempts the "analyst [mistakenly] tries to normalise the subject's behaviour in accordance with a norm, a norm that is coherent with the analyst's own ego. This will always thus involve the modelling of one ego by another ego, by a [supposedly] superior ego" (1954, p. 285).

Instead, the analyst's position is to assist the child in asking and trying to answer various forms of the question "*Che vuoi*?" such as "Who am I?", "What does the Other want from me and for me?", "What is my role in my family?", and "How can I satisfy myself as well as the

Other?" The analyst's role is to listen to the child and to be open to what is particular about the meanings and functions of his symptoms. A symptom, after all, is always an attempt to solve a problem.

The silent and sometimes not-so-silent demand of the parents is often that the analyst patch up the problem, do so quickly, and avoid making them talk about things that they would rather keep swept under the rug. By the time the parents bring the child to analysis, the child (as the symptom of the family) has often in their opinion caused quite enough trouble. In the parents' fatigue, they would rather the child conform to their conscious preferences than have to face their own unconscious investments in the child's symptom. As Lacan said:

> It should be obvious that analytic discourse does not in any way consist in making what isn't going well go away, in suppressing what isn't going well in ordinary discourse … The discourse that proceeds only by true speaking is precisely what is disturbing … It's enough for someone to make an effort to speak truly for that to bother everyone. (1974, February 12th, 1974)

In other words, the analyst is the bearer of bad news that feathers must be ruffled if there is any hope of the symptom taking flight.

Many clinicians (e.g., Greene, 2014; Kazdin, 2009) are tempted to take a moralising, teaching, or preaching stance with the child when presented with manifestations of the child's aggression (e.g., rivalry, not wanting to share, bullying, and various hateful impulses that may be directed to the parents). At times the child's aggression can be quite difficult to bear when it is aimed at the analyst in the transference. That being said, the analyst must be able to tolerate this kind of transference in order to allow the progressive articulation of the fantasy of the child and of her parents. This does not mean that the analyst should let himself be physically hit or hurt by the child. If the child does so, the analyst could potentially terminate the session while providing a rationale for doing so. The analyst might consider giving the child an opportunity to put her thoughts into words before she leaves if it is appropriate to the situation. Violent acting out is always open to and is even a call for interpretation (see for example Lacan, 1958 in his discussions of acting out).

Another aspect of working with children that can be difficult to handle is their not being toilet trained or having "accidents" in the analyst's session room. When a child visits the restroom during a session, it may be a communication to the analyst or a response to something anxiety-provoking that arose in the session. The analyst should take note of what was happening or being said just prior to the child's request to visit the restroom and then make use of that information as appropriate to the individual case. Similarly, when the child urinates or defecates during the session—in which the child brings the partial object into the room—it might (but not always) have a meaning in relation to the session material or within the transference.

How can we speak of a demand for analysis being made by the child if it is the parents who request the treatment? Who is making the demand, and for what? This question should be asked in each particular case, and it is helpful if both the demand of the parents and the demand of the child can be articulated. Although typically the initial demand for treatment comes from the parents or the school, and the child may never even have heard of analysis or therapy, in order for the treatment to work, the child must develop an investment in the treatment or a demand of some kind that the analyst help him with a problem.

This brings us to the important question of the framing of the first session in instantiating the child's relationship to the analyst and to the work itself. If the analyst decides to let the parents participate in the first session, it is very important to begin the session by addressing the child directly before letting the parents speak since this dramatically increases the probability that the child will tell the analyst what is troubling him. In this vein, I find it also helps if the analyst explains who she is (e.g., someone interested in hearing more about the child's understanding of his suffering and who can help the child come up with a solution that works best for him) versus who she is not (e.g., someone on the side of the parents) and what the child can expect from the treatment. When the analyst speaks to the parents first, this communicates to the child that the analyst is there for the parents and not for him, or that the parents have more authority on the problem of the child than the child himself. Instead, the analyst's invitation gives the child the freedom to symbolise *his* problems and creates an initial sense of trust that the analyst's presence is for him (alternatively, the analyst may choose to speak to the parents on the phone or even in person on their own prior to the first session with the child, so that only the child is invited into the room for his first session).

When working with adolescents, I prefer to obtain the parents' perspectives in a way that also facilitates creating trust with the adolescent by speaking briefly with the parents on the phone prior to the first session about their child and the nature of the problem (after all, the parents need some contact with the analyst to be convinced that they should bring their child to see the analyst). This allows me to subsequently see the adolescent alone on the first session. Upon meeting the adolescent, I ask for his input on how to involve the parents (or not) through giving the adolescent several choices and helping the adolescent think through the potential pros and cons of each choice.

A parallel issue is that of the child's confidentiality in relation to his parents, teachers, and others involved in his case. Just as in work with adults, if the child knows that the analyst communicates freely with the parents and shares details of what he says in sessions, he will restrict what he says. The child may even request that the analyst say certain things to his parents and intervene on his behalf. Since in psychoanalysis the analysand's ability to say whatever comes to mind is the fundamental rule, restrictions on the child's free speech can significantly compromise the treatment.

I find it best to emphasise the importance of the child's confidentiality to the parents while at the same time making sure the parents understand what kind of work I am doing with the child so that they do not prematurely terminate the analytic work. After all, in conducting analysis with children the analyst must handle not only the child's transference but also that of the parents and others involved in the case. I therefore try to adopt a stance in which, without giving them advice, the parents feel they are listened to and taken seriously. Of course, if a parent has her or his own demand for analysis she or he can be given a referral to another analyst. Thereafter, it is sometimes helpful to get updates from each parent in a way that honours the child's desire for their involvement in the treatment; after speaking with the child about his preferences, the analyst might speak to the parents on the phone at regular intervals or upon request or in person with the child or on their own. This can be especially helpful in instances in which the child is prone to leaving out significant events in his life or is not old enough to put them into words. Information from the parents about, for instance, a fight the child got into on the playground, can help the analyst highlight related aspects of the child's play on the occasion of the subsequent session.

In my experience, it is helpful to attend to the child's desire for treatment by asking at the first session's conclusion if he would like to come back. Sometimes I am more specific and add "to talk about" or "to work on" "your sister making you angry" or whatever specific signifiers have been uttered by the child about his troubles. If the answer is "yes," then this moment marks the child's demand for and initial investment in the treatment. Some analysts ask this question at the end of every session.

If the answer is "no", I prefer to enquire about the reasons for the child's refusal, which may assist in deciding how to respond. For example, the child might say "I am missing soccer practice now because of this", in which case the analyst could try to work with the child and parents to find an alternative session time. Alternatively, the child might say that it's embarrassing to talk about problems. In response, the analyst might acknowledge that it can be embarrassing but that oftentimes if children do not talk about them the problems do not get solved and can even get worse. In other words, the analyst does not take the "no" at face value.

Donald Winnicott's (2008) innovative work with the Piggle is a very good example of the importance of utilising the child's desire for analysis in the constitution of the analytic frame. Because the Piggle and her family lived too far to commute back and forth from their home to his office for regular sessions, Winnicott made it clear that the sessions would occur only upon the Piggle's request. In the intervals between sessions the parents wrote letters to Winnicott describing how the Piggle was doing. The Piggle knew about these communications and often sent drawings and messages of her own in the letters. She asked her parents to take her to see Dr Winnicott whenever she had some trouble about which she wanted to speak (and play). Although the case was criticised on account of it not being a "real" or "full" analysis, it was a successful treatment. Had the Piggle not been enlisted by Winnicott to request each session instead of the parents arranging meetings at regular intervals or in accordance with their desire, the outcome of the treatment may not have been as favourable. The analytic frame, then, should be adapted to the particular situation of each child. De-contextualised theoretical arguments about a universal meaning of "analysis" are beside the point.

Inventions

In children who are subjects (versus psychotic or as yet unformed), the in-between world of the session room is one in which the child's fantasy

($\$ \lozenge a$) (Lacan, 1963, p. 774) may appear in various play-acted scenarios. For example, a boy pretends he has found a magic wand (standing in for the phallus as *objet a*) which allows him to play the role of a powerful unbarred master. The child will also depict herself (perhaps through identifying with one of her characters) as the *objet a* (Lacan, 1961, p. 682) for her parent. For instance, a beautiful princess (ideal ego; Lacan, 1949, p. 94) gets lost in the forest and her distraught mother and father send out a search party for her (*objet a*) and even join in the search themselves. In her travels, she happens upon a bear cub who has lost its mother and she (ego-ideal; Lacan, 1961, pp. 667–683) helps reunite mother and cub. The analyst might intervene by highlighting the distress of the parents insofar as it is the fantasied answer to the question, "*Che vuoi*?" (Lacan, 1960, p. 815) of what does the Other want and can she or he afford to lose me? The child may feel in reality that her parents would not miss her enough if she were to become lost and so she play acts a wish fulfilment of being their irreplaceable lost object (*objet a*). In contrast, it may be that the child's fear of becoming lost belies a wish to become separated and independent from her parents, or that she wishes she could tell her parents to "get lost". The aim in working with child subjects, as with adults, is one of a *creative deconstruction*—to decrease the subject's alienation and invent solutions that allow the child to shift in her relationship to the Other (Lacan, 1959, pp. 547–553) and have some breathing room of her own.

On the other hand, in cases in which the child's structure has not yet been formed and there is a danger of psychosis, the analyst's work is one of a *creative construction*. Working within the narrative of the child's play, the analyst might help the child see the mOther as desiring and the law giving Other as existing and having authority. In cases in which the child seems to have no special place in the Other's heart, the work will centre around such a construction that is convincing to the child. In helping the child to construct a fantasy, we are isolating an *objet a* whose alternating presence and absence opens the way for the child's desire. In instances of already-formed psychosis, the analyst assists the child through the play in finding ways to stabilise his imaginary order and create a special place for himself.

Is scansion an appropriate aspect of the analytic frame when working with children? In terms of the "standard" frame, Lacan was famous for his variable-length session, such that each session is retroactively framed by the scansion or cut (Lacan, 1956, pp. 313–314). This element of surprise helps to capture something of the analysand's jouissance—or an element of non-meaning—in the last words that were spoken. Those last words, such as a previously unavowed desire, are highlighted by the cut and the analysand's unconscious is put to work.

School-aged children, like adults, are used to set times for events and even if they cannot yet "tell time", they will still ask "how much longer?" If the analyst practises fixed-length sessions with a child, there may be times when the last ten minutes, for example, consist of the child biding her time until she is allowed to leave. She may have become tired or hungry, and the analyst's demand that she continue to stay until the prescribed time has passed is not only fruitless in terms of the progression of the analysis but also an onerous demand akin to those placed on the child by various authoritative Others in her life. Even if the child analyst typically practises fixed-length sessions (in cases in which the child is more or less engaged during the entirety of the session), he might consider letting the child leave if she expresses a desire to do so. Of course, the analyst should always ask why the child wishes to leave at that moment, since there may be a desire hidden behind the demand, and it may end up that the child had wished to avoid symbolising something difficult but with the analyst's prompting is able to remain in the room and begin the work of symbolisation.

On the whole, scansions with children, as with adults, can be quite helpful. In work with older children who make significant use of speech during their sessions, scansion functions in much the same way. In work with younger children, highlighting via scansion for instance a key signifier or a manifestation of aggression does communicate its importance to the child, and the effects of the intervention are often detectible in subsequent sessions. That being said, children can be so engaged in their play, that they want to "finish the story" before leaving the room. It can be difficult for them to tolerate the abrupt nature of the scansion. Especially when working with children who have not yet achieved subjectivity or children who are psychotic, the aspect of surprise that goes along with scansion is not necessary (as the work is aimed toward construction instead of deconstruction) and can cause an excess of anxiety. In these cases, the analyst might suggest that a certain action in the play is important and seems to him to be a good note on which to end, but to then allow the child to quickly finish her narrative if she wishes or suggest that she remember where she left off so that she can continue from that point at the next session.

What happens during sessions? The child should be told at the first meeting that the analyst is interested in hearing about her problems, about troublesome thoughts or feelings, difficult events or interpersonal interactions, and dreams—even if they seem boring, not relevant, or only a few aspects of the dream are remembered. In the initial or preliminary sessions, whether the child is a subject, psychotic, or undergoing the process of structural formation, the analyst does a great deal of "listening" prior to making any substantive interventions. The analyst wants to get to know how the child sees herself, what or whom she wishes she were like, what she thinks her parents think about her and want for and from her, and her thoughts and feelings about each of her family members and other key figures in her life—friends, teachers, and foes. Depending upon the child's developmental level, she may symbolise her troubles through play or drawing in addition to speech, and the analyst intervenes through highlighting key signifiers in whatever form they are spoken or appear.

Especially when working with pre-adolescent children, many clinicians use board games or cards (Bellinson, 2002) employing the rationale that it brings into the session the child's relation to taking turns, winning, losing, and playing by the rules *vs.* creating their own rules. Nevertheless, playing these games typically involves a lot of concentration on something that does not have to do with putting the symptom into words. Although this is a tempting option when children do not seem to have much to say or when they complain of being bored, playing these games can stagnate the treatment because it significantly limits the amount of symbolic communication that occurs. Unlike playing make-believe with toys, in which the child creates a story and through that narrative stages aspects of his life—pairing symbolic communication with affective engagement—playing card and board games and the like with older children serves more to hinder symbolic articulation than to foster it. In my experience, it may sometimes become necessary with older children who do not offer much in the way of words to guess at what they are feeling, and offer it as a hypothesis with which they can agree or disagree and hopefully elaborate.

The contents of the child session room are a central part of the analytic frame insofar as the play items and how the child makes use of them are the stuff of signification, repetition, remembering, working through, and interpretation. In order to set the scene, the room should be furnished with child-friendly items such as blankets, sleeping bags, and child-sized chairs and a table. In the way of toys, the analyst should have a variety of items available from which the child may choose to express herself. To name a few main categories, toys should include human figures who may represent the child or individuals in her life, props related to the Law, to various types of jouissance (e.g., plastic food or play instruments), to illness, help, and healing, to the body's functions/drives (e.g., play poop), to communication (e.g., toy phones), props specific to the patient population (e.g., fake needles, pills, and pill bottles for children with relatives with substance abuse problems), dress-up clothes, toy animals, toy transportation methods, and art supplies. As I have alluded, certain types of toys correspond to crucial aspects of human experience that may come to the fore in the analytic work. It follows that having, for example, a full-length mirror available, is helpful in bringing out imaginary, symbolic, and real order experiences that correspond to Lacan's Mirror stage.

An important related question of the analytic frame is that of who cleans up the toys after the session. Cleaning up bears relevance to the position of the analyst and also to the specificity of the symptom of the child. When the child and the analyst clean up together, the child gets the message that the analyst wants her to be responsible for cleaning up her "mess"—perhaps both materially and psychologically. The desire of the analyst as Lacan understands it becomes compromised should the analyst implicitly request that the child "be good" by "cleaning up". Instead, the position of the analyst may be embodied by scheduling a few minutes in between sessions to clean up on his own. This, of course, also has effects on the treatment. For example, the child might express aggression toward the analyst by making a big mess and even might comment on how long it will take the analyst to clean it all up.

In playing with the child, the analyst enters the in-between space of the child's imaginary world. As depicted so well by the famous *"fort–da"* game (Freud, 1920g), this world is one in which even traumatic events can be re-enacted not only safely but with enjoyment. The game was invented by Freud's grandson at one and a half years of age in order to master the suffering that arose when his mother was occasionally absent. The boy played with a wooden reel with a string attached to it by holding onto the string while throwing the wooden reel over the edge of his curtained cot so that the reel disappeared. Then he uttered a sound "o-o-o-o" that resembled the German word *"fort"* which means "gone". Freud noted that his grandson experienced a kind of pleasure at this part of the game, which may have been that of mastering a traumatic loss over which the boy had no control. On occasion, the game progressed by the boy pulling in the reel by way of the string, upon which he triumphantly proclaimed "*Da*!", the German word meaning "there". In the game, the boy had the power to make the reel, standing in for the mother, reappear.

Through play, therefore, the child creates solutions to achieve mastery over her suffering. Relationship dynamics, key signifiers, and key themes related to the symptom are repeated again and again in the play narratives of the child. The analyst engages in the in-between make-believe world in a way that values the subjective truths being enacted there. As such, the analyst will find himself truly playing his part(s) by speaking in different play voices, walking differently, and so on. As Lacan said, the analyst "would do better to take his bearings from his want-to-be than from his being" (1958, p. 589), such that instead of being "himself" or being true to his personality, the analyst plays the role of the Other and speaks and acts within the symbolic axis.

The position of the analyst is at stake when the child makes demands or requests of the analyst. One such demand I frequently encounter is the child's request that the analyst display her drawing on the wall. This request often mirrors what a child has done at home. Either the child will ask her parent to put a drawing up on the refrigerator or in presenting the parent with a gift of a drawing, the parent responds by saying it is so good or special that he wishes to display it prominently in the house. The child through her request that the analyst display her drawing is seeing the analyst as an Other like a parent from whom she wants love. She is asking that the analyst think of her in between sessions when he looks at the drawing. What is more, insofar as the child is aware that the analyst also works with other children, her request likely has to do with rivalry. The child wants to have a special place in the heart of the analyst as Other. This in and of itself is nothing new; it is transference. However, in this case the child demands that the analyst show a proof of love.

Most importantly, if the analyst assents to the child's demand he will be giving an answer to *Che vuoi*? which diminishes his role as analyst and places him in a similar position as a parental Other. This, of course, is potentially detrimental to work with children who are subjects. On the other hand, for children who are in danger of becoming psychotic it may be temporarily stabilising to have the sense that they have a special place in the session room and that they exist for the analyst in-between sessions. Nevertheless, if an analyst says "yes" to one child, then other children will be upset if they are not allowed the same privilege.

If the analyst refuses to display the child's drawing on his wall, he might consider keeping a photo album with large photo sleeves in which to keep the drawings. The drawings, after all, symbolise the child's conscious and unconscious narrative and so perhaps their proper place is the in-between world of the session room. With this solution, the child can request to look back on previous drawings (and the analyst can reference prior drawings, for example by saying "This is like the dog you drew a few weeks ago, only this new one has a hurt leg") and also have the sense that the analyst thinks of the drawings as important and worthy of commemoration.

Whether handling this or other challenges, the child analyst adapts to the specificity of the case. Just as there is not a cookie-cutter analytic frame in our work with adults, neither is there such a rigid frame in our work with children. Psychoanalysis takes the individual as its starting point, and the conditions for the possibility of analytic work differ depending upon the child. Each psychoanalysis is the joint invention of the child and the analyst.

References

Bellinson, J. (2002). *Children's Use of Board Games in Psychotherapy*. New York: Jason Aronson.

Freud, S. (1911–1915 [1914]). Papers on Technique. *S.E., 12:* 85–174. London: Hogarth.

Freud, S. (1920g). Beyond the Pleasure Principle. *S.E., 18:* 1–64. London: Hogarth.

Greene, R. (2014). *The Explosive Child: A New Approach for Understanding and Parenting Easily Frustrated, Chronically Inflexible children*. New York: Harper.

Kazdin, A. (2009). *The Kazdin Method for Parenting the Defiant Child*. New York: Houghton Mifflin Harcourt.

Lacan, J. (1949). The Mirror Stage as Formative of the *I* Function as Revealed in Psychoanalytic Experience. In: *Écrits: the First Complete Edition in English* (pp. 75–81). B. Fink (Trans.). New York: W. W. Norton & Co., 2006.

Lacan, J. (1954). *Freud's Papers on Technique. The seminar of Jacques Lacan, Book I*. J. Forrester (Trans). New York & London: W. W. Norton & Co., 1991.

Lacan, J. (1955). Variations on the Standard Treatment. In: *Écrits: the First Complete Edition in English* (pp. 269–302). B. Fink (Trans.). New York: W. W. Norton & Co., 2006.

Lacan, J. (1956). The Function and Field of Speech and Language in Psychoanalysis. In: *Écrits: the First Complete Edition in English* (pp. 197–268). B. Fink (Trans.). New York: W. W. Norton & Co., 2006.

Lacan, J. (1958). The Direction of the Treatment and the Principles of its Power. In: *Écrits: the First Complete Edition in English* (pp. 489–542). B. Fink (Trans.). New York: W. W. Norton & Co., 2006.

Lacan, J. (1959). On a Question Prior to any Possible Treatment of Psychosis. In: *Écrits: the First Complete Edition in English* (pp. 445–488). B. Fink (Trans.). New York: W. W. Norton & Co., 2006.

Lacan, J. (1960). The Subversion of the Subject and the Dialectic of Desire in the Freudian Unconscious. In: *Écrits: the First Complete Edition in English* (pp. 671–702). B. Fink (Trans.). New York: W. W. Norton & Co., 2006.

Lacan, J. (1961). Remarks on Daniel Lagache's Presentation: "Psychoanalysis and Personality Structure". In: *Écrits: the First Complete Edition in English* (pp. 543–574). B. Fink (Trans.). New York: W. W. Norton & Co., 2006.

Lacan, J. (1963). Kant with Sade. In: *Écrits: the First Complete Edition in English* (pp. 645–670). B. Fink (Trans.). New York: W. W. Norton & Co., 2006.

Lacan, J. (1969). Note sur l'Enfant. In: *Autres Écrits*. Paris: du Seuil, 2001.

Lacan, J. (1974). *Le Seminaire XXI. Les non-dupes errant*. C. Gallagher (Trans.). Unpublished.

Winnicott, D. W. (2008). *The Piggle: An account of the Psychoanalytic Treatment of a Little Girl*. London: Penguin.

CHAPTER TWO

Transference in analytic work with children and adolescents: the space and time of demand

Hilda Fernández Alvarez

> [T]he analyst is he who sustains demand, not, as people say, to frustrate the subject, but in order to allow the signifiers with which the latter's frustration is bound to reappear.
>
> (Lacan, 2006, p. 516)

Coordinates

"Tell me how this therapy is different from others I have attended before?" Manuel, fourteen years old, for the third time starts the session with this question whose insistence lingers over a good portion of our meeting. Just before we start this session, I get a message from his mother who states her concern about Manuel not wanting to come back. During the session, he asks me to explain how this therapy is supposed to help him because he believes it is not. He compares it to the previous therapies in which his diagnosis ("anxiety disorder") was explained to him and suggestions on how to go about resolving it were provided. I ask him questions that enquire about the knowledge he has of his own symptom and the reasons he believes he is in this therapy. He reluctantly answers, protesting that I want to distract him so that he forgets his point. To my silences, he demands that I say something. He looks frustrated but remains responsive.

How do we conceptualise and handle the occurrence of demand, a central aspect of transference, in psychoanalytic work with children and adolescents? A "pressing exigency" (Lacan, 1960–1961, p. 189) that addresses someone, the place of demand is particularly challenging in the treatment of children and adolescents, as a result of the often cross-firing demands originating with those who bring the child to treatment.

Following Lacan in *Seminar XI* where he defines the unconscious as "a movement of the subject that opens up only to close again in a certain temporal pulsation" (Lacan, 1964–1965, p. 125), in this text I understand the unconscious as a topologic throbbing system that opens and closes in certain spatial-temporal coordinates to reveal its truth through slips of the tongue, dreams, parapraxes, jokes, and transference.

How do we situate the spatial-temporal conditions of the demand within transference, the object/subject polarity, and the conditions that open and close the unconscious with regard to the analytic work with children and adolescents?

In this chapter I reflect on some aspects of working with young subjects who presented with neurotic positioning. I will leave aside any discussion of psychotic or perverse subjective positions, as well as the treatment complexities of institutionalised children, as those vast themes exceed the limits of this chapter. With the help of some clinical vignettes and using four Lacanian constructions, I will approach the ways in which the unconscious manifests through transferential demand. First, I introduce the topological model of the Moebius strip, often referred to by Lacan, to explain the structure of the unconscious and how it reveals itself in language. Second, I use the L Schema, introduced in *Seminar III* (Lacan, 1955–1956, p. 14) to account for the four elements involved in the intersubjective dialectic. I will use the L Schema to instantiate the imaginary aspect of communication and its demand for symmetric satisfaction. Third, I will make use of the graph of desire, which Lacan presents in *Seminar VI* (Lacan, 1958–1959) to locate the places where the unconscious closes and opens. Finally, in the last section of this chapter, I will refer to Lacan's 1945 text "Logical Time and the Assertion of Anticipated Certainty: A new Sophism" (Lacan, 2006, p. 161), to illustrate the logical times in which the interpretation of demand arises.

I think that the conceptualisation of transference and its management with younger populations should observe the same theoretical principles as those observed with adult subjects, albeit the techniques utilised are diversified—play and art therapy, work with a third party, special attention given to flexibility and sensible tact, etc. I understand the work of the analyst/therapist as consisting of a presence that positions itself to listen and respond in such a way as to allow possible articulations of unconscious truth, so that the young subject emerges as a desiring subject. These interventions happen within a space and a time.

"Space is the everywhere of modern thought" (Crang & Thrift, 2000, p. 1). The social sciences influenced by structuralism have experienced a spatial turn that extends to our current moment. Such a spatial turn could not be more tangible than in Lacan's work and his development of psychoanalytic theory, as evidenced by his graph of desire, various schemas (L, R), mathemes (discourses), Borromean knots and topological models such as the torus, Moebius strip or Klein bottle. Such spatial representations involve an abstract, mathematical space, but they are in no way bereft of embodiment, as they are conceived originally as maps to approach the slippery subject of the unconscious within the analytic experience.

Lacan's core aphorism "the unconscious is structured like a language" engenders the topological concept of extimacy, which "is an inherently spatial process of psychical apprehension" (Kingsbury, 2007, p. 253).

Lacan utilises the Moebius strip as a model of the unconscious since "its outside continues its inside" (Lacan, 1964–1965, p. 156), a boundary that has no back and front, where the external/internal are not exclusive or distinct but rather continuous. If we think of the Moebius band as the surface of language threaded by the signifying chain, we can locate the spaces in which the subject of the unconscious arises in the course of an analysis. The unconscious is always accessible, as "it is in the surface that depth is being seen" (Lacan, 2006, p. 503), but is only apprehended in certain coordinates. The subject of the unconscious is constantly slithering through spacing and timing and in this chapter I aim to demonstrate how.

Transference

"Until next time" says Nieves, eight years old, smiling coquettishly after she has used the washroom at the end of a session. She has been drawing a layered picture where a devil is burning a hanging woman.

Later, when I need to use the washroom I find that Nieves has defecated in the paper bin instead of in the toilet.

Nieves is a girl with a very pretty face, vivacious eyes covered by glasses, and rosy cheeks. She is brought to treatment by the mother because both parents, separated but friendly to each other, are concerned about Nieves being highly dependent on the mother and extremely seductive toward the father. Nieves appears confident, gently controlling, and mature for her age; she complains about blushing often (erythrophobia) and about some interpersonal issues at school.

In the next session, Nieves puts music on and performs an intricate dance that she clearly has been rehearsing. After her dance, I tell her, "You brought me today this beautiful dance and last time you left me a piece of *caca*". By intervening in this way I wanted to bring into discussion, through a direct signifier, the residue left behind in the previous session while highlighting what appeared to be, in both instances, gifts addressing the analyst. Nieves looks at me defiantly and says "I did not do that" and changes the topic quickly, resisting bringing the theme into discussion for a number of sessions. How do we conceptualise the "weight of sexual reality" in this transference? (Lacan, 1960–1961, p. 155).

Transference for Freud has to do with repetition, love, and resistance (Freud, 1912b; Freud, 1915a). In Freudian terms, transference is a regression of the libido that revives unconscious portions of infantile complexes and then repeats them on the figure of the analyst. In children, clearly, these unconscious complexes—i.e., Oedipus, castration—are still in the course of being construed and therefore the possibilities of intervention are generally promising. Or to say it differently, the situation is hopeful when a young subject has the opportunity, early in their life, to (re)write part of their history, through analytic interventions, in order to reposition themselves in language and experience life in a less painful way.

There are abundant theoretical nuances regarding child transference in the literature from all schools of psychoanalysis. I approach child and adolescent transference as I do with adults, with the proviso that the work with young people often involves interviews with the child's caregivers and/or parents' which has effects upon and in the transference. Mathelin underlies the beginning of treatment as the privileged moment which brings up "the issue of demand and desire" within the transference "often present even before the first session" (Mathelin, 1999, pp. 22–23). Addressing transferential material with those significant others, in a best case scenario, will adduce some "passwords" or key signifiers and significations that have contributed, within the libidinal economy of the family, to the encryption of the symptom in the child's body. It is crucial to situate the child's place as object of love, desire, and jouissance for his parents and/or caregivers, as it indicates the discursive position of the young subject in relation to the symptomatic constellation in which he is involved.

Stavchansy summarises it beautifully:

> All subjects—whether girl or boy—"write" their singular version of jouissance, and in their relationship with the Other (familial and institutional), they occupy a position that articulates something of the jouissance that they obtain from the object, and from the jouissance that allows them to be the object for the Other. In this way the child counts himself, as singular, and different from all others. (Stavchansy, 2015, p. 21, my translation)

Freud works with transference love as a resistance, while recognising its "character of a 'genuine' love" (Freud, 1915a, p. 168). If every demand is a demand for love, how does that relate to resistance in treatment? In the clinical cases we are discussing, could we conceptualise Manuel's reluctance to talk and the "gift" from Nieves as demands for love? And if so, would that involve a manifestation of a resistance within transference? I will try to answer affirmatively to these questions in this chapter.

Dolto approaches transference in children this way:

> The ease with which the child begins to think, to live imaginatively with us, to release his internal world through his drawings, to recount his dreams, which he often tells his family he doesn't remember, to confess to mistakes, or to spontaneously tell us secrets that he never revealed to anyone before, this ease, this confidence are the basis of the therapeutic effect: this is what *transference means*. (Dolto, 1971, p. 113)

Lacan brings a *twist* to the concept of transference, as his unconscious is topologically hidden in language and we find a passageway through transference. In *Seminar XI*, Lacan defines the unconscious in relation to transference as: "That which is inside the subject, but which can be realised only outside, that is to say, in the locus of the Other" (Lacan, 1964–1965, p. 147). In front of another who is invested with knowledge—the subject supposed to know—the door of transference opens in the analytic work with children. Transference typically starts with the parents saying: "I don't know what to do with this child"; although children also establish transference with regards to knowledge, for example Nieves asks me: "What can I do not to blush anymore?" Let's see how demand landmarks the transferential openings.

Demand

Demand is a central concept in analytic treatment because it actualises transference love, situates desire and brings to the forefront resistances that pave the way to interpretation. The management of demand depends on the singular space and time in which it is asserted.

Apart from the obvious examples of schedule changing, reduction of fees, and so on, demand in the analytic sense extends its connotations to the subtle but structural requirements of intersubjective communication. Each of us demands by the very fact that we are immersed in language, and such demand asserts itself ultimately to prove we are beloved and worthy. Why not reassure such a needed thing within the analytic treatment?

Satisfying some demands is vital at times when the person is at risk of subjective destitution, suicide, psychotic breakdown or active trauma. But demand is ambivalent—while asserting it, the subject, in order to safeguard desire, does not really want the demand to be satisfied. Thus, whatever the analyst gives the analysand as a loving response would be ultimately dissatisfying.

While most subjects want the Other to satisfy their demand, so as to reassure their place as object of desire, such satisfaction both traps in a compulsion to repeat and alienates from the possibility of desiring as subject. As objects we cannot desire, we can only enjoy. Such is the impasse of desire as it is viewed by Lacan; the desiring subject realises that he "cannot reach this object [cause of desire] *as object*, except in some way by finding himself as subject, subject of the word", substituting himself for a signifier that is missing—the phallus (Lacan, 1958–1959, session of 1st January, 1959, my emphasis).

After several silences and questions, I offered Manuel an interpretation in the form of a question: "Maybe you want to know whether or not

I like you?" Manuel gave me a big smile and from his seated position on the couch tentatively lay down. I moved into the "analyst's chair" and he started laughing, surprised at the "crazy way" he was speaking after I invited him to free associate. Some aspects of the paralysing weight of the other's gaze emerged and it was the beginning of some important articulations about his symptom.

Albeit ambivalent, the subject compulsively demands by the very means of speaking. Lacan's L Schema elucidates how communication occurs when the sender receives back from the receiver his own message in an inverted form. In this schema we can locate the specular aspect of demand which stems from the Other but is articulated from the ego's locus.

The L Schema helps us in understanding how Manuel's demand unfolds:

- S (*Es*=Id): This locus designates the place of the subject of the unconscious and the inexhaustible insistence of the drives. In Manuel's case this could stand for his erotic body in adolescent metamorphosis rendered unutterable.
- a′ (*autre′*=small other): This space corresponds to the imaginary other addressed in communication. It could explain the place where Manuel positions the analyst to whom he demands a specific response. This demand masks a beyond that if satisfied would maintain the status quo.
- a (*autre*=Ego): This locus corresponds to the ego, where Manuel properly voices the demand to know. Such request aims to elucidate his

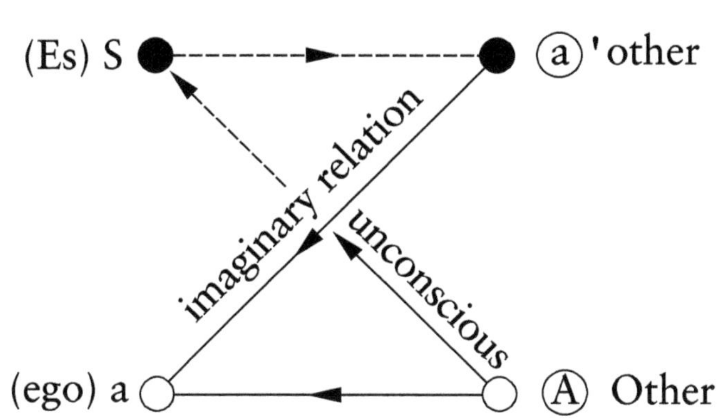

Figure 1. L Schema.

existence through a diagnostic category (anxiety disorder) as a way to reassure his being worthy of love.

- A (Discourse of the Other): Refers to the origin of the unconscious articulation of discourse. In Manuel's case, this place revealed an overwhelming object-gaze. Silencing the automatic response of *a′* allows a starting point for decoding (not repeating) the discourse of the Other (A).

Hence, as it happens in most analyses, Manuel reveals resistance through the transferential demand. By asking to be recognised as beloved, he attempts to suture the issue of his lack and to elude the questions of his castration complex. Had I satisfied such demand, the pressing issue of the Other's censoring gaze that hurdles his desire could not have been revealed.

Demand and the Other

Whereas need and object correspond (food to hunger, liquid to thirst, evacuation to intestinal pressure, etc.) object and drive are not coincidental (Freud, 1905d, p. 182). Hence, the drive aims at the pleasure of the organ (mouth pleasure, anus pleasure, genital pleasure, and so on) rather than at object of satisfaction. Demand then having dissociated itself from need, is intransitive; it does not aim at any specific object besides obtaining a proof of love from the other. Demand, Lacan says, is situated between love and desire (Lacan, 1960–1961, p. 198).

Demand articulates differently according to which representation of the drive insists (oral, anal, phallic, etc.) and what semblance of *objet a* is involved. At the level of the oral, a demand "to let oneself be fed" emerges from the Other and the child responds by asserting his demand to be fed (Lacan, 1960–1961, p. 201). This is exemplified by the typical phrasing of some parents when referring to their young children: "she does not *let me* feed her, unless …". The demand of the Other is inverted and appears, redoubled, as the baby's demand. Such a subtle, but powerful dialectic, will remain present in every intersubjective exchange.

At the level of the emergence of the anal object, the demand from the Other is educational, and asks the child "to hold in", to control and retain. The phallic demand from the Other asks the subject to be the phallic object to the Other's jouissance. In *Seminar X* Lacan adds the scopic and vocal dimensions to the list of the semblances of *objet petit a*. At the scopic level, it is the might of the Other that demands the desire of the subject, who consequently responds with an enduring insistence to be recognised. The vocal object *voices* its demands as superego proper and materialises through the incorporation of moral commands. It is important to note that in these "libidinal stages", the child represents himself in the Imaginary through these signifying objects that are located in the real register—breast, excrement, phallus, gaze, etc., thus, "above all he *is* these objects" (Lacan, 2006, p. 513).

In the case of a child, his desire expressed as the desire of the Other means here that the baby will want to be the absolute object for the mother and that he will also want what she wants. He is a little lover, passionately in love. But he is in love with a mother (to be understood as the primary caregiver) whose desire is overwhelming: "the mother's desire is not something that is bearable just like that, that you are indifferent to. It always wreak[s] havoc. A huge crocodile in whose jaw's you are—that's the mother" (Lacan, 1969–1970, p. 112).

Thus anxiety reveals itself when confronted with the giant "praying mantis" of the undecidable desire of the Other—another of Lacan's animalistic metaphors. The demanding nature of the Other might lead to anxiety as the Other's desire reveals no knowledge about "which object *a* I am for this desire", pushing the subject to question his position as desiring subject (Lacan, 1962–1963, p. 325).

In this way, demand brings to the forefront issues of object/subject positionality, which are relevant for the psychoanalytic treatment of anyone, but more so for children as the signifier *child* "is a site of hope and a locus of fear [therefore] childhood discourses and practices typically operate as moral forces of regulation" (Poyntz, 2013, p. 6). Children are among those preferred objects/bodies made docile through "the three great methods" of discipline posited by Foucault: "establish rhythms, impose particular occupations, regulate the cycles of repetition" (Foucault, 1975, p. 149), all implemented by institutional practices, specifically those of family, education and mental health.

Space markers: the graph of desire

Lacan's graph of desire can serve as a map upon which to locate how the subject emerges when demanding. The graph, as developed by Lacan in *Seminar VI* (Lacan, 1958–1959), could be thought of as made

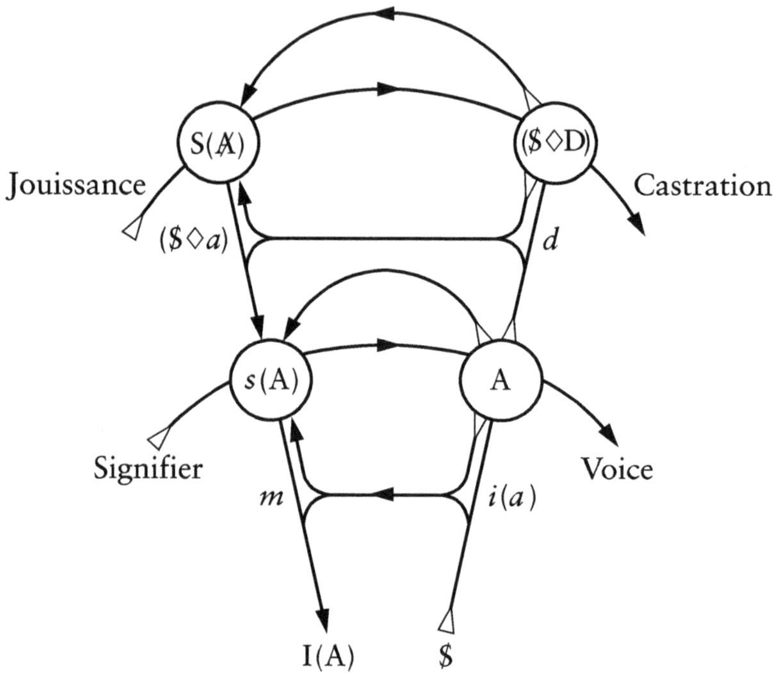

Figure 2. Graph of desire.

of Moebius lines whose circuits fire simultaneously when a subject speaks, unfolding multi directional lines that delimit the spaces that produce a psychic reality located in the registers of the Symbolic, Imaginary, and Real.

A very brief account of the above graph is needed to situate the place of demand in relation to the Other. The inner circuit of the first level in the above graph is parallel to the L Schema and situates the predominantly imaginary interchanges between the child's ego, the image of himself and his radical narcissistic identification with the other. The second level shows the signifying chain that goes, forward and retroactively, from s(A)—signifier of the Other—to (A) indicating the place where a subject articulates his statement (*enoncé*). The third level of the graph is the unconscious proper that goes, forward and retroactively, from S(Ⱥ)—lack of the signifier in the Other—to ($<>D)—the locus of the drive—where demand is articulated. This vector indicates that the signifying system is lacking and therefore the subject appears hidden in the enunciation (*énonciation*). This lack of consistency in the Other, which leaves the subject unsure of what he is for the Other, prompts the articulation of a demand ($<>D). Such demand has historically emerged from the Other, and as a result, will conform to a lexicon of enjoyment that lacks signification and leads the subject to respond with fantasy ($<>a) and with the insistence of demands that harbour a desire impossible to be fully articulated.

An element of utmost importance to the understanding of the graph as an effective map of the appearance of the subject of the unconscious is the recognition of the way in which the temporal pulsation—opening/closing of the unconscious—makes such a subject disappear in the statement (*enoncé*) while appearing in the enunciation (*énonciation*). Such a dialectic of subjective presence and absence is in direct relation to a certain timing which will be discussed in the next section.

The action of Nieves—leaving a piece of excrement exposed to my gaze—is formulated as an acting out in demand of interpretation, whose clarification took us a number of months and involved some work with the mother. I learned that Nieves had done the same at home a couple of times. Acting out, Lacan tells us, is "wild transference" and therefore calls for interpretation (Lacan, 1962–1963, p. 125).

Nieves' demand can be located in the upper right side of the graph ($<>D). The demand here is not mediated by the word or the imaginary/symbolic communication, but rather stems from the Real (a body residue, with no agency, confronts the gaze of the analyst). Nieves, as subject, was hiding and thus the demand required to be answered, albeit in a different way altogether than in Manuel's case.

While in the lower vector (statement) Nieves presented as pleasant and seductive, "see you next time" hiding her true intention, on the upper vector (enunciation) this young subject of the unconscious speaks through her action and leaves behind a remainder of her own body—*objet petit a*—demanding to be interpreted.

Previous to the session I am discussing, Nieves' transference had appeared "positive" for a number of months. She enjoyed attending sessions, was pleasing and tried to soften her evident push for control. But then after this event, she brought out some hostility towards the therapist through judgmental remarks about the therapist's style and taste in decorating the office. The elucidation of Nieves' demand/acting out was informed by several determinants. The mother was very invested in finding a romantic relationship but had not been successful;

Nieves consequently played the part of the ideal ego, admired for her intelligence, confidence and beauty. At the same time, identifying hysterically with the mother and wishing to provoke a "masculinity" in the father, who was perceived as passive and weak, Nieves histrionically embodied the (little) woman her mother was desiring to be, and she played this out with the father in a very "traditional" oedipal situation.

Nieves' acting out is framed within the anal, phallic and scopic demands. The therapeutic work produced an articulation of this event as:

- The girl's demand for space as subject. Trapped as an imaginary phallus (-phi) in the intense parental demand for love, the young subject was overwhelmed by her own seductive and domineering drives; also, by the phallic image she identified with for the parents, resulting in hardly bearable feelings of hate and social inadequacy. Her material residue constituted the symbolisation of a needed limit—psychical distance from her parents—to alleviate the pressure of such demands.
- The piece of excrement was a contravention of the prescription "hold in", to be in control, to talk mainly about "good things", which appeared to be the mother's demand. This protest was transferred to the figure of the therapist in the following sessions, allowing work on her hostile tendencies.
- Leaving for the therapist what could be read as a gift from her own self, Nieves repeated her compulsion to seduce at the same time that she demanded to be loved. She told me once that she would be a treasure or a trophy if she were an object. "Oblativity is an obsessional fantasy" (Lacan, 1962–1963, p. 321). My bringing her action into question brought about the articulation of hate tendencies that were for her unacceptable and central to her enjoyment. We discovered an obsessive element emerging within a young hysteric subjective position.

Timing

As I have tried to demonstrate, there is a "law of placement" in transference, to use a Bahktinian concept (Holloway & Kneale, 2000, p. 74), but also a specific timing. When Lacan discusses the presence of the analyst, as cause of the unconscious, he clarifies how transference and interpretation are paradoxical. The temporal pulsation of the unconscious opens through transference but interpretation closes it up again (Lacan, 1964–1965, p. 131).

The interpretation of demand arises within a specific logical time. Lacan uses a new sophism through which he exemplifies points of doubt and certainty, processes of verification that will conclude in an action (Lacan, 2006, p. 161). He proposes these logical times that he also calls scansions or hesitations: the instant of the glance (fulguration time, the moment of "insight"); the time for comprehending (meditation, hypothesis, and intuition), and the moment to conclude (assertion of oneself in the making of a judgement).

The last piece of case material I want to use here illustrates how logical time operates within the interpretation of demand. I see Mandy for only three sessions. She is twenty-eight months old, and is brought to therapy a few months after her baby brother was born. Mandy regularly pinches her little brother's face and body resulting in the baby's crying and the interruption of his sleep. The mother is exhausted and is asking me to help. In the first session, after tentatively touching some toys, Mandy handles a doll, she touches it carefully, almost caressing, and then rapidly pinches the doll's nose. I asked her "what is that?" and she repeats the action several times saying "this, this, this" and then adds in a baby's angry voice: "So he has a *dood* [good] reason to cry." She plays with other toys and at some point brings the same doll and places my hand on the doll's body, saying "Pinch him". I do not move, gauging how to react, while she persists in demanding that I pinch the doll. I hesitate in complying but remain calm asking her to "tell me Mandy, what you want me to do to the doll?" She starts crying very profusely and calls her mother very loudly. I invite the mother to enter the play room and Mandy sits in her lap and cuddles with her, looking at me, from time to time, with an upset demeanour, asking that they leave, which we both agree in doing, arranging another session in two days. At the next session Mandy appears content. We play ball, draw a bit and all of a sudden she appears to have realised that I am pregnant. She looks at my belly and I say "You are looking at my body". She continues gathering some toys and after a few minutes says "big belly" and she smiles covering her mouth as if she was mocking me. I asked her if she remembers her mummy's belly when she was pregnant but she does not answer. She lines up about five dolls and pinches them all over their bodies, then places my hand on the doll's belly while saying "do it". I ask her "what for?" and she continues saying "do it". Fearing another scene that would interrupt our session, I softly touch the doll's body and she, in an authoritarian voice, says "sweet and gentle". At the third session, Mandy appears happy to be there and walks around the playroom confidently. During an active game consisting in running around to meet in the middle of the room, she slaps my belly playfully. I remark on this and she keeps doing it, alternating the playful tapping on my belly with the gentle repetition of a softer "sweet and gentle". The mother cancelled the next two sessions informing me that the problem had disappeared. I would say that Mandy's frustrated demand resulted in:

- A movement that surpassed the imaginary request of symmetry—"do it!"—permitting the emergence of a certain symbolic authority, with which she had identified through her father, but which was temporarily absent as the father had become disinterested in the family, overwhelmed by the birth of an unplanned second child.
- Mandy's jouissance, a profound jealousy of her baby brother that reminds us of Lacan's intrusion complex (Lacan, 1938, p. 23), was therefore limited with the analytic intervention. Such a limit relocates authority; she moves from a jouissance, imaginarily engendered, towards the assertion of a symbolic law.
- In this way, Mandy also could tolerate ambivalence as she exemplified in the playful approach to the therapist's pregnant belly.

When demand appears within analytic transference—and by that I mean addressing someone invested with the subject-supposed-to-know who can listen and receive it analytically—the subject will face a cut in the signifying chain, an instantaneous glance which reveals a realisation that something of the unconscious has opened. In the case of Manuel this moment coincides with his smiling at my interpretative question; in the case of Nieves with the moment in which I bring into the dialogue the residue she left behind; with young Mandy it is the moment I refused to pinch the doll. The instant of the glance typically encounters a resistance to analysis and consequently closes the unconscious.

The time for comprehending allows the analysis of those frustrations in relation to the subject's enjoyment, love, and desire. The analytic aim then is to dialectically reduce the moment of comprehending to the moment of conclusion, which precipitates an act. Such an act is not a disarticulated impulse, but rather a return to another fulguration moment in which the subject grounds his subjectivity by acting upon his desire. The moment to conclude is not the "I got it" of a notional insight, but rather the embodiment of a disclosed unconscious truth elevated to an act of subjective assertion.

In the case of Manuel, his moving to the couch opened the possibility to interpret his demand, yet he is still working to find a way to assert himself in view of his history and the internalised judgemental gaze of the Other. With Nieves the time to comprehend took a number of months and her resistance to talk about the "gift" was intense. She was not able to reach any conclusion, specifically about the self-identified symptom of erytrophobia, until the mother started her own therapy and Nieves could reposition herself in the family dynamic. In the case of Mandy, the moment to conclude appears to be when she is able to incorporate a boundary to her own jouissance through the saying "sweet and gentle".

Thus, timing refers to the way unconscious phenomena rise in certain discursive loci bringing about an enigma that questions the subject in his act. No one is ever too young to elude the questions related to how to act as subject with regard to those traumatic aspects of the repetition of the Real.

Final observations

In this chapter my aim was to discuss the analytic conceptualisation and management of demand in the treatment of children and adolescents, therefore it was important to focus on the child's psychic reality rather than on the more complex mode of relations within a social environment. Responding to demands is hardwired into our social make up and therefore the analyst has to rely on her desire, as analyst, rather than on her set of social and moral values to intervene. The analyst is aware that the opacity of the subject's desire is contingent on his radical demand to be recognised and loved, and that it is the ultimate analysis of this demand which will make possible the assertion of a subjective desiring act. If the resistance to analysis is mainly on the side of the analyst, the desire of the analyst—to take the analysis to its last consequences—will be what allows the event of the analysis to take place under the ethical principles from which it obtains its therapeutic power.

References

Crang, M., & Thrift, N. J. (Eds.) (2000). *Thinking space*. London: Routledge.

Dolto, F. (1971). *Psychoanalysis and Paediatrics: Key Psychoanalytic Concepts with Sixteen Clinical Observations of Children*. F. Hivernel & F. Sinclair (Trans.). London: Karnac, 2013.

Foucault, M. (1975). *Discipline and Punish: The Birth of the Prison*. A. Sheridan (Trans.). NY: Vintage 1995.

Freud, S. (1905d). *Three Essays on the Theory of Sexuality*. *S. E., 7*: 123–243. London: Hogarth.

Freud, S. (1912b). The dynamics of transference. *S. E., 12*: 97–109. London: Hogarth.

Freud, S. (1915a). Observations on transference-love. *S. E., 12*: 157–171. London: Hogarth.

Holloway, J. & Kneale, J. (2000) Mikhail Bakhtin: Dialogics of Space. In: M. Crang & N. Thrift (Eds.). *Thinking space* (pp. 71–88). London: Routledge.

Kingsbury, P. (2007). The extimacy of space. *Social & Cultural Geography, 8*(2): 235–258.

Lacan, J. (1955–1956). *The Seminar of Jacques Lacan Book III The Psychoses*. J. -A. Miller (Ed.) & R. Grigg (Trans.). NY: Norton, 1997.

Lacan, J. (1958–1959). *The Seminar of Jacques Lacan Book VI Desire and Its Interpretation*. C. Gallagher (Trans.). Acessed 10th February, 2016, available at: http://www.lacaninireland.com/web/wp-content/uploads/2010/06/Book-06-Desire-and-its-interpretation.pdf.

Lacan, J. (1960–1961). *The Seminar of Jacques Lacan Book VIII Transference*. J. -A. Miller (Ed.) & B. Fink (Trans.). MA: Polity, 2015.

Lacan, J. (1962–1963). *The Seminar of Jacques Lacan. Book X Anxiety*. J. -A. Miller (Ed.) & A. R. Price (Trans.). NY: Polity, 1998.

Lacan, J. (1964–1965). *The Seminar of Jacques Lacan. Book XI The Four Fundamental Concepts of Psychoanalysis*. J. -A. Miller (Ed.) & A. Sheridan (Trans.). NY: Norton. 1998.

Lacan, J. (1969–1970) *The Seminar of Jacques Lacan Book XVII: The Other Side of Psychoanalysis*. J. -A. Miller (Ed.) & R. Grigg (Trans.). NY: Norton. 2007.

Lacan, J. (2006). *Écrits*. J. -A. Miller (Ed.) & B. Fink (Trans). NY: Norton.

Mathelin, C. (1999). *Lacanian Psychotherapy with Children. The Broken Piano*. S. Fairfield (Trans.). NY: The Other Press.

Poyntz, S. (2013). Eyes wide open: stranger hospitality and the regulation of youth citizenship. *Journal of Youth Studies*. Accessed on 20th February 2013.

Stavchansy, L. (2015). *Autismo y Cuerpo. El lenguage en los trazos de la perfeccion*. Mexico: Paradiso Editores.

CHAPTER THREE

Seminars on child psychoanalysis

Françoise Dolto

with translation and introduction by Olga Cox Cameron

Introduction

"The best-known psychoanalyst in France." Elisabeth Roudinesco, the historian of French psychoanalysis, has no hesitation in according this title to Françoise Dolto and not to Lacan. And yet, with the exception of *Dominique* and a couple of other books, not much of her work has been translated into English. Her weekly radio programmes and her highly readable books and recordings made her a household name in France in the seventies, eighties, and beyond, although she was by no means an establishment figure in the wider psychoanalytical community. Following the investigation by the IPA (International Psychoanalytical Association) in 1953 of those analysts who had split from the SPP (*Société Psychanalytique de Paris*), Winnicott who interviewed her, while deeming her to be thirty years ahead of her time, was negative. His report states that "her patients and students were entering into an uncontrolled—and consequently—harmful transference with her, that she had too much intuition and not enough method to be a training analyst, and finally that she ought to be kept at a distance from the young lest she "influence them" (Roudinesco, 1986, p. 319).

The seminar excerpts presented here allow us to see that Winnicott was not wrong in recognising her formidable intuition, something we lesser beings cannot aspire to. But they also permit us to see that this extraordinary clinical intuition is based on a close respectful listening as well as a clear-eyed recognition that sometimes psychosis can be the only valid exit for a child faced with certain familial impasses.

Given how often psychoanalysts fall into transferential traps and become locked into political splits, Dolto presents as an exceptionally independent thinker. Born into the *haute bourgeoisie* in 1908, in the eyes of her family her path seemed clear. Music, cookery, and housework were acceptable interests for a girl. She managed under this regime to train as a nurse, but her insistence on sitting the *Baccalauréat* and commencing medical studies rendered her "unmarriageable" and caused so much bitterness that she was obliged to leave home and work as a nurse to pay for her studies.

Her psychoanalytic lineage links her with France's first psychoanalysts. In 1934 she began analysis with Jules Laforgue and her medical thesis, later published as *Psychanalyse et Pediatrie* was supervised in 1939 by Pichon, co-author with Damourette of the article on Negation so often cited by Lacan in his seminars. At about this time she began to practise as an analyst, specialising in children and psychotics. Horrified at what she saw in psychiatric hospitals as a student and by the hierarchical jostling of the medical profession, Dolto preferred to remain an outsider and for thirty-eight years ran a weekly clinic at the Hôpital Trousseau but was never on their payroll. In 1938 she came upon Lacan's work on "Family Complexes" (Lacan, 1938) and later attended his seminar at the Hôpital Sainte Anne. They became lifelong friends and she supported him over many decades in his successive battles. It is said that he would regularly send her the analysands and supervisees he found too hard to handle. According to Dolto herself they were never close, but she was very appreciative of the fact that Lacan's analysands worked better with children than those of any other Parisian analyst (Dolto, 1989, p. 149). Unsurprisingly this admiration in no way compromised her staunch independence of spirit. In 1979, a row which involved Michèle Montrelay's proposal to hold a seminar on male sexuality, and categorically refused by Lacan, saw Dolto siding against him, and rather acidly suggesting that in a society of analysts one should not have to ask "daddy" for authorisation to act. According to Roudinesco Lacan got up in a fury and left in silence (Roudinesco, 1986, p. 650).

As you will see in these excerpts from the "Seminars on Child Psychoanalysis", Dolto is a clinician. Like Winnicott she believed that psychoanalytically informed intervention in early childhood can prevent later troubles. To this end she founded the Maison Verte in 1979, an informal meeting place where parents and children could spend time and which functions as an intermediary space between the family and the wider socialised world. Her books and her radio programmes reflect this same very practical application of psychoanalysis to immediate difficulties; in many instances offering parents the possibility of finding a way forward, but even more strikingly, when this is impossible giving to the child the necessary tools to tolerate or exit certain impasses.

Simone Weil defined prayer as "attention". This is what Dolto brings to the psychoanalytic encounter. One never meets "the" obsessional or "the" psychotic in her work, but only and always a speaking subject whose speech may be warped by a suffering which is nonetheless somewhere inscribed in it. As practitioners of the talking cure, we have at least as much to learn from seeing Dolto in action as we have from the great theoreticians.

References

Dolto, F. (1989). *L'Autoportrait d'une psychanalyste, 1934–1988*. Paris: Coll. "Points", Le Seuil, 1992.

Lacan, J. (1938). Les Complexes Familiaux dans la Formation de l'individu. Paris: Navarin, 1984.

Roudinesco, E. (1986). *Jacques Lacan & Co.: A History of Psychoanalysis in France, 1925–1985, Vol. 2*. J. Mehlman (Trans.). Chicago: University of Chicago Press; London: Free Association Books, 1990.

Extracts from seminars on child psychoanalysis*

From seminar 1: "Childs play"

PARTICIPANT: When a child asks me to play with him, what should be my position?

FRANÇOISE DOLTO: If it is he who is in charge of the game, what does he ask to play?

PARTICIPANT: It is very often this game with two letters and hyphens.

FRANÇOISE DOLTO: One letter is you, one letter is himself, and he establishes a hyphen between the two.

PARTICIPANT: Or else he asks riddles: "What is it that is green?" or "Who hangs out of trees?" Should I answer?

FRANÇOISE DOLTO: Say to him, "What should I answer? I am not here to play."

---

*Editors' note: we have extracted four segments from the first two seminars on child psychoanalysis and sub-titled them in order to allow each segment to be read coherently "outside" of the dialogue of the original piece.

PARTICIPANT: He says, "You don't want to answer."

FRANÇOISE DOLTO: "No, I don't want to answer. You do not pay me to answer you, and I do not pay you to answer me. I am paid to listen to what is going badly for you. Is it that you can't play with anyone?" Very often, children take a doll and play, doing both roles themselves, mother and child.

PARTICIPANT: True, they end up playing alone, but it is very stressful.

FRANÇOISE DOLTO: The stress is that of resisting the erotisation. But there are games of shop which are very important because they are oral and anal games. For example, if a girl says to you, "I'll be the butcher", that is exactly why she comes to you because that is what she is, blocked, and you will be the customer.[1] "Now Madam, what do you want?" I respond like a character out of Molière, saying in a low voice, "What should I say?" She: "You say, you want two slices of this". Then you say in a monotone: "I want two slices of this". Exactly what she has said to you, without the addition of any affect of your own. Then you say again in a low voice and in an aside: "What should I say? What would a customer say", you explain to her, "But I am a stupid customer, you tell me what to do". Bit by bit the scene will progress. In the end, she will be creating the game while using you, the analyst, to express what this game with herself signifies. It is always an oral and anal game. Very often there is no payment. The shopkeeper is happy to sell her goods, but the customer goes off without paying.

Many children will not tell you that you should pay. So, it is for you to say, after some time, "Do you think this is what happens with real shopkeepers?" By introducing payment and the value of money you teach the child that nothing is free. It is a game which opens on to others things. I remember one little girl who used to say to me. "The customer always takes this many portions." I asked her, "Why does she take that number of portions? For whom?" and she said, "It's for her husband", I answered: "How many children does she have?" There was always a portion missing for one child. In fact, she was casting the customer in the role of her mother. There were four children in reality, but she always bought portions for three only. It was the customer who was responsible for not wanting the youngest little brother to live (a responsibility she transferred on to me as customer).

It (the game) can represent the point of departure for an underlying association which is to be decoded, or on the other hand, it can be a denial of reality. It is always the same task when reality forces the subject to block off his imaginary life. He cannot go on, but becomes a being who has totally submitted to the wishes of his educators and is no longer truly living.

On the other hand, if his imaginary life has taken over and denies reality he can no longer adapt to everyday life which simultaneously requires a sense of reality and the preservation of the imaginary life which surrounds it like a nimbus.

Our task always is to put at the disposal of the child easily understood symbolic expressions which will allow him to encounter other human beings with whom he can communicate when this is not happening in his own circle.

For example, a baby cannot communicate as fully as he might like with his mother. We have had proof of this at the Maison Verte which is a place where small children socialise.

The babies there communicate with each other far more than with their mothers, and with such delight! They need this communication which is specific to them since they are tuned into the same auditory register, and, doubtless, to the same fantasies. Several times we have observed mothers, jealous of their three-month-old babies who are lying on the floor side by side cooing at each other.

It is quite extraordinary: as soon as a mother tries to join in, the babies immediately fall silent. It proves that at their level of human evolution babies have ways of communicating fantasies which their mothers forbid them already without realising it. Because the mothers require them to be in the Real while they need to communicate fantasies. Or because the mothers impose their own fantasies on them which are not the fantasies of babies with other babies.

In these games of shop, these games which involve complicity, what is the child seeking? He is looking for someone at his own level. It is for us to place ourselves there but without bringing our own fantasies into play. We must maintain the position of analyst who seeks to discover where the child is denying reality, or on the contrary where the child is too much in a reality which obliges him to be sadistic in the same manner as the world around him.

"The role of the child psychotherapist"

PARTICIPANT: **Basically, how would you define the role of a child psychotherapist?**

FRANÇOISE DOLTO: Our role consists in validating the desire which is expressed, and in seeking to discover what the child is in the process of repeating concerning this desire, which he has not been able to express in his daily life in his own milieu. We must also discover the affects surrounding desires which have been repressed because of a Super-ego imposed by educational forces. If its affects cannot find expression either directly or indirectly, this desire will disturb both somatic and mental functioning in the child, and will create anxiety. This is exactly the schema set forth by Freud in *Inhibition, Symptoms and Anxiety.* In a child, inhibitions can go so far as to stop growth and interfere with vital processes. Our role is to restore this circuit. Certainly not to normalise, which is meaningless.

Above all, it consists in allowing this Imaginary and this Real which are contradictory to find expression and to co-exist more or less peacefully. For all of us the task is to assume this Imaginary and this Real and we do so via the symbolic life which is not simply and only verbalised. Everything is language.

From seminar 2: "The child as symptom ..."

PARTICIPANT: **When a child is a symptom of his parents, should one take him into therapy and send his parents to other psychoanalysts? Or should one rather commence therapy with each of the three of them?**

FRANÇOISE DOLTO: The parents should go to see other therapists. Otherwise in the unconscious of the child's analyst, the parents will meet up with each other as if they were somehow twinned with their child. This would be very bad.

If the parents themselves need to be treated it is because in producing this child they have seriously disturbed him by transferring on to him their own earliest lived experience. It is a transference relation instead of a true relationship. When this happens, because the real-life parents are playing out a falsified object—relation by repeating their past upon their child, it is necessary for the psychoanalyst to listen to them in the interests of the child in order to get an idea of the projections to which the child is subjected in his or her day-to-day upbringing.

But the psychoanalyst must never involve herself with the child's upbringing in the present. The analytic focus is on drives from the past, on body—images from an earlier era. The analyst is there only to facilitate the transference from the past and to allow some kind of catharsis of current repressions.

Certainly it is a question of facilitating the return of the repressed in the patient, so that it can be "catharsised" thus allowing the aggressivity which cannot be sublimated to be expressed in words. This process eases the inhibition of the other drives insofar as they are susceptible to sublimation outside the framework of the treatment.

This is why the parents, since they constitute the real milieu of the child, can stand in need of help in order to live through their child's return to health. Indeed the parents, having without realising it spent years living with a problem which they have themselves created in their child, can find themselves in a strange state of renewed suffering in their bodies and in their relationship once these problems disappear.

Obviously you cannot say to the parents in the first session that the child is their symptom. They come in good faith bringing a child which they and their society fear is disturbed, because he or she is disruptive in school, or because physically he or she suffers from functional problems: problems of language, of motor function, anorexia, encopresis, enuresis, stammering, etc. The role of the psychoanalyst is first of all to meet with the parents, allowing plenty of time especially the first time. Then to see the parents and child together allowing all of them to express themselves freely. Finally to see the child first with one parent then with the other.

If it is really a case of the child as symptom this will become obvious. Either the child will be completely uninterested in these interviews, will leave the room, allowing the parents to become aware of their own difficulties or else the child will ask his parents to leave, and the upset parents will need help in coping with this sudden weaning and the independence which their child has demonstrated.

This is why I say that one should first be a psychoanalyst working with adults before becoming a child psychoanalyst.

Otherwise one cannot understand that the suffering projected on to a child since birth which makes her the symptom of her parents, itself implies the parents' need for treatment, and that is precisely what they are seeking through the medium of their child. It is surprising to hear many child psychoanalysts who are not psychoanalysts working with adults say: "Poor child, with a mother and father like that" or "the child must be got away from that mother", or "this man is not a father", etc.

They are expressing a massive negative transference on to the parents which results from their own anxiety as therapists, and which means that it would be impossible for them to work with this family.

The public authorities, by which I mean their representatives, are not psychoanalysts, and this is why they have set up consultations for children, assuming that children can be treated for their inability to adapt to society without the involvement of their parents. As a result these consultations set up to treat children quickly reach an impasse.

It is all the more surprising in view of the fact that the law makes parents responsible for their children for a longer time nowadays than heretofore since the young are not expected to work until they are at least sixteen and have no means of escape from potentially harmful family surroundings other than delinquency.

As regards the forcible separation of a child from his or her parents by the authorities as in the placing of a child in care, or because parents sign away their rights, the after-effects of this type of separation will very seriously mark the life of the child and also his or her future descendants.

Parents and children can be helped separately and together to understand the necessity of separating from each other, and can with the support of therapists, approach the social services of their own free will, in order to avail of whatever resources they need to do this. But this decision should never be taken by someone outside the family group.

I want to go back to something I was saying about the negative transference of many therapists towards what they call "bad parents".

I will give you an example. If the child comes into the session with a little car saying it is broken or with her doll saying "she gets on my nerves all the time. She wets the bed, she bites everyone, she won't sleep, she won't eat, etc.", would you take care of the car or the doll and tell the child's parents they had better get her another car or another doll and give these toys to some other child since this one is unable to look after them properly?

This rather absurd example more or less illustrates the well-intentioned attitude of these therapists. This holds true for children up to the age of six or seven, ill because of projections on the part of parents who are themselves neurotic, or have returned to a celibate state and are at war with each other *via* the child.

Beyond the age of seven or eight, after a certain number or interviews with the parents and with the child, the therapist can recognise whether the child wants help for himself independently of the parents. As a result of their interviews with the psychoanalyst who should be as positively disposed towards them as towards the child, the parents often become aware of their own need for help. At this point the psychoanalyst should convey to them that she can only take on one member of the family since it is not possible to have several members of the family in therapy together.

If it is only the child who is seeking help, it is possible to establish a therapeutic contract with him even if the parents have not yet decided to undertake their own analysis; it is perfectly possible for the child to start personal work on his own. The repercussions of this work will have a liberating effect on the parents if the child succeeds in finding his or her place in society but this will not happen without a backlash of anxiety.

This is where the psychoanalyst needs to be sufficiently human not to become locked into an attitude which radically excludes the parents. The difficulties experienced by the parents because of the child's therapy—psychological difficulties or problems of temperament—will drive the child himself to ask the therapist to respond to the parent's request for an interview.

This request is similar to the case conferences required by institutions where there are children from the institution in therapy.

Obviously at this point there is no question of seeing the parents without the child, but there is nothing to prevent an interview with the child present in order to hear what they have to say. Family meetings like this can allow parents to take the measure of the positive transformations in their child. But these transformations also create suffering in the parents, since they can see the help which the child requires of them and which they are unable to give her. The psychoanalyst reflects back what each one is saying, thus opening up communication in the family which can be continued outside of the interview. This is important because when a therapeutic contract is set up between a child and the therapist with the consent of the parents, it can happen that the parents and the child stop talking to each other about the problem at issue as if the psychoanalyst had ousted the parents from their position as educators.

These meetings allow the therapist to make it clear that the day-to-day care of the child is entirely in the hands of the parents (at the moment when the therapeutic contract was set up with the child the parents may not have been able to grasp this).

It should be repeated at these meetings that the parents are the primary educators and that they remain entirely free in their attitudes and in their statements *vis- à-vis* this child.

In actual fact the growing number of consultations for child guidance give parents the impression that therapy has replaced parental upbringing. It is our task as psychoanalysts to redress this imbalance and when treating a child to refuse the role of educator or pedagogic counsellor with the parents. I want to emphasise that I am speaking here of children over age seven who have personally entered into a contract with the analyst and commenced treatment.

Sometimes an incident which occurs in the transference can cause a child to forget the conditions of her contract even though these were clearly spelt out to her and to her parents at the beginning of treatment.

The anxiety and the negative reactions of the parents which necessitate these meetings are sometimes brought about because the child enacts upon the parents the negative transference which she doesn't bring to the sessions.

How often do we hear parents tell us in the course of these meetings that every time something unpleasant for the child happens at home she resorts to roaring: "I'll tell my analyst". It is only on hearing this that one realises how inhibited these parents can feel in their reactions *vis-à-vis* their child because of this threatening and fantasy laden cry.

Let us beware of seductive transferences from the child which put us in the place of the parents in fantasy. But are these so very different from the transferences of married men or women who make use of their fantasy relation with us, the therapist, in order not to have relations with their real partner, and even create a break-up because of love for their analyst.

With children as with adults, perhaps even more so with children because of the absence of the genital sexual relation necessary for the body, one must be vigilant lest in the name of transference a perversion of family relations should occur—or indeed for that matter a perversion of the analytic relationship.

Another problem to watch out for in your analytic listening to the parents, is the possible resemblance of this child to people whom the parents dislike in real life. It is extremely important to verbalise this for the child. "You look like Aunt Thingy whom your mother cannot abide.

You are going to have to surmount this handicap. You have her eyes, her face, spiky hair like hers." Once it has been put into words, it becomes a reality and children can take it on board and cope with it. While it remains unsaid, children don't really feel like themselves because a whole part of their being disappears on account of their resemblance to something in the body of the other which the mother, for whatever affective reasons, cannot endure.

This happens too in the unconscious of adoptive children: they have to surmount the handicap of not being the flesh—and—blood children of their parents. For this reason they do their best to resemble them, especially when they are small.

A little boy whom I saw recently said to me: "You see, because I didn't grow in my mummy's tummy she wants me to be even more like my dad because she loves him." He was in the middle of the Oedipus complex and very jealous, but he still wanted to be like his father. In resembling him he could compete with him in order to possess the mother. Every kind of imitation via partial objects served his purposes—tics, obsessions, everything he could lay hold of. Up until the day when the psychoanalyst said to him that he seemed to believe that his adoptive father was his birth-father. The child simply answered: "Well yes, if that's the case I don't really need to have the same mannerisms as he does."

Once he realised that there was no point in competing in this way everything changed. For every child, adoptive or not, the resolution of the Oedipus complex consists in assuming one's own identity and renouncing earlier identifications with the object of pleasure or the object of desire of one or other of the guardianship parents.

The love of adoptive parents for their child which is not "guarded" by the knowledge that she is flesh of their flesh can create further pitfalls for the child. The very earliest filial sentiments of the parents *vis-à-vis* their own parents will be played out in the early childhood of their adoptive son/daughter just as it would have been with a child which they had themselves engendered. All of this occurs in unconscious fantasy.

The unconscious need of the adoptive child to be even more visibly, more bodily, their child than a birth child, touches on a corresponding need in the adoptive parents, who place all of their hopes in this child who is destined to carry on their name and to bring to fruition all the love and effort which they have invested in him. What we call the difficult age appears even more difficult in the case of an adoptive child whose apparent ingratitude can provoke even greater blame than that of a birth child.

A birth-child is the child of the parents' need though sometimes not of their desire, at least not of their conscious desire. He or she can be the child of the father's rutting and the mother's submission; but in the case of an adopted child the parents cannot deny that he is a child whom they chose and desired for a long time before they got their wish.

From the moment he entered their life as a couple the adopted child has occupied such a large place that when he begins to detach himself from his adoptive family, he is much more severely condemned than a birth-child would have been.

The biblical command, "Honour thy father and thy mother", is very difficult because it completely contradicts the notion of the love for one's parents, a love which implies dependence. To honour one's parents is to attain one's full stature, to succeed in life under their name, perhaps to succeed better than they did. This ethical precept is in each person's heart whether or not he or she is educated, and it often runs counter to what each of us thinks we owe our parents because of our infantile dependent love which we have not yet left behind.

Helping aged parents when they are no longer able to look after themselves is also in the heart of each one a response to the help they gave us in childhood. We can often confuse this with dependent love, which is so close to hate, when this love has blocked our access to our own identity. To put it briefly, the pre-genital trap always recurs in the post-genital era, that is to say in old age.

One last problem to be pointed out. It can happen in the course of analysis that a child will say to you, "You are my mummy". You must answer categorically, "Your mummy from when?" He can in fact live a transference to his mummy from two to three years of age, but not his present-day mummy. Each day he must cause his mother to die and resuscitate her the next day as he does with himself indeed. The mummy of the past is dead. He can therefore transfer her on to something else. But his current mummy is alive and it is with her that he has to learn to sort things out.

"The field of our listening ..."

PARTICIPANT: I would like you to say something further about the first sessions which set up the treatment, and about what our role should be.

FRANÇOISE DOLTO: It is in fact very important to get across to patients and to parents what not to expect from us. In going to see a psychotherapist parents often tend to see the psychotherapist as a teacher from whom they are to receive a lesson in psychotherapy, or at least some type of lesson. Or they see her as a particular type of doctor who is there to cure a symptom which is troubling them in either a real or an imaginary manner because it is an obstacle to their child's integration into society. Obviously, our role consists in making them understand that this has nothing to do with their child's body or with how others relate to this body but concerns something completely different.

We are not here to attend to the body or its problems, even if these problems have been recognised as physical in origin, and are being treated as such by a doctor. This is not the field of our listening, our wavelength.

One sometimes comes across psychoanalysts, especially young psychoanalysts, who urge the parents to put a stop to their child's medication if the child is stupefied by a whole panoply of drugs. It may indeed be a pity that the child is debarred from contact with others because of this pharmacological cotton wool, but it is not our role to speak of this.

Our task is to concern ourselves solely with this symbolic being. This is our castration as analysts. Besides, some children really need medication. Their bodies need "veterinary" help, to survive.

I remember a woman paediatrician in analysis with me who specialised in the treatment of children who were true epileptics, and whose attitude to these children changed in the course of her analysis.

She now gives them complete responsibility for their own medication from about the age of five or six. She says to the parents in front of the child: "You do not need to concern yourself with your child's medication. If he wants treatment I will sort out the problem of medication with him." She requests only from the parents that they will allow the child to come and see her any time he wants to or that he can telephone her. "If you feel you want to lessen the dose you can telephone me. I will tell you whether or not the time is right. If you have done it and you are worried about it you can come and see me. I ask one thing only of you—never increase the dose on your own."

Obviously she doesn't always ask for a consultation fee and she is on a government salary.

She has obtained extraordinary results. "I am able to prescribe the minimum dose since the child is perfectly capable of telling me how he feels and if the dosage is harmful rather than helpful." This technique has taught her a good deal on the way the risks of medication vary from one person to another.

It is indeed a big step to establish in the parents a castration between needs (the medication corresponds to a bodily need) and desires.

This woman understood that it was a question of giving a human being responsibility for his own body. She had the necessary knowledge of his illness and its medication for this. She did not undertake psychotherapy in the classic sense: nonetheless her approach, to his anxieties is another form of therapy.

The impotence of many doctors in cases which are not organic betrays itself sometimes in astonishing ways. I am thinking for example of many autistic children crammed with stupefying medication by their doctors, although tests reveal no organic problem.

I have seen the same thing with children who are not deaf but for whom doctors prescribe a hearing aid all the same because they refuse to hear. From the moment some form of true communication is established with the therapist these children pull out their hearing aid.

Note

1. Translator's note: play on words in French: *boucher* = *bouchée* = blocked.

CHAPTER FOUR

Dolto, Klein, and Lacan in a polylogue or the Agora effect in the Maison Verte-UK

Bice Benvenuto

The French psychoanalyst Françoise Dolto, though a most prestigious figure worldwide because of her very original approach to the mind of the contemporary child, is not so well known in the English-speaking world due to most of her books still not having been translated into English. She pioneered the idea of a call-in place on the street, open to anyone who was accompanied by a child. The creation of La Maison Verte in Paris in 1979 marked a new impact of psychoanalysis in the social and a passage from nineteenth-century bourgeois rituals of private and enclosed consulting rooms to the streets, to meet ordinary people and their children. Dolto's invention of bringing the psychoanalyst to the street entailed quite a shift of the analyst's position when working with the unconscious. This relocation of the analytical setting has not repaid Dolto with too much consideration from the psychoanalytical establishment, including the Lacanian one, even though she was theoretically very close to Jacques Lacan, with whom she founded the Société Française de Psychanalyse (1953) and later the École Freudienne de Paris (1964).

We know, after Lacan, that psychoanalysis is not merely a one-to-one verbal enterprise; indeed its effects are polyphonic. The Freudian subject, for instance, is split between different psychic agencies, while the unconscious struggles to speak through the edicts of consciousness, and in addition the superego is simultaneously the representative of an external demand and of an internalised one (Freud, 1911b). Likewise, the Lacanian subject is divided by different registers, not least the Symbolic, which both ties us to, and separates us from the others and parts of ourselves. Our interiority from the beginning seems to be a complex inter-relational field of both internal instances (needs, drives, pleasure) and external, social ones. It is no coincidence that in child analysis members of the child's family are now often welcome in the session and included in aspects of the work. This allows the child to speak to the relevant others upon whom their psychic formation still depends and opens up the possibility for different psychic instances to find a voice in an inter-subjective polylogue. I shall try in this chapter to also outline a polylogue between Dolto, Klein, and Lacan regarding their theories on early infancy.

I shall also give a description of the way the Maison Verte (MV) approaches the inter-subjective field, based on my experience of setting it up and working in two such places: La Casa Verde, established in Rome by Associazione Dolto in 2004, and the Maison Verte-UK, established in 2013 by a group of child psychoanalysts, mostly of Lacanian orientation, in Finsbury Park, London (*cf.* Benvenuto, 2009). After the creation of the first Maison Verte by Dolto in the fifteenth *arrondissement* in Paris in 1979, hundreds of centres inspired by it were opened in France and all over the world. Dolto left anyone free to use the idea of a place for primary socialisation by building their own project and finding their own name. This means that MV inspired centres, even though all adhere to some standard format, differ noticeably according to the more or less psychoanalytical or socio-pedagogical orientation of the team involved. The Maison Verte-UK therefore claims its own difference, which consists in considering the MV work more than just an application in the social of certain psychoanalytical background ideas but an actual theoretical and clinical turning point for psychoanalysis itself.

From the claustrum *to the* agora

Lacan, in his 1938 text on family complexes contemplated the Oedipus complex in sociohistorical terms, and already envisaged the social decline of the paternal Imago with the advent of the nuclear family, from which today's family types derive: single parents, blended and step-families, same sex parents, etc. (Lacan, 1938). The most significant example is the legal use of sperm banks, with which the name, as well as the very existence of the father, is effaced with the consent of the law. As if the father were implicitly no longer acknowledged as the psychic representative of the law in our culture. Such a symbolic vacuum seems to require a new psychic impact from external sources through an increase of social measures and networks, whether virtual or real; it needs more and more contemporary substitutes for the old patriarch!

We need to reflect on these transformations of family ties, which have deep effects on the psychic development of children. While we are losing many of the rites of passage of the extended family that marked our psychic and social life until the last century, new ones are either too uncertain or not emerging at all. There are gaps in the structure of today's family that are fertile ground in both disadvantaged and well-off families for the suffering caused by new silent symptoms spreading in the contemporary era: depressive syndromes, feeding problems, addictions, juvenile delinquency.

Whereas Freud saw civilisation as a source of repression and, therefore, of psychic discontent (Freud, 1930a), Dolto saw it also as a main source of its cure, a source at once of loss and psychic enrichment. This is why, in contrast to the 1960s anti-psychiatry movements, which waged a war against it, the Maison Verte doesn't condemn the social, but welcomes it, in the form of people dropping in, children and grown-ups, immigrants and natives, the sick and the healthy.

But what is the link between very young children and the social as it works in the Maison Verte's theoretical and clinical strategy? What is crucial about the invention of a place that welcomes primary relations freely played out in a wider public context, away from the *claustrum*, the mother-child's or analyst-analysand's closed cloister? The Maison Verte *is* not a one-to-one Socratic dialogue, nor a group therapy, but relies instead on the polyphony of the public square, the open assembly, an experience I would call the *Agora* effect.

First of all the Maison Verte offers a threshold to cross, even only accidentally, as you don't have to be necessarily conscious of some sort of demand or suffering related to your child or to yourself. The offer, a Maison Verte in the neighbourhood, will have created a demand for it. A certain disengagement from desire is a peculiarity of contemporaneity. Today's market-culture, by filling us with objects it imposes as desirable, has created a sort of obstruction of desire and, therefore, of a subjective freedom to choose (Salecl, 2010). For example we have come to readily accept mental health's medical drugs and short CBT (Cognitive Behavioural Therapy) treatments that are regularly prescribed as quick fixes to suffering. Hence the Maison Verte does not rely on its guest's conscious engagement with psychoanalysis, but offers the possibility of crossing its threshold almost by chance.

Once beyond the threshold, the hosts (child psychoanalysts, trainees and volunteers, called "MV-welcomers" in the Maison Verte-UK), welcome the guests and write the children's names and the adult's role (mum, granny etc.) on a blackboard. With their first name on the blackboard the children have entered the Maison Verte's space. It will be up to them and their carers to use it as they wish, even by not accepting it at all. Once beyond the threshold, even if the adults usually give it a try, this does not mean the child does. After all they were carried there in mummy's arms; it was not their choice. Negotiating between this new space and mother's body describes the process the Maison Vert elicits, the *Agora* effect indeed.

Welcoming Nicholas

Nicholas, a boy around eighteen months old, comes to the Maison Verte with his mother. He plays mostly by himself in a detached way and hardly says anything. He does not interact with anyone who addresses him, not even his mother, who tries to excuse (mainly to herself) his behaviour: he's just shy! Once two people joined the three of us on a large baby mat and tried to play with Nicholas with a little doggie toy, which he kept grabbing and then anxiously pushing away. When I joined the game and the dog fell on my lap I placed it next to Nicholas and said: "Here's the doggie sitting next to you, Nicholas", and then, pointing to each person who was sitting in semi-circle on the mat: "Here's M … Here's J … Here's your mum sitting next to you … and here I am, Bice, who is talking to you." Nicholas was staring at me with great intensity, as was everyone else sharing the mat. Then he leaned on his mother's body trying to hide his face against her, who smiled as she put her arm around him. He was being shy at last, as his mother had wished! By hiding his face Nicholas showed that, even if only for a moment, he had been affected by the presence of others, from whom he found refuge in his mother's body.

Up until then, in spite of having been welcomed in the Maison Verte, Nicholas had never really entered it. We had his name on the blackboard, but he had not put his face on the line. By way of his autistic behaviour, which so anguished his mother, he was defending his own cut out space from both the surrounding space and his mother's, as if they did not exist. By calling his name and that of the people who were sharing the same mat, I was putting him on the map of the place. He suddenly found himself caught out as part of the mat assembly, as much as all the others were as well. Even if only for a moment, a sense of space had opened where he could not pretend to be invisible and unable to see others. Having his presence named together with that of the others, he felt the need to take refuge in his mother's body. Solitary autistic defences had given way to ordinary shyness, when children acknowledge their own presence in the face of others. Having been introduced to a slightly larger space, mother and child could find their own in this first reciprocal close contact they had ever had in the Maison Verte.

The exponential growth of autistic features and syndromes is still a riddle for today's child psychiatrists, neurologists, and psychologists. Parents, like Nicholas' mother, dread mentioning the word when their child seems to show some form of delay or early features of a defensive and rigid relation to human space. Nicholas had cut out his own solitary space, a small circuit, in which even his mother seemed to feature only as one among a few selected objects. Autism seems to be the world of de-humanised objects, including the children themselves. When Nicholas kept grabbing and throwing the doggie away, he was showing he was setting himself aside from the mat assembly. When I placed the rejected toy next to him and named it, I was cutting out also a circuit, a gathering place, where both humans and objects were all included. In pointing out that people and objects can sit next to each other, and still respect each solitary space, we were welcoming his autism. So he could evade it for a moment.

The mat assembly worked for Nicholas like the Greek public square, where you went to be present in the presence of others whose words resonate because they concern you as a member of the *Polis*, whether you like it or not. In the *Agora* effect words resound even in the puzzling autistic vacuum. Might it not be the case that autism is itself a resound of a more extended vacuum, the one left by that process of mutation of the paternal function I was mentioning earlier? Might not autism be one of the most startling effects of such a symbolic vacuum? This is a fundamental question the Maison Verte-UK is working on theoretically at the moment.

Polylogue Dolto–Klein–Lacan

This process of opening a larger space that includes and makes sense of the smaller mother/child two-body relation, is for Dolto more than a process of socialisation, it is one of humanisation. She questions the fundamental role of the object in object-relation theory by highlighting the infant's relation to the fundamental humanity of others, *in primis* the mother, who is not an anonymous carrier of a series of objects (breasts, nipples, inside of the body, etc.) but a real addressee of her baby's relation to her body. Objects in themselves cannot be relational; they are defined by the fact that, even if we use them, they do not relate to us. Therefore, the infant already relates to a human mother who does not simply carry the needed objects but is both their very flesh and the representative of a larger world within which the baby has already been assigned a place. The *Id* is relational for Dolto, as much as it is not at all alien to a symbolic universe.

While Klein sees the breast as the object *par excellence*, both Lacan and Dolto see the new-born as already marked by an original coexistence *in utero* with the mother, whose placenta was the source of nourishment and pleasure. Birth shatters the coexistence with the body of the mother and inaugurates the principle of separation with what the new-born feels is a part of themselves. Therefore, for Lacan the very first encounter is not with the breast or any other object or person but with the loss of a part of oneself (Lacan, 1994). When babies claim themselves back by crying, a breast comes in the way of their want, offering itself as an external object in the place of the enveloping placenta. By satisfying the need for nourishment, the placenta is the first auto-erotic object; that is, attached to the foetus' pleasure.

If the Kleinian baby takes in the mother's nourishment as moved primarily by a greedy and envious will to destroy her breast, the Doltoian baby is moved towards the breast primarily by a search for pleasure in nourishment; that is by an auto-erotic will to exist. Here we have a radical turn away from Kleinian thought, even more than Lacan's, who subscribed to Klein's status of the infant's body felt as being in pieces. In fact, for Klein, as well as for Lacan, the body of the infant has no cohesion, it does not feel whole. Such a fragmented body seems to be totally dominated by the death drive that reverberates in the infant's delirious phantasies of a destructive and sadistic nature. The only feeble counterpart to these feelings and phantasies is a still potential and shapeless Ego, which is developing very slowly. Still, this weak Ego alone will be the vehicle towards the life drive. For Klein, the life drive, which strives for cohesion, also coincides with what is good in an always uneven struggle with the evil of the death drive. There is an explicit Manichaeism of the drives in Klein, especially at the beginning of life, when the undisputed master is death.

Dolto's psychoanalytical ethics takes a different turn by focusing on Freud's early conception of the death drive, which is not an active force that wants to annihilate the envied object; it rather works as a limit, a bridle on the cohesive activity of Eros; it is inertia, pleasure's mortification. It is rather more on the side of deep sleep and ecstatic enjoyment, feeling nullified in the hands of another. But the death drive gathers force from the building-up of repression, which blocks the flow of libido; that is, of pleasure. In this perspective, where Klein sees cannibalism even in the foetus feeding on the maternal placenta, Dolto sees a primary desire to live. A certain degree of aggressiveness is not a prerogative of the death drive alone, it is needed by life itself in order to subsist in the face of all kinds of real and imaginary threats to our existence. The life drive runs on beyond the good and the evil of human morality. Dolto's ethical stance is her swinging the scales towards a desire to live and fighting for it, rather than an apparently peaceful, obedient giving up, which is indeed closer to death.

Can Alice hear?

Alice, a two-and-a-half-year-old girl, comes to the Maison Verte with her mum. They are like an enclosed unit in which the mother leads their activities and makes sure that every single toy, crayon or piece of paper is tidied away soon after use. Alice, unlike most children at the Maison Verte, does not wear casual comfortable clothes but pretty long dresses that prevent her from moving freely or getting dirty. Alice is partially deaf because of a recurrent serious ear infection, much the focus of her mother's anxiety. One day mother and child were playing on the baby-mat whilst Alice was keeping an eye on a small group of children who were climbing on a set of steps, showing great joy upon reaching the top. Alice could not resist: she stood up and made for the steps. But she was stopped by a little girl, who hugged her and would not let her go. Her mother kept asking Alice loudly to hug the child back. Alice seemed paralysed but would not hug the child. M., one MV welcomer who was witnessing the scene, said with a soft voice, in an interrogative way: "Maybe you were about to do something else rather than hug little Jeanne?" These words were like the breaking of a spell: all at once mother stopped shouting, Jeanne loosened her grip and Alice pushed herself forward to reach the top of the steps, triumphantly. She'd made it indeed! She had taken hold of her own body, in spite of her awkward long dress, of Jeanne's tight embrace and of her mother's freezing prescriptive words, and put it on a podium. Alice had not given in to her death drive, to its inertia and deafness. She could re-acquire her missing sense thanks to the soft utterance of somebody else's words which, by addressing her potential capacity to choose and move, had opened up a new sound-field for Alice's ears.

Sensing and appearing

There is a subtle common thread between Klein and Dolto, the evidence of an original *sensitivity* of the infant's mind that Klein called *feelings* (1975). The English term "feeling" covers several meanings such as affects, sentiments, and even love, but in a more concrete way it can mean *sensing*. This is the term Dolto chooses to describe the baby's earliest perceptions.

Sensing, besides being the activity of the senses, is a primary *making sense* of the world. If, as Lacan says, we are born into language, we are also born into the discourse of the flesh and its senses. We cannot exile the body from our mind and consider it, or parts of it, an object; neutral matter for our minds to mould. The living body can never be an object, or just a series of objects. According to Lacanian theory, there are in fact two kinds of body: a visible one, the image of the body that a mirror returns to us, and an invisible one, made up of the parts of the body that are excluded by the narcissistic mirror image. The infant's body, though still a premature and rather fragmented one, is not neutral matter. It is endowed with the senses that give it a sensorial cohesion and a way of communication through sensorial body codes exchanged with the mother. Messages are exchanged through smell, touching, gazing, hearing, especially the voice of the mother. The concept that the infant's body is plunged from the beginning in the water of language, its new amniotic liquid that places it in a larger background, would be an empty one if we didn't take into account that, beside language with its universal system of signifiers, there is a sensual order with its universal codes pertaining to living matter. Although there is a homology between language and sensorial codes, as they both pre-exist and inhabit the subject (Brennan, 2004), they are also destined not to align with each other except in certain privileged fertile moments (*points de capiton* or anchoring points). I think in this case Alice experienced one of those crucial points where somebody else's words aligned with her sense of hearing.

Dolto thinks that a cohesion of the infant's body, the unconscious image of the body (Dolto, 1984), is offered by *sensing* rather than by *appearing*. The unconscious image of the body, as she conceives it, is not the Ego image, which relies on sight, the sense closest to consciousness. The body image, the most important organiser of primary narcissism, is unconscious. It does not belong to a self-reflective subject; it is rather linked to the individual's unconscious history, to the forms of her libidinal relation with relevant others. She conceives the unconscious image as a psychic *topos* where language meets the real of the body, always an outcast even in psychoanalysis.

An archaic unconscious body image develops through the consistency of a repetitive sensual relation with the first carer. This is a basic image, linked to the primary functions of survival such as breathing and sucking, which resists change. But almost at the same time the baby looks at the mother's face while sucking at her breast, or the bottle, and turns her head to respond to other people's smiles. This shows also the presence of a dynamic image, which is pushing the baby towards the others in order to achieve pleasure beyond the need for food, beyond existing in a pure erotic state of being (a state very close to Heidegger's poor world of animals such as the tick, all absorbed in its blood sucking). The dynamic of desire is then reflected in a changing image that opens onto a shared pleasure with others who will add meaning to their exchange. This turning of the head from the mother in order to lend an ear to other stimuli is what we are witnessing with Alice. The MV welcomer's words had appealed to her desire to exist beyond her mother's deaf space, which was holding her tidily and tightly to an archaic static image of her body, which could hardly move and hear further away sounds. The Maison Verte had functioned for her as a sound field, where her own image had acquired its missing ears, and could narcissistically triumph at the top of the podium.

Dolto liked the idea of having a mirror placed on top of a small ladder in the Maison Verte so that children could admire their triumph in climbing to the top. The mirror experience is for Dolto not always a happy one, because children are confronted with a scopic image that does not reflect their own unconscious image. In Alice's case, there was no mirror; her "jubilation" did not arise from a reflective visual experience but from having successfully claimed the unconscious cohesion of her body as separate from her mother's and reflected by the gaze of the others. The week after I could hardly recognise Alice who had her hair cut short, wearing tight jeans and trainers! She spent the whole session at the MV playing with the mirror, ecstatically admiring this new image of herself.

Before acquiring a mirror image Alice had needed words she could hear, which could offer new elements in her psychic organisation. Said and unsaid words are incarnated in the body as we are marked from the beginning by the words of those who welcome us (or not) into the world. This is already the core of a social link, but one that can easily degenerate into a loop-knot, a seducing lure as well as an oppressive enclosure of an exclusive two-body relation. For language to determine the human dimension it needs dissonances, more voices; a signifier does not work alone, it needs at least another one in order for the child to be included in the symbolic network of language. Words help the drive to detach from a compulsive repetition that loops you to your mother's erotic enjoyment as well as to her masochistic suffering. By enlarging the drive circuit in a wider context words open up a gap, a distance from the object, which affords more complex satisfactions.

Where play meets words

The question is what kind of words were involved in the two examples I have given. Children come to the Maison Verte at an age when they can hardly speak; rather they are spoken about by their parents. At the Maison Verte we speak to the children and babies, even to the foetus inside the pregnant mother, and not about them or in their place. One can speak to their separate existence, to their forming unconscious, thanks to the fact that all children, even toddlers and babies who hardly utter comprehensible words, play. What appears as playing to adults is in fact children's life activity, their way of living and communicating. This is why the Maison Verte-UK's motto on the wall reads "Where Play Meets Words". When playing, the MV welcomer's words do not construct interpretations, as is the case in individual child analysis where the analyst holds mostly the positions of the witness, but are authentic play actions, interventions rather than interpretations.

Lacan came close to this notion when he identified the mainspring of psychoanalysis in the "analytical act". Constructed interpretations that still need to be filtered by the Ego, leave their place to interventions, free floating responses to the other's speech and actions. More than well formulated verbal interpretations, the unconscious needs the living immediate response of the other. Of course, the risk of false responses, commonplace chat and power abuses occur here like anywhere else. By not undertaking a one-to-one therapy, abuses and suggestions can always be challenged by someone else, child or adult.

Much of the welcomer's way of playing rather agrees with Winnicott's idea that, only if you are involved in the game, can your verbal interventions reach the child's unconscious (Winnicott, 1971). When play involves the unconscious of both child and adult, then words become play actions, acts of speech. When I spoke to Nicholas, as my contribution to the game with the doggie, my words had come as a surprise to all, especially to myself.

Dolto's wager was that an analytical position before the child's words and play could be maintained in a setting that is not an individual psychoanalytic session. Here, the others who surround the child in their daily life—parents, siblings, grandparents, nannies, and so on—are also invited to speak. Speech is entrusted to the guests, also to other mothers and children, in a way that assures there will always be a potential third party they can address or be addressed by. If a certain degree of anxiety is released by articulating what bothers you, the presence of a listener can challenge and change a pathogenic perspective.

The nanny

Frank and James, two brothers aged one and two, would come with "The nanny", as she proudly introduced herself. She was a very experienced one indeed; at once stern and attentive, and the children seemed to love her for it. She used to spend most of the time sitting near the baby area while the children looked very comfortable moving about confidently and independently. She was an "unmoved mover", in the same place, always there for them. A quick cuddle, a biscuit, a smile from her would set the children moving freely among other guests and hosts.

Only once did the children come with their parents, when I was not there, and I was told that it was a very different scenario. The two brothers were very much left to their own devices, crying and not knowing what to do with themselves as if, without their prime mover, they had lost their sense of orientation; a well-known place had become uncharted territory. But sometime later I witnessed a stormy session when Frank and the nanny came to blows. We immediately noticed their furious faces as they entered the room. Frank started to push his nanny while she reacted by pulling his ear, all of this in silence. When Frank spat on her, she decided they should leave and made for the pushchairs. Absolutely nothing like their usual sober idyll. People around were silent too, as there was no possibility of communication with their fury or with the nanny's wounded pride. I dared approach them as they prepared to leave and ask what was happening. "Frank has been like this since I came back this morning from my leave." She replied.

"Have you been away?"

"Yes, I was on leave for two days."

I turned towards Frank and asked him if he knew his nanny would not have come for two days. Frank replied with a rendering "No-o-o …" and began sobbing. The nanny looked startled.

"So, you were waiting for your nanny who never came. Did you think she'd left you?"

He replied "Y-e-e-s …" still sobbing.

I said to the nanny who still looked puzzled, "It seems Frank is upset because he was not told and believed you would never come back … he missed you." The nanny's usually stern face looked moved as she put her hand on little Frank's head. They started to move back inside the room, where she sat at her usual place, her self-esteem seemingly restored. Some dark clouds were still hovering over their unusual silence though. Why, I wondered, had Frank reacted with such despair to what was, after all, only an ordinary absence of the nanny?

It was only the following week that the nanny told me that she was going to stop working with Frank and James in a few weeks, as the family was moving to a different area. By now, she assured me, the children had been told about it! This late piece of information suddenly showed me a new meaning for the previous week's drama. Frank must have been aware of his family's plans to move, including the consequence of having to lose his nanny. No surprise that when she did not turn up the previous week, he had believed she had already gone, so that his grief for his nanny about to go, started before the event itself, a sort of *avant-coup*. When I asked Frank how he felt about moving to the new place without the nanny, he said he was going to have a big garden and his own bedroom. I do not think it was a denial of his grief; he had already gone through his mourning, first when she had not turned up and later at the Maison Verte. As the children had not been informed of changes in the family that concerned them, Frank had to interpret and fill the gaps of non-forthcoming information.

Frank's case is exemplary of the difficulty adults have putting into words what concerns the child. It's not easy to tell the truth. Lacan says that it cannot be said whole. But we can pick up elements of an unsaid truth, such as an uncanny silence or startling sobs, devoid of those words our psyche needs to feed on. The Freudian afterwardness or *après-coup*, a concept Lacan gave great prominence to, occurs when a trauma from the past is reactivated by one occurring in the present. This is confirmed also in this case, where the unconscious knowledge that the nanny was about to leave was reactivating a possible earlier trauma, something that seems to have prevented parenting taking place in this family. This was highlighted by the children not knowing what to do with themselves when they were with their parents who could not even tell their children their life was about to change. So, what could be worked with at the Maison Verte were the missing words to say it, which Frank had turned into spit and, then, gulped down through his sobs. The trauma in this case was not the nanny's accidental absence, but the unsayable unconscious knowledge of the imminent catastrophic loss of the nanny who was parenting him. Therefore, her recent leave had made present her future absence leading to his uncharacteristic behaviour that had alerted and urged me to find words that could address, through his present trauma, his past and future ones. In this way he was given the opportunity to prepare himself to make up for the absence of the nanny by looking forward to his very own room and a big garden … and, I would add, to claiming back his own parents, whom he will have to deal with at last. Coming and playing at the Maison Verte gave Frank also the opportunity to let his unconscious message float free in a place where someone could hear it, where he could, by expressing rage and grief, mourn and bid farewell to the removed mover of this first stage of his life.

References

Benvenuto, B. (2009). Speech, listening, welcoming in Francoise Dolto's work. In: Hall, G., Hivernel, F., & Morgan, S. (Eds.) (2009). *Theory and Practice in Child Psychoanalysis. An Introduction to the Works of Françoise Dolto* (pp. 163–190). London: Karnac.

Brennan, T. (2004). *The Transmission of Affect.* Ithaca: Cornell University Press.

Dolto, F. (1971). *Psychoanalysis and Paediatrics Key Psychoanalytic Concepts with Sixteen Clinical Observations of Children.* F. Hivernel & F. Sinclair (Trans.). London: Karnac, 2013.

Dolto, F. (1984). *L'Image Inconsciente du Corps.* Paris: Le Seuil.

Freud, S. (1911b). Formulations on the two principles of mental functioning. *S.E., 12*: 213–236. London: Hogarth.

Freud, S. (1930a). *Civilization and its Discontents. S.E., 21*: 57–146. London: Hogarth.

Klein, M. (1975). *Envy and gratitude and Other Works 1946–1963.* London: Hogarth.

Lacan, J. (1938). *Family Complexes in the Formation of the Individual.* C. Gallagher (Trans.), London: Karnac.

Lacan, J. (1994). *Le Séminaire Livre IV. La Relation d'objet.* Paris: Le Seuil.

Salecl, R. (2010). *Choice.* London: Profile.

Winnicott, D. W. (1971). *Playing and Reality,* London: Routledge.

PART II

CLINICAL STRUCTURES
(EDGES, LIMITS, BOUNDARIES)

CHAPTER FIVE

Psychoanalysis with children, the work with the parents, and the clinical structures

Leonardo S. Rodríguez

Five-year-olds

A lady telephoned me not long ago.

> "Doctor, my son has a problem. Do you have any experience with five-year-old boys?"
>
> "Madam, most of the children with whom I work are five-year-old boys."

These children suffer from anxiety hysteria, probably the most common form of neurosis in our times among people of any age (Rodríguez, 2016). One hundred and sixteen years after the publication of his inaugural paper on Little Hans, Freud's words are still pertinent:

> Anxiety-hysterias are the most common of all psychoneurotic disorders. But, above all, they are those which make their appearance earliest in life; they are *par excellence* the neuroses of childhood. (Freud, 1909b, p. 116)

Many things have changed since the Professor offered the young Herbert Graf what might be considered as the first interpretation in the history of psychoanalysis with children (Freud, 1909b, pp. 41–43). What has actually changed in the matters that specifically concern the psychoanalyst who works with children?—i.e., human desire, love, jouissance, the structure and functions of the unconscious, symptoms, fantasies, the composition, and functions of the family: in brief, what has changed in the phenomena, problems, and questions with which we operate, which our conceptual efforts attempt to elucidate and our praxis aims at effectively transforming? (Rodríguez, 1996).

The impressive scientific and technological advances and the significant socioeconomic and cultural changes that we have witnessed in our own lifetime should presumably have had an impact upon the ways in which subjectivity is constituted and upon both creative and morbid human productions, as well as our conceptions of childhood, the education of children and young people, and maternal and paternal functions.

In industrially advanced and in developing countries the social status of children and women has generally (but not universally) changed in the direction of an increased awareness of their human rights, and in some places (but not everywhere) there have been actual improvements in their living conditions. That the child is "a subject in his own right and in the full sense of the word" according to the very apt expression of Rosine and Robert Lefort: "*l'enfant est un sujet à part entière*" (Rosine Lefort & Robert Lefort, 1984, p. 3, my translation) does not only apply to the child in the analytic experience and to the ethics and praxis of psychoanalysis. The formula condenses a psychoanalytic contribution to the social and cultural standing of children; but it is also an effect of cultural evolution upon our own field, its ethics and its praxis.

That motherhood has become a matter of choice for a larger proportion of women and no longer an imposition upon virtually all women capable of becoming mothers has also, among other things, modified the status and subjective position of the women with whom we work, and who come to see us *qua* mothers or prospective mothers.

The position of the father has been affected in significant sections of contemporary societies quite markedly, particularly as regards the presence, responsibilities and actions of the *real* father—as distinct from the symbolic father, which is a function of the cultural law, and from the imaginary father, which corresponds to the significations of what is said about the father (both symbolic and imaginary), in particular by the mother, but not exclusively.

The institution of the family, which continues to be necessary for the constitution of the human subject, has undergone legal and ethical alterations that were simply inconceivable just a few years ago: same-sex marriage; the procreation, adoption, and raising of children by parents of the same sex; one-parent families (which have always existed, but which are now increasingly the result of a positive choice); "open" marriages in which the parents are more than two, with a variable combination of the sexes—and a few other familial arrangements. The changes in the constitution of the family are linked to the increased social acceptance of different sexual identities and orientations—something that as socially acceptable positions was—again—unthinkable not long ago (Rodríguez, 1996).

This is only a cursory reference to the changes that have affected human communities in our part of the world; a more precise account of those changes, their causes and their effects would be necessary if we were to gain an insight into their relevance for our discipline. It is reasonable to expect correlative changes in the individual speaking beings that inhabit our world. The interlocutors of these speaking beings have changed in their ways, the language that they employ has changed, and the parameters of the discourses—which are social bonds—that participate in their constitution as subjects have also changed.

I referred to "our part of the world" in the previous paragraph because the changes in question have not occurred, or have occurred only to a minimal degree, in large parts of our planet, and the same can be said of the considerable number of fellow human beings who live in "our" part of the world but who have maintained, to this day, their traditional cultural morality as regards sexuality and the composition of the family.

As for our specific conceptual and clinical categories, have the sociocultural changes that we have experienced in our lives, in the organisation of our own families and in the lives and families of our patients resulted in actual structural alterations in the clinical structures and their concrete manifestations, namely, symptoms, sexual identity, and the ways in which people deal with these manifestations?

Despite the changes in our living conditions over the last hundred years, the psychopathological organisations which human beings are capable of producing have not changed in their structure, and new types of symptoms have not appeared. It is true that some symptoms, syndromes, and clinical presentations have increased in their statistical frequency, as social conditions and technological advances have promoted particular individual and familial disruptions. That is the case with the addictions to both illegal and medically prescribed drugs, and the addictions linked to the availability of pornography through the internet (*cf.* Rodríguez, 2007). It is also the case with the so-called "eating disorders" better described as "disorders of desire" (Rodríguez, 2009), and with the so-called "personality disorders" and "borderline personality disorders". These conditions are not new from a psychoanalytically informed diagnostic point of view, but they have been "promoted" as nosological entities by the last versions of psychiatric classifications of "mental disorders" (*cf.* Rodríguez, 2005). We can think of other clinical presentations whose diagnostic status remains problematic.

The extraordinary expansion of the use of psychopharmacological agents in psychiatry and general medical practice has contributed to the increase in the frequency, for people of all ages, of the diagnoses of depression, anxiety states, panic attacks, "bipolar" disorders, hyperactivity, and deficits of attention. These conditions have also been known for a long time, well before the advent of modern psychopharmacology, but it is not a coincidence that they began to be diagnosed more frequently in medical practice once the relevant pharma-cological agents indicated for their treatment became readily available and known to the general public.

The etiological factors behind the reported increase in the cases that fall into the category of "autism spectrum disorders" remain unclear. It is conceivable that a plurality of factors is involved in the genesis and development of cases that belong to this spectrum—and I would not disagree at this point with the prevalent psychiatric usage of the term "spectrum" (Rodríguez, 2001; 2008). At any rate, a plurality of etiological determinations (or "overdetermination", to use Freud's term) is the norm, rather than the exception, in the causal constellation of every psychopathological organisation, whether we refer to entire clinical structures or individual symptoms.

The parents' demands and the child's desire

It is usually the mother who telephones to ask for a consultation for the child or in relation to the child. These days, on occasions it is the father who takes the initiative. This represents a change, at least in my experience, as until not so long ago it was the mother who as a rule requested the first consultation.

In all the cases with which I have dealt over forty-six years the request is fully justified: the child is suffering to a very serious degree. The child is *disturbed*, and not only disturbing. The parents are certainly disturbed in relation to the child's disturbance, but also beyond it. Beyond their distress at the perception of their child's disturbance, they do not know what *their own* disturbance is really about: it has to do with their own unconscious and its sources remain opaque to them. The disturbance in the child has unconscious determinants, but it also has to do with *the parents'* unconscious: the *transindividual* status of the unconscious is fundamentally grounded upon the primary familial bonds (Lacan, 1956, p. 214; Rodríguez, 2013). The etiology of the disturbance in each of them (the child, the mother, the father), although involving a number of fundamental signifiers and experiences common to all of them, is strictly singular and cannot be reduced to a familial or collective etiology.

Usually the parents have some idea as to the causes of the child's disturbance, particularly if this has to do with the child having become a nuisance at home, or at school, or both. This is a frequent presentation: the child has been persistently naughty, or worse; he or she has become an embarrassment and a danger to others and him or herself. No approach has been effective: punishment, leniency, conversation, silence—nothing has worked. Violence on the part of parents makes things worse, and they know that. And because they know it, they feel guilty and impotent when they exercise violence. Violence is always physical: so-called "verbal" violence is a form of physical violence. Insults, threats and other offensive verbal expressions are integral parts of discourse—albeit at the very limits of language in action. As discourse, they involve a physical materiality that literally hurts the body (and the spirit) and breaks it in various degrees.

I have worked with very intelligent, well-educated parents who behave like very dumb and ignorant people in their relation to their children and their problems. I have known parents who have adopted courageous positions in relation to the defence of human rights in the community, but who against their own better judgement use corporal punishment and verbal abuse to "educate" their children and "cure" their symptoms. They feel embarrassed when telling me what they have done to their children, because they know very well that a violent, punitive approach is not only ineffective but also unethical. They know very well that in "our" part of the world corporal punishment and other methods of torture have been abolished and made illegal in prisons, work places, schools, and all other social settings (of course, the corresponding transgressions occur all the time); and they cannot explain why it is that they are capable of inflicting physical and mental pain to a child systematically, and not just at a moment of "losing control". Yet the horror at the recognition of the morbid, fundamentally masochistic satisfaction and consequent sense of guilt involved in the administration of corporal punishment interferes with their perception of the child's suffering and of their own tragedy, and with the transmission of a truthful account of the facts to the analyst.

On the other hand, according to my experience most of those parents who have lost their way when facing the child's suffering are the same ones who bring their child to an analyst and are prepared to sustain the narcissistic injury inflicted by the recognition that there is something fundamentally wrong with the child, that they have something to do with it, and that remaining ignorant as to the causes of the problem and impotent to find a solution only aggravates the child's suffering and their own pain. Certainly, there are also parents who are incapable of tolerating the narcissistic blow derived from what they regard as parental failure and the concomitant sense of guilt. But even these parents may be open to changing their subjective stance through the work with the analyst.

There are, of course, many parents who bring a child to analysis and who do not actively engage in any form of overt physical violence, verbal or otherwise. Nevertheless, there is always a dimension of violence in the internal and external affective struggles involved in human conflicts. From early in life the human body registers and suffers subjective conflicts in the form of anxiety, fears, conversion symptoms, psychosomatic phenomena, and the physical tension and anxious states that accompanies obsessions and compulsions—which are never purely "mental", in that the whole of the body is compromised by them (Rodríguez, 2009).

These considerations, and the simplest reflection on our daily labours, bring us to the question of the analyst's work with the parents. There is no established technique for this work. Perhaps Anna Freud and her school (at the Hampstead Clinic) have been, among all the analysts that work with children, the most committed to a systematic approach to working with the parents in parallel to the treatment of the child designated as "the patient", broadly following the principles that Anna Freud established for working with children (A. Freud, 1946; Burlingham, Goldberger & Lussier, 1955; Hellman, Friedmann & Shepheard, 1960; Levy, 1960). A number of psychoanalytic authors, including myself, have questioned the ethical and clinical principles that guide the orientation of Anna Freud and some of her followers (Klein, 1927; Lacan, 1988, pp. 62–70; Rodríguez, 1999, pp. 36–53). There are testimonies of the work with the parents by analysts of other orientations: Kleinian, neo-Kleinian, Winnicottian, the authors of articles in *The Psychoanalytic Study of the Child*, and others. Maud Mannoni and Françoise Dolto, among the analysts with a Lacanian orientation, have provided clear accounts of their work with parents and the conceptual reference points that guided it (Mannoni, 1973a, 1973b; Dolto, 1974, 1995, 2009, 2012).

Even if we maintain differences with the psychoanalysts who have not followed the ethical and conceptual principles established by Jacques Lacan, we must recognise that there is something to learn from all the analysts who have endeavoured to work with children and their parents. Lacanian analysts do not form a monolithic group, and divergences are to be found between different Lacanian authors. In their work with the parents of children who have become analysands, all of them had to be creative in their technical approach, and inventive in the application of the psychoanalytic body of knowledge to unique familial constellations and very diverse and contingent modalities of relation between patients, parents and members of the extended family.

Psychoanalysis works with subjects

Strictly speaking, we do not treat children in psychoanalysis, but subjects. Strictly speaking, we do not treat parents either—but subjects: human subjects who come to work with us in their capacity as parents, but who are primordially and fundamentally subjects who are having difficulties in assuming the position of mother or father. It is possible to come to understand the sources of these difficulties. This requires analytic exploration and interpretation, which means the development of a transference relation. In my experience, the parents of the child brought for analysis present themselves less as parents than as children. Their own children often reproach them for being "so childish". This childish presentation is in fact a symptomatic formation—on occasions a consolidated symptom. "Child", "adult", "parent" and similar words do not designate analytic concepts. They represent for us fields of enquiry: questions rather than explanations or conceptual reference points. Of course, we must be familiar with the developmental dimension of human history (both ontogenetically and phylogenetically), as well as with the legal and informal cultural norms that define the rights and responsibilities of children, adolescents and adults.

It is impossible to differentiate in a categorical manner the analytic work with the subjects/parents from analysis proper. In my experience, some of the interviews with the parents "progress" onto analysis proper, and the parent becomes an analysand in his or her own right. This does not mean that the interviews with the parents who do not engage in a full analysis are of a lesser analytic quality, less "deep" or less efficacious.

The analytic work with a child and his or her parents shows clearly that it is not a question of "blaming the parents". Apart from not explaining anything, such a naïve approach (extended among the general public, but also present among some analysts) has the paradoxical effect of covering up the actual contribution by the parents to the specific pathology manifest in the child, and consequently their assumption of the responsibility that genuinely belongs to them.

I work with each parent who wants to work with me individually. I do not work with parental couples. I used to do so, many years ago, until I realised that the presence of a partner interferes with the subject's capacity to engage in the psychoanalytic discourse, which is a unique, irreproducible method of speaking that discourages censorship and promotes the emergence of unexpected truths. All the parents with whom I have worked agree on this point, as they can easily recognise that the child and each one of the child's problems have a different subjective significance and resonance for each of them.

The child-analysand's desire, the parents' desires and the analyst's desire

I have maintained this ethical and technical position in consonance with what is simultaneously an ethical principle, a clinical method and a technical orientation: the concept of the analyst's desire, Lacan's original contribution that designates what is incomparable about an analyst's work—the respect for the singularity of the individual human subject in his or her capacity as a speaking being.

Lacan's "Note on the Child" remains an enlightening text on the links between familial impasses, the child's symptoms and their co-relation with the position that the child occupies in the mother's subjectivity, as well as the clinical consequences that may be extracted from those links—all this, despite its brevity: less than two pages (Lacan, 1969).

Among other cases, the analysis of children brought to the treatment because of hyperactivity and deficits of attention have illustrated in my experience the pertinence of the initial paragraph of the "Note":

> In the conception developed by Jacques Lacan the child's symptom is found to be in a position of answering to what is symptomatic in the family structure.
>
> The symptom, which is the fundamental fact of analytic experience, is in this context defined as the representative of truth.
>
> The symptom may represent the truth of the family couple. This is the most complex case, but also the one that is most open to our intervention. (Lacan, 1969, p. 7, see also Rodríguez, 1998, pp. 141–145)

Lacan then refers to subjective and familial situations in which the conditions are not so favourable:

> The articulation is much reduced when the symptom that comes to dominate stems from the subjectivity of the mother. In this case the child is concerned directly as the correlative of a fantasy.
>
> The distance between identification with the ego ideal and the portion taken from the mother's desire, should it lack the mediation which is normally provided by the function of the father, leaves the child open to every kind of fantasmatic capture. He becomes the mother's "object" and has the sole function of revealing the truth of this object.
>
> The child *realizes* the presence of what Jacques Lacan designates as the *objet a* in fantasy.
>
> [...] He saturates the mode of lack in which the (mother's) desire is specified, whatever its special structure—neurotic, perverse or psychotic.
>
> In it he alienates all possible access by the mother to her own truth, through giving it body, existence and, even, the requirement of protection.

> The somatic symptom gives the greatest possible guarantee to this miscognition [*méconnaissance*]; it is the inexhaustible resource that, depending on the case, may testify to guilt, serve as a fetish, or incarnate a primordial refusal. (Lacan, 1969, p. 7)

This is a very precise definition of what is essentially at stake in the intergenerational transmission of psychopathology.

Colette Soler's remarks in her book on Lacan's contributions to the questions posed by femininity are pertinent at this point:

> We cannot fail to be aware that at the level of the organism's vital needs and the care it calls for, what occurs is what Lacan calls an "object-relation *in the real*". (Lacan, 1961, p. 548; Soler, 2006, pp. 115–116)

And she adds:

> Is motherly love thus an empty word? Certainly not, but like every other love, it is structured by fantasy. This is not to say that it is imaginary—far from it—but that in a very real way, it reduces the partner to being only the object that the subjective division calls to. Furthermore, the mother-child relation carries to a higher power the alienation inherent in love, since the newborn is not first a subject, but an object. The child is a real object, in the hands of the mother who, far beyond what is required by her care, can use him/her as a possession, an erotic doll from which she can get jouissance and to which she can give jouissance. (Soler, 2006, p. 118)

That the symptoms of the child have their genesis in the concrete experience of bodily jouissance that he or she has in the course of family life—primarily with the mother, but not only with the mother, and then not only with members of the family but also with other significant others—does not mean that the analytic experience requires necessarily the participation of the mother or the father, or of the person who takes responsibility for bringing the child to the analytic session (sometimes a grandparent, or an aunt, an uncle, a family friend or a legally appointed guardian). That the child in analysis is treated as an analysand in his or her own right and in the full sense of the term means that the word of the child is necessary, but also that it is sufficient for his or her engagement in the analytic discourse. The aim of the work with the parents is not the gathering of information about the child and the family history. The child will expose all the unconscious history that an analysis is capable of generating. Rosine Lefort insisted that the children whom she analysed at Parents de Rosan did not have parents or any other person that could give an account of the child's history at the time of the treatment; and yet the four children whose cases she published engaged fruitfully in an incomparable analytic experience (Rosine Lefort & Robert Lefort, 1988, 1994, 1995). The aim of the work with the parents is to help them to get to know how they, *qua* subjects who speak, are engaged in the psychopathology of the child, its etiology, its evolution and its aggravation, on the basis of their own psychopathology. Since Freud "psychopathology" means differential clinical structures, or the subjective positions that human beings necessarily come to occupy in the course of their humanisation.

It is true, however, that psychoanalysis with children offers a privileged position to the analyst, which enables him or her to learn, from the testimonies of children and parents, the points of contact of the unique tragedies that each of them experiences differently—so close and so alien as they are in relation to each other in the traumatic avatars of their desires and their jouissance.

I have treated a number of children who presented with hyperactivity and deficits of attention, and for whom their symptoms made life rather miserable. I am referring to genuine cases, properly evaluated and diagnosed. I say this because I know of cases of children whose diagnosis of "ADHD" (Attention Deficit Hyperactivity Disorder) is established without due consideration of the clinical facts by practitioners who are convinced of the biochemical etiology of this condition to the exclusion of other factors.

Hyperactivity and parental malaise

The first of the cases I treated, one of the first children with whom I have worked, many years ago, when I was an apprentice of psychoanalysis working at the child psychiatry department of a teaching hospital in Buenos Aires, was that of a three-year-old boy. The boy entered the consulting room ahead of his parents, like a tornado, jumped on top of my desk, and from there onto a filing cabinet, pushing toys and small pieces of furniture in the course of his frenetic run, paying no attention to my hopeless attempts to calm him down by verbal means, to then run away from the room before his parents had time to enter. Staff members found him some ten minutes later at a distant section of the hospital. That was hyperactivity!

"He is like that all the time, doctor", the active child's mother told me. "What can we do?"

If only I knew …

I was able to work with the child and separately with the parents, and after a few weeks the hyperactivity had gone. We worked with each of them around what was symptomatic in the family structure, as Lacan would put it. In this work I had the good guidance of our supervisor, an experienced and astute psychoanalyst who discussed difficult cases with a small group of us, young psychoanalysts-in-formation. I presented the case of the hyperactive boy the evening of the same day of my first encounter with him. The Professor said to me:

> "There you have a decent case of hyperkinesia, Rodríguez. Tell me, what are the sleeping arrangements in that family?"
>
> I did not know; they had not told me, and I had not asked.
>
> "Ah, Rodríguez, that is the first thing you have to ask in a case of hyperkinesia—and in any other case, for that matter."

In all the cases of hyperactivity (which used to be called "hyperkinesia"), with or without deficits of attention, that I have seen over the last four and a half decades, plus a good number of other cases that I have supervised or that colleagues have presented in clinical seminars, the wise clinical advice of the Professor has never failed me. When I worked in the shantytowns of Buenos Aires, I knew many families with six or more children living in one room and sharing one or two beds—without any pathogenic effect deriving directly from the absence of "private" space. It is not a question of the physical arrangements of people and furniture within the house. It is, rather, a question of the child's position *vis-à-vis* the sexuality of the parents: typically, the child is propelled to compensate for the lack of sexual satisfaction of an unhappy parental couple, by literally sleeping *between* the parents, usually under the pretext that he or she is scared in his or her own bed and wants the parents' company. In fact, as analysis uncovers, the child fears the effects of the "promotion" to a physical position of sexual excitation without resolution and with the mark of the transgression of the prohibition of incest on top. The fear is not the cause, but the effect of the incestuous arrangement, a hopeless attempt to make up for the impossibility of the sexual co-relation.

On the whole, the clinical prospects in most cases of hyperactivity and deficits of attention are favourable, as typically the situation to which I have just referred corresponds to the prototype described by Lacan in the first paragraph of his "Note on the Child" (Lacan, 1969, p. 7). The symptoms of hyperactivity and deficits of attention are derivatives of the anxiety induced by the non-metabolised surplus-jouissance that literally, and materially, invades the child's body; and the deficits of attention may well serve a function. As a rule there is no failure of attention, but a *displacement* of attention towards the source of unhappiness: maternal and paternal dissatisfaction and impotence.

I am not claiming that this typical description is applicable to all cases of hyperactivity and deficits of attention. It is well known that neurological and other organic factors play a part in the etiology of a good number of cases. What I am describing is the testimony of an analyst who works with children and their parents and who has listened to their experiences, in the context of a discourse that offers the opportunity to hear truths that no one can say or hear elsewhere. For all the merits of the advances in pharmacology, clinicians who employ psychotropic agents as the only form of treatment should consider the human-made factors that contribute to the genesis of human conditions linked to anxiety: "the signal of the real", as Lacan defines it—the affect proper to an encounter with a real something in the face of which there is no recourse (Lacan, 2014, p. 160).

In the same connection, already sixteen years ago I wrote these lines:

> The child, depleted of his symptom (in so far as this is reduced to a pure deficit), becomes the object of medical practices and the psychopharmacological industry, thus realising in his own organism what the discontents of our civilization demands: nothing other than conformity presented as biopsychosocial stability.
>
> If the surplus-jouissance of the symptom is captured by the discourse of science and technology, and if it becomes surplus-value for the pharmaceutical industry, then the task of rescuing the truth-value of the symptom is left to the analytic discourse. (Rodríguez, 1998, p. 57)

There is a price to pay for humanisation—for becoming human by virtue of the Other's desire and the demands imposed by the Other's jouissance. The primordial maternal discourse, whose traces get inscribed in the unconscious as the foundational *lalangue*, is oriented by the mother's fantasy and the erratic, contingent influence of her preferred modes of jouissance (Rodríguez, 2013). The best and the worst for which humans are known are first transmitted in that intimate and precious relationship. Nowadays the maternal functions tend to be shared by others: the significant others—the father, siblings, grandparents. In many societies this sharing has been the norm for centuries.

Children have something to say about what is done *with* them and *to* them, as well as about what they are capable of doing themselves. And there are analysts who are willing to listen to them, who desire to know their original stories, and who can help them to make a difference in their lives and the lives of their parents.

References

Burlingham, D., Goldberger, A. & Lussier, A. (1955). Simultaneous Analysis of Mother and Child. *Psychoanalytic Study of the Child, 10*: 165–186.

Dolto, F. (1974). *Dominique: Analysis of an Adolescent*. London: Souvenir Press.

Dolto, F. (1995). *When Parents Separate*. Lincoln, MA: Godine.

Dolto, F. (2009). *Une Psychanalyste dans la Cité. L'Aventure de la Maison Verte*. Paris: Gallimard.

Dolto, F. (2012). *Psychoanalysis and Paediatrics*. London: Karnac.

Freud, A. (1946). The Psycho-Analytical Treatment of Children. In: the *Writings of Anna Freud*, volume 1. New York: International Universities Press, 1966–1980.

Freud, S. (1909b). Analysis of a Phobia in a Five-Year-Old-Boy. *S.E.*, 10: 3: 3–149. London: Hogarth Press.

Hellman, I., Friedmann, O., & Shepheard, E. (1960). Simultaneous Analysis of Mother and Child. *Psychoanalytic Study of the Child, 15*: 359–377.

Klein, M. (1927). Symposium on Child-Analysis. In: *The Writings of Melanie Klein*, volume 1. London: Hogarth and the Institute of Psycho-Analysis, 1975.

Lacan, J. (1956). The Function and Field of Speech and Language in Psychoanalysis. In: *Écrits* (pp. 197–268). B. Fink (Trans.). New York and London: Norton, 2006.

Lacan, J. (1961). Remarks on Daniel Lagache's Presentation: "Psychoanalysis and Personality Structure". In: *Écrits* (pp. 543–574). B. Fink (Trans.). New York and London: Norton, 2006.

Lacan, J. (1969). Note on the Child. R. Grigg (Trans.). *Analysis, 1990, 2*: 7–8.
Lacan, J. (1988). *The Seminar, Book I, Freud's Papers on Technique, 1953–1954*. J. Forrester (Trans.). Cambridge: Cambridge University Press.
Lacan, J. (2014). *The Seminar, Book X, Anxiety*. J.-A. Miller (Ed.), A.R. Price (Trans.). Cambridge, UK & Malden, MA: Polity Press.
Lefort, Rosine & Lefort, Robert (1984). L'enfant: un Analysant à Part Entière. *L'Ane, 16*: 3.
Lefort, Rosine & Lefort, Robert (1988). *Les Structures de la Psychose: L'Enfant au Loup et le Président*. Paris: Seuil.
Lefort, Rosine & Lefort, Robert (1994). *Birth of the Other*. Urbana and Chicago: Illinois University Press.
Lefort, Rosine & Lefort, Robert (1995). *Maryse Devient une Petite Fille: Psychanalyse d'une Enfant de 26 Mois*. Paris: Seuil.
Levy, K. (1960). Simultaneous Analysis of Mother and Child. *Psychoanalytic Study of the Child 15*: 378–391.
Mannoni, M. (1973a). *The Retarded Child and the Mother: A Psychoanalytic Study*. London: Tavistock.
Mannoni, M. (1973b). *The Child, his "Illness" and the Others*. London: Penguin.
Rodríguez, L. (1996). The Family and the Subject: a Lacanian Perspective. *Analysis, 7*: 21–33.
Rodríguez, L. (1998). The Mother, the Child, the Truth and the Symptom. *Analysis, 8*: 56–58.
Rodríguez, L. (1999). *Psychoanalysis with Children*. London & New York: Free Association Books.
Rodríguez, L. (2001) Autistic speech. *Analysis, 10*: 124–136.
Rodríguez, L. (2005). Persona non grata. Paper presented at the Conference of the CFAR (Centre for Freudian Analysis and Research), London, 24th June 2005.
Rodríguez, L. (2007). Sexual Malaise in the Twenty-First Century. *Analysis, 13*: 91–97.
Rodríguez, L. (2008). Autistic Transference. *Journal of the Centre for Freudian Analysis and Research, 18*: 135–155.
Rodríguez, L. (2009). Body Parts. *Analysis, 15*: 63–74.
Rodríguez, L. (2013). Discourse and *Lalangue*. *Analysis, 18*: 151–166.
Rodríguez, L. (2016). Hysterics Today. In: *Hysteria Today*. London: Karnac CFAR Library, pp. 1–25.
Soler, C. (2006). *What Lacan Said about Women*. J. Holland (Trans.). New York: Other Press.

CHAPTER SIX

From childhood psychosis to neurosis

Cristina R. Laurita

Lacan's theories and remarks on the structures indicate that clinical structures (psychosis, perversion, and neurosis) once formed are unchangeable. That is, although shifts are possible with regard to the discursive position one occupies (e.g., an obsessional may become hystericised during analysis), the structure itself does not change. According to Lacan, a neurotic will not become psychotic, and a psychotic will not become neurotic. Verhaeghe affirms this, noting that "[a]cross the three structures themselves no transition is possible" (Verhaeghe, 2004, p. 460).

For Lacan, the structures are determined by the operation of the Oedipus complex and the installation of the paternal function. In the Lacanian diagnostic schema, everything hinges on whether or not the paternal function, or Name-of-the-Father, has been installed. Indeed, as Fink explains, "either the paternal function is operative by a certain age or it never will be" (Fink, 1997, p. 82). Moreover, I believe that the binary nature of the paternal function (i.e., it is either installed or not) needs to be conceptualised within a temporal context having to do with child development. Although Fink does not flesh this out, he does endorse that "[t]here is, of course, some question about the maximum age at which the paternal function can be instated—that is, the age beyond which one's psychical structure cannot be further modified" (Fink, 1997, p. 82).

In this chapter I will argue that there must be a critical window during child development during which the resulting clinical structure might still be malleable and can potentially change. This logically follows, because psychic structures develop and are not biologically given. The potential implications of these ideas for analytic practice with children are of paramount importance.

Taking this as my starting point, the focus of my chapter is two fold:

1. When and how might a psychic structure be considered still malleable (during childhood) and potentially transform into a different one? This is a theoretical supposition, but perhaps one that can be supported with clinical evidence and material to verify its plausibility.
2. How, from a clinical point of view, might one direct the treatment so as to facilitate or bring about such a transformation?

In what follows I will draw upon a case vignette that I believe illustrates an accomplishment, through the clinical work, of a critical shift in a child, from a psychotic to a neurotic structure. This is not meant to be prescriptive, or to universalise a set of interventions but rather to speak to larger clinical and theoretical issues from the particularity of a case.

I worked with a child whom I will refer to as Thomas for close to two years (he was approximately six years old at the beginning of treatment and eight when the treatment ended). When Thomas was first referred to me, my initial impressions of him came by way of how he was spoken about by others. The child's school and parents told me that Thomas had a "behaviour problem" and that they wanted me to help the family "better manage" his behaviours. Among the long list of behaviours that they wanted eradicated were: Thomas sticking his finger in the automatic pencil sharpener, eating pieces of plastic bags and whole post-it notes, squirting juice on himself and describing himself to the "lunch aide" at school as "worthless", fighting with other children, twice hitting children over the head with his lunchbox, threatening to kill two children with a knife, and frequently complaining to his teacher that he was scared of his father and hated him.

During my initial meetings with Thomas's parents, it was abundantly clear that they were "tired of him". His father declared that he considered Thomas to be "just a bad kid" and felt the situation was hopeless. Although they had adopted Thomas when he was a baby, his father had been giving serious thought to putting him back up for adoption: "He's taking over. I can't even be in the house anymore. It's either him or me." The parents were on the brink of divorce. His mother scowled and demanded that I "fix" Thomas.

In my first few meetings with Thomas, he said very little. There was minimal eye contact and it was as though I was not even in the room. At times he barely moved, appearing to be frozen and immobile, and at other times he was unrestrained and chaotic. Over time, I came to learn that he was presenting that way due to experiencing hallucinations. That is, Thomas often went into a kind of fight-or-flight reaction to the hallucinations that scared him, and that is what generated his alternately frozen and frenetic ways of being, both inside and outside of sessions.

I encouraged Thomas to speak with me about the hallucinations, saying: "You may feel as though the voices and images are very scary and powerful, and that you want to just hide or run away from them, but words can be much more powerful. Let's work together to talk about the voices and images. Talking can help build a shield against them, protecting you from them." Thomas's entire body and being noticeably calmed and settled as he listened to me say this. In response to this intervention, and as he came to trust me more over the course of our sessions, seeing me as a benign figure who wanted to help him, he began speaking about the hallucinations.

During one session, he revealed that he sometimes heard a voice of "someone laughing at him", and although he didn't understand why, he felt certain that it was about him. This is what Lacan refers to as psychotic certainty—he feels certain that the hallucination is about him, even if he doesn't understand anything else about it (Lacan, 1955–1956, p. 74). Thomas frequently experienced the auditory hallucinations at night, but also sometimes during the day. Indeed, the two incidents of hitting children over the head with his lunchbox became more comprehensible once Thomas told me that he believed the children were laughing at him and mocking him. In reality, the children were laughing but not at him; however, Thomas registered their laughter as equivalent to the hallucinated mocking laughter. The visual hallucinations seemed to be images of a human figure, and although the nature of them was never fully elucidated, both the visual and auditory hallucinations did go away by the end of treatment.

My early attempts to engage Thomas in play were met by him repeating a simple sequence with action figures: he would tell me to be one of the figures and he would take another, saying, "Okay, now they fight." He would make quick work of immediately crashing his action figure into mine, knocking it over quite forcefully each time, and sometimes throwing it across the room. He repeated this sequence with two more action figures, and so on, content to spend a great deal of time repeating this arrangement, and always with Thomas as the "bad guy". I asked Thomas, "Why all the fighting?", to which he responded: "Just because. They fight." What marked the early stage of treatment was therefore a demand: to fight.

I imagined that Thomas might be showing me something through this play sequence in which the signifier "fight" seemed to insist. I spoke with his parents, who endorsed frequent arguments between them, and together we began to wonder if Thomas had overheard or witnessed them. Perhaps Thomas was re-enacting through play something about his parents' fighting (i.e., "they fight") that could not yet be symbolised for him.

We recall that his father's declaration that "it's either him or me" was an indication that the father/son relationship was marked by a tone of imaginary rivalry—a kind of Hegelian fight to the death in which only one could survive. In fact, this dynamic characterised most of Thomas's relationships—as I remarked earlier, he had been getting into fights at school and had even threatened to kill some of his peers. In his contentious and downright rivalrous relationship with his father, he wanted his father gone. Thomas would even cry when his father returned home from business trips and say he wished he would leave again. In many ways, Thomas indeed seemed to have succeeded in taking the place of his father, even to the extent of literally sleeping in the same bed with his mother every night, as his father was relegated to the guest bedroom. In the mother's discourse, too, the father was either absent or demeaned, as she often criticised and ridiculed the father, saying to Thomas: "We don't need him, anyway; it's much more fun when it's just the two of us." When the mother's desire does not extend beyond the child, and takes the child as its sole object, her desire is not metaphorised and there is a resulting absence of a fully functioning paternal function or paternal metaphor, as in psychosis (Lacan, 1959).

This failure of the mother's desire to extend beyond the child, and the absence of the father, was also evident in the story of Thomas's adoption. Thomas had been adopted when he was young, and the only thing he knew about being adopted was a story his mother repeatedly told him: "You were supposed to be mine, but you were born on the wrong side of the country, and so I had to take two planes, a train, a bus, and a car to come get you and take you with me." The father's desire is not present in this story; it is all about the mother. Moreover, it is a story about a child who is supposedly destined to be the mother's. "You were supposed to be mine." His existence may have become stamped with being for her, as opposed to something like a mother's general wish to have a son so as to raise him to grow up to be a good man who will contribute something to society. The latter would instead have offered him a place within the Symbolic, as opposed to one in which he is caught up in the maternal orbit.

This story may have left a signifying stamp, such that being "on the wrong side" may have come to operate as a master signifier or S1 with which Thomas identified. That is, the story implies not only that he is trouble, his mother having had to make a tremendous effort to retrieve him, taking multiple modes of transportation to find him, but also that there was a kind of error—that he was "on the wrong side" of the country and that he was with the wrong mother.

In light of this, it is perhaps not without significance that among the laundry list of behaviours the parents and others had been complaining about was that Thomas just seemed to be doing everything *wrong*. He was constantly missing the mark, which is why I chose the pseudonym Thomas, to play with "to miss". Much to everyone's chagrin, Thomas consistently did the exact opposite of what he was supposed to do. To name just a few examples among many: he would eat pieces of paper rather than write on them; aim distinctly outside the toilet bowl and miss the bowl every time during urination; and in baseball, he would run the bases in the wrong direction and cheer for the other team. The latter, along with him always choosing to be the "bad guy" in the action figure battles, was a perfect example of him being on the wrong side. This highlights the determining role of the signifier and the relevance to the pattern of living out his existence as being on the wrong side.

I will now address what I consider to be three key stages in the treatment, by way of which a shift from psychosis to neurosis may have been effectuated for Thomas.

Crocodiles

Over the course of many sessions, Thomas pretended that a toy crocodile in my office—which he said was a mother crocodile—was on a rampage. She went wild, thrashing about, making threatening-sounding animal noises, devouring or trying to devour all of the crocodile children. It was brutal, and no one was spared (I have found it very striking, and not without significance, that quite a few psychotic children I have worked with have, of their own accord, gravitated towards the toy crocodiles in my office and enacted a similar play sequence). Eventually I put forth an intervention in this play sequence, by introducing a male figure with a stop sign who came between the crocodile mother and her prey, saying "No!" and stopping her from gobbling them up. This was an attempt to represent through play, and perhaps install by way of clinical intervention, a version of the Name-of-the-Father/paternal function. That is, the male figure with the stop sign might represent through play the law or paternal function and possible barring of the mOther.

In *Seminar XVII*, Lacan famously refers to the mother as a crocodile and compares the phallus to a kind of stick in the crocodile's mouth, which prevents the mother from devouring the child:

> A huge crocodile in whose jaws you are—that's the mother. One never knows what might suddenly come over her and make her shut her trap. That's what the mother's desire is. Thus, I have tried to explain that there was something that was reassuring. [...] There is a roller, made out of stone of course, which is there, potentially, at the level of her trap, and it acts as a restraint, as a wedge. It's what is called the phallus. It's the roller that shelters you, if, all of a sudden, she closes it. (Lacan, 1969–1970, p. 112)

The installation of a no/Name-of-the-Father in the phallic function involves prohibition but also allows for accession to the Symbolic and the realm of desire and lack, by pointing to a direction of the mother's desire outside the child. One might argue that this was absent in Thomas's family, but perhaps the possibility of instituting the paternal function can be introduced in analysis with a child through interventions in play such as those described here. As Fink suggests, "It seems likely that appropriately oriented analytic work with young children can, up to a certain point, bring about the establishment of the paternal function" (Fink, 1997, p. 82).

What paralleled this individual analytic work through play with Thomas was work with the mother in which the primary focus was helping her to actually develop desires outside the child. It is not uncommon for periodic individual meetings with a parent to occur alongside a child's treatment, not as a form of individual treatment for the parent but rather to support and better facilitate the overall trajectory of the child's treatment. Concretely, this meant encouraging Thomas's mother to pursue other activities she could enjoy, other relationships, to consider dealing with her marital problems in couples treatment with a different clinician (though she never did pursue that), and to attend to and cultivate other aspects of her identity other than being a mother. As a result, both mother and child began to find some breathing room. In play, the crocodile children were spared and formed a family as the crocodile mother married the male figure with the stop sign, who became the "crocodile children's daddy".

Reconstructing the adoption story/the Other's desire

The original adoption story that Thomas's mother told him had left little room for wondering or desire. That is, it presented more of a closure or an answer to any possible question of being for the subject: "You were supposed to be mine." Hoping to carve out a space within which he could come to be, outside of the identification of being for his mother, and being hers, I began to introduce a gap or space, in the form of engaging Thomas in wondering about his biological parents. Hoping to carve out a space whereby desire could be directed outside his mother, this involved opening up for him a space of someone else's desires, other than that of the adoptive mother. I held this space open. He said he had never thought about his biological family before, and he was noticeably intrigued.

A desire for knowledge was sparked in Thomas and he began learning about his geographical homeland of origin, asking questions about the weather there, wondering what his biological parents were like, how he might be similar to them or dissimilar, and so on. Carefully coordinating this work in advance with his adoptive parents, Thomas and I together wondered about what his biological parents might have wanted for him in giving him up for adoption. This was tantamount to installing constructions on the level of the fantasy of the parents, which Thomas himself began to generate. Thomas's desire for knowledge didn't stop there; in school, he became quite curious and an active learner, suddenly asking questions in class and manifesting a curiosity and inquisitiveness that neither his parents nor teachers had ever seen in him before.

In addition to reconstructing the adoption story and the Other's desire, the overarching technique of slowly carving out a space within which Thomas might come to be as a desiring subject, outside the mother and the imaginary dyad, was done in a variety of forms across many sessions. Another form this took was Thomas literally writing a story with me, entirely of his own invention, with accompanying pictures that he drew, entitled "The Lonely Boy". This story became a kind of displaced autobiographical narrative for Thomas, in the form of a story with a fictional character who happened to look and act a lot like him. He wrote about a boy who was lonely and who was lost. The boy did not have a home but wished for one.

Around this time, many of Thomas's strange behaviours began to cease—for example, he stopped running bases in the wrong direction and stopped missing the toilet bowl during urination—and instead, signs of sadness and mild depression emerged. Along with this came introspection, thinking about things and wondering—about others but also himself—and a growing awareness of an internal world of his thoughts and feelings. Thomas's sadness was not a symptom to be eliminated or medicated away; it was instead a rather positive (and temporary) development. That is, his feelings indicated an experience of lack and the advent of desire—feeling sad about what he didn't have in his life and, for the first time, wanting things to be different. At this point in the treatment, Thomas began verbalising a wish to have more friends. Really, he had never had any friends at all, much less expressed a desire for them. His mother had been his only playmate up until then and he had been content with that. Now he was a lonely boy; his mother was no longer enough for him. Thomas had become a desiring subject.

To be lonely is indeed a very different form of "missing". Whereas previously Thomas always missed the mark and was on the "wrong side" of everything, including doing everything wrong, he moved away from this identification and began instead to miss *people*. That is, he began feeling lonely, and wishing for relationships and human connectedness, which is a manifestation of a development of lack and an opening of a space of desire. To be lonely implies lack, and it is only from lack that a desiring subject can come to be.

Building a nest: a place for the subject

Sometime later, Thomas became interested in the stuffed animals in my office, the porcupines in particular. The baby porcupine began to repeatedly stab others with its quills, seemingly without reason or purpose. Thomas enacted this over and over again, with the baby porcupine viciously going after countless other animal characters somewhat indiscriminately. This play sequence seemed marked by a repetition of a sort of unrestrained jouissance (perhaps outside the symbolic order and more of a throwback to the theme of a fight to the death/it's either him or me). As the play became locked in this repetition, Thomas appeared to be enjoying it a bit too much—with a wincing expression on his face emblematic of the combination of pleasure and pain that Lacan tells us characterises jouissance beyond the pleasure principle—and so I put a stop to it: "No. No more hurting people."

By stopping this sequence within the play I hoped to install a symbolic limit, a kind of "no" to bar and delimit an unrestricted jouissance as had been manifesting in the porcupine play. The intention behind this was similar to that of my intervention, described earlier in this chapter, of having a male play figure with a stop sign prevent the crocodile mother from continuing to attack and gobble up all of the crocodile children. Here Thomas was having the porcupine repeatedly attack its prey just as the crocodile mother had ravaged hers. The interventions described were an attempt to represent within the play, and perhaps symbolically install, a version of the Name-of-the-Father/paternal function and to set limits to jouissance.

Then, Thomas made the baby porcupine sit curled up into a ball, quills down in order to trick others into thinking he was just a rock. As the other animals went to sit down, the baby porcupine would put its quills back up, stabbing the others by way of this sneak attack. Eventually we worked with a construction involving the idea that the baby porcupine was lonely but going about things all *wrong*. "He doesn't know how to be with the other porcupines; he doesn't know how to make friends", Thomas stated.

In the next session, Thomas played that the porcupine figured out a way to retract his quills ... sometimes. He said the porcupine learned that he could choose. At the same time as the quills became things that can rise and fall (phallus as object), Thomas began to play that the father porcupine had fallen ill and may be dying. There was an alternation in play between the father porcupine dying, and then becoming resuscitated, and then dying again, and then resuscitated, and so on—an alternation reflecting not only ambivalence in Thomas about his own father, but also perhaps the fragile status of the Name-of-the-Father for him at that point (the father is alive, then dying, alive, dying again, etc.). In the end, Thomas decides that the father will survive, which seemed to me to mark a hopeful moment in the treatment, in terms of his prognosis.

In subsequent sessions, Thomas had an idea: "Let's build a nest together for the baby porcupine." He and I proceeded to spend many sessions working on building the nest (also at this time Thomas began to engage with me much more and used the words "we" and "us" with far greater frequency). He worked intently and for long periods of time without distraction, putting great care and attention into every detail of the nest, wanting to get it, in his words, "just right". Given the emphasis in his own adoption story on being in the wrong place and on the wrong side of the country, and his pattern of doing things all wrong, this effort to get it "just right" took on particular significance. That is, there was a shift to making a place for oneself, and one that is governed by a feeling that things are "just right"—an act through play that may have paralleled and signified the possibility of Thomas beginning to create a place for himself in the world.

In the midst of this work on the nest, the transference deepened. Thomas looked at me intently and asked me a question, for the first time in the treatment: "Are you a mother?" I expressed warm interest in his question. He continued: "I think you are, and I think you have a son—someone like me." I considered there to be a strong contrast between this and how Thomas presented at the beginning of treatment. Indeed, this sounds like a decidedly more neurotic structure—wondering "What does the Other want from me?" (Lacan, 1960, p. 693). Moreover, it perhaps implies the presence of a benign and caring Other, and a relation marked by a desire for a child to grow, develop, be cared for, and to eventually separate and leave the proverbial nest. There had been a shift from play sequences involving fights to the death or the threat of being devoured by the mother crocodile to instead a caring maternal presence who neither devours nor suffocates him, but rather creates a kind of metaphorical "nest" for him, a safe place within which he may grow up (and eventually leave the nest, of course—separating from the parental Other and coming to be as an autonomous subject). Instead of hallucinations, unrestrained jouissance, and relations marked by imaginary rivalry and a fight to the death, there is ambivalence, and the possibility of relationships marked by care, working together on a project, and so on. Also around this time I learned that Thomas had made a friend, a neighbourhood boy his age, and that they got along well and played nicely together—ordinary things—and that no one was getting hurt.

When he decided that the nest was finally "right", Thomas named the baby porcupine, giving it a name one syllable away from his own. This work of completing a nest, a place within which one can come to be, and then the act of naming, seemed to bring to a resolution an important process for Thomas. At the end of treatment, Thomas announced: "I'm the porcupine. Well, I was the porcupine." Thomas's final words to me, as he threw himself into my arms for a big hug at the end of our final session together, as treatment ended due to the family relocating, were: "I'm really going *to miss* you."

References

Fink, B. (1997). *A Clinical Introduction to Lacanian Psychoanalysis: Theory and Technique.* Cambridge, MA: Harvard University Press.

Grigg, R. (Trans.). New York: W. W. Norton and Company (1993).

Lacan, J. (1955–1956). *The Seminar of Jacques Lacan: Book III, The Psychoses, 1955–1956.*

Lacan, J. (1959). On a Question Prior to any Possible Treatment of Psychosis. In: *Écrits: The first complete edition in English* (pp. 445–488). B. Fink (Trans.). London & New York: Norton & Co., 2006.

Lacan, J. (1960). The Subversion of the Subject and the Dialectic of Desire. In: *Écrits: The first complete edition in English* (pp. 671–702). B. Fink (Trans.). London & New York: Norton & Co., 2006.

Lacan, J. (1969–1970). *The Seminar of Jacques Lacan: Book XVII, The Other Side of Psychoanalysis, 1969–1970.* R. Grigg (Trans.). New York: W. W. Norton and Company, 2007.

CHAPTER SEVEN

Rapunzel: a necessary unravelling

Elizabeth Monahan

According to the tale of Rapunzel, once upon a time there lived a husband and wife who wished for many years to have a child together (Brothers Grimm, 2014). They were very happy when the wife finally became pregnant. However, the pregnant woman developed a desire for salad leaves which could only be obtained by her husband stealing them from the garden of a fairy called Gothel. The husband entered into a curious contract with Gothel which involved handing over his new born daughter to her in order to ensure an immediate and never-ending supply of leaves for his wife. The baby, duly taken by the fairy, and named Rapunzel (after the salad leaves), grew up to be the most beautiful child under the sun. However, on her twelfth birthday she was locked in a tower. The only way in or out of the tower for the fairy was to climb up Rapunzel's long golden braid which was let down rope-like, for her, upon her demand. As the story goes, Rapunzel had a lovely singing voice and one day her singing was heard by a Prince riding in the forest who fell in love with her. Hiding in the forest, he discovered how Gothel gained access to Rapunzel and copying her gesture, he was able to climb up to "woo" Rapunzel. As time went by, Rapunzel discovered she had become pregnant and Gothel punished her by cutting off her long golden tresses and banishing her to a desolate land. The hair braids were left hanging out by Gothel and the prince unwittingly climbed up, only to encounter the fairy who informed him that Rapunzel was lost to him forever. In his despair he threw himself out the window; "surviving yet blinded" by his fall, he wandered around miserably until years later he ended up in the desolate land where Rapunzel lived. One day he recognised her voice and she recognised him. Her tears unclouded his eyes and he could see again. He led her to his kingdom where they were joyfully received and they lived for a long time afterwards, happy and contented.

In this chapter, I will describe the trajectory of the work with a girl—whom I will call Elva—who came to me when she was fourteen years old and worked with me for three years. She knew the story of Rapunzel from her childhood days and during the course of her analysis came to realise that there was a resonance for her with the fairy tale. Something of what she was feeling: her fears and anxieties, became represented in the themes and motifs of the fairy tale, and recast, and worked through, in her associations, and in her drawings which she brought to me during this time. By the time she came to see me, her parents had sought help from her GP, the Child and Adolescent Mental Health Services (CAMHS), and her school, because of their concerns following periods of hysterical outbursts, depressed behaviour, a possible eating disorder, cutting herself, and a serious communication issue with her parents.

Initially she was a reluctant visitor to my clinic and spent many sessions sitting with her signature Rapunzel-like hair hanging down completely hiding her face. Her hair was a substantial and consciously managed screen and lure or so it seemed to me. I doubt that Elva was using her hair to attract me, but I am sure her hair was used as a lure in other circumstances. With me it was more about hiding in plain view just like the letter in Edgar Allen Poe's *The Purloined Letter*. As Lacan remarks, the point is to protect what must remain hidden from inquisitive eyes, precisely by leaving it out in the open. This "lure" as Lacan identifies it is that which involves a being "caught in the trap of the typically imaginary situation of seeing that he is not seen, leading him to misconstrue the real situation in which he is seen not seeing" (Lacan, 2006, p. 22). So with her hair down I could see her "not seeing" and she could imagine hiding from the world. A screen both reveals and occludes, so in another way, her hair was a lure to the gaze of the Other, it specifically attracted this gaze. Slowly, very slowly over a number of sessions she began to build a dialogue with me, with furtive glances, moving her hair, to see my facial expression, or watch for any other reaction to her initially monosyllabic answers. Gradually, a positive transference began to build and despite her best efforts at maintaining a substantial resistance to any form of interaction, Elva began to speak without being continually prompted.

Elva was poised at the very pivotal moment in her life of leaving her childhood behind and had begun to free herself from total dependence on her parents, as she was emerging out of her latency period. She found this new phase a different and bewildering time. In the third of his *Three Essays on Sexuality*, Freud maintains that before the onset of puberty, "the germs of sexual impulses are already present in the new-born and [that] these continue to develop for a time, but are then overtaken by a progressive process of suppression" (Freud, 1905d, p. 176). Freud continues: "with the arrival of puberty, changes set in which are destined to give infantile sexual life its final, normal, shape. The sexual instinct has hitherto been predominantly autoerotic; it now finds a sexual object" (Freud, 1905d, p. 207). This (re-)emergence of sexual interest in Elva's case was confusing: it both interested and disorientated her. Her new sexually orientated relationships with her male peers seemed impossible to manage within her parents' rules, and sublimation of libido into sports, music, or some other form of acceptable activity was largely absent.

I learned that she felt as though she was continually in trouble with her parents and adults generally. Just as Rapunzel had been locked in her tower, Elva felt herself to be locked into an isolated existence in her room by her need to start separating and distinguishing herself from her parents. Her mother was no longer recognisable to her as the "cuddly mum" of her childhood, rather, she appeared changed, false, angry, and uncommunicative. In fact, her mother appeared to Elva as a personification of Gothel from the tale of Rapunzel, as witch, rather than fairy (some versions of the fairy tale render Gothel as witch, rather than fairy). It is interesting that the meaning of the name Gothel is "God-Mother" coming from a German dialect. But in this case, at this stage for Elva, it was more of a "God-damn Mother".

Elva has two sisters: eight and thirteen years younger than her. Uninterested in her much younger siblings and avoiding helping or integrating herself in the normal household tasks, she passed the time listening to music, smoking out of the window and chatting online using various forms of social media. When she became overwhelmed with anxiety, she resorted to cutting herself. Some part of her wanted to talk, especially to be listened to, but what she found unbearable was what she heard as endless diktats or imperatives all trying to "fix her" when she herself wasn't sure what, if anything, was broken. Noticing her anxious and withdrawn behaviour her mother brought her to her doctor who referred her to the CAMHS team in the area where she lived. However, as she was always seen by two people from the CAMHS team, she experienced this intervention more like an interrogation than a dialogue. What she heard was a demand for answers, and this confused and frightened her as she could not articulate why she was angry, or acting out, or had suicidal impulses. For Elva, the entire process felt like a reprimand and proved not at all helpful in alleviating her anxious or depressive bouts.

Initially in our sessions conversation centred around safe subjects such as, what book she was reading for school, who she liked in the book and why, what was going on in school with her friends, etc. Gradually a picture began to emerge of Elva finding herself in situations where she felt completely overwhelmed by an anxiety she couldn't understand, that had no known object for her. It couldn't be pinpointed to any one thing, person or place, and she could not find the words to explain it. It was a traumatic experience of feeling something unbearable, like drowning or utter powerlessness. In order to manage or mediate these bouts of oppressive emotion, Elva resorted to cutting herself and controlling her food intake. She found that managing her symptoms through her body and acting out in other ways permitted a temporary alleviation or momentary suspension of her psychical pain. She sometimes said she wished to return to the time when she felt close to her mother. However, alongside this she was very ambivalent about remaining a child: on the one hand not wanting to be a child, and on the other, not wanting to relinquish that safe place with Mum. However, this static position, this "in-between" of her two worlds, had a lethal aspect which she also recognised. She was incapable of resolving the simultaneous attraction to, and confusion about her situation. To stay in this "in-between" would be to "die of boredom" but to change, to grow up, would mean identifying with her friends as a "party girl", a position which also caused her overwhelming anxiety.

It became clear, as the weeks and months went on, that Elva was trying to find a way out of "dying": dying of boredom, dying to get out, dying to grow up, dying with a hangover, dying to meet the right boy, dying or wanting to die, in order to have a simple life again. In all of this, what is sketched is an adolescent's attempt to resituate her subjectivity, to figure out who she is, what place she will hold for the others in her life, and for herself. Finding herself in an unfamiliar and uncomfortable position caused a psychical alienation from the position she had inhabited called "child", which now belonged to the older of her siblings, while the younger sibling was occupying the position of "baby". Elva's reality was changing: she was growing up, and her bouts of anxiety increased in frequency and seriousness. It became common for her to express "guilt", or of not being "good enough", but even with prompting she could not explain the origin of these feelings. She brought her diary—which she put on the table during one session and left for me to read but with some of the pages taped together so that I couldn't read all of the entries. The first thing she checked at the following session was whether these taped pages had been opened. The diary was full of drawings, prose, and poems, like this piece:

Unanswered Questions

I DON'T know what is going on with ME any more.
My head gets SAD and I'm weighed by an emptiness I can't fill.
No amount of sleep can fix my tiredness. The shocking passing thoughts wondering if I jumped would I DIE.
Could I fly. Reminding me of how I was. Craving in a sick way, I want it back.
I want the DARKNESS ENVELOPING me. But then I'm fine and I feel as though I'm Faking IT to myself. WHAT AM I?

During the third year of our work, Elva brought me some of her drawings to look at. She was beginning to re-engage in school, in particular with her art class which was the first subject she started to enjoy. One drawing which she brought to me on paper rather than in her note book is a representation of how she was feeling about her mother at this time (Figure 1). It is immediately noticeable that her mother is masked and appears witch-like. Talking about this drawing Elva sees that while her mother's appearance is distinctly unhappy, possibly angry, she is still however administering to Elva, fixing her hair while Elva covers her ears so that she cannot hear what is being said. As is the case with dreams, pieces of art can only be psychoanalytically interpreted by the dreamer or artist themselves. I pointed out that she drew herself not listening and without eyes to see: I conjectured that she was blind to

Figure 1.

the situation. However, this did not resonate with her at that time. She discussed how angry she was while drawing, but couldn't pinpoint the anger other than to say her mother was part of it. It occurred to me that she was trying to create some perspective between herself and her mother while simultaneously re-humanising her mOther from the position of a threatening Other to a less threatening administering mother. What she didn't discuss about the pencil drawing is that she has no facial features at all: not alone blinded, but unable to speak.

In Elva's life, just as in the story of Rapunzel, the father is largely absent. In the story the father steals the salad leaves (Rapunzel) for his wife, makes the deal with Gothel, and then doesn't reappear in the story. As Lacanians, when we think about "the father", we are not so much concerned with the person of the father, but rather with the father as function, as the symbolic function that facilitates, and allows, the transition through the Oedipus complex. In Elva's story there is a marked absence of the symbolic father, the father that functions to install the paternal law. So while he does exist, there is a lack in his role as law giver, as a person with authority to whom one appeals and from whom are taken the insignias of the ego ideal (Lacan, 1957–1958). As Bettelheim says of the fairy tale father of the Princess, her real father is depicted as benevolent, but helpless to come to the rescue of "his lovely girl" (Bettelheim, 1995, p. 112).

Of course, Rapunzel's dilemma wouldn't be possible without the action of the father—he is the problematic and largely absent piece of her narrative. In the fairy tale he causes the problem and sets the entire plot in motion by stealing to come up with the object the mother desires and then disappearing leaving Rapunzel to accept the consequences. In sessions Elva rarely talked about her father. She concentrated on the rows with her mother, or with her friends, about what is going on in school, who is talking to whom, what party is on. This was the material she brought on a "good day". During a session when she was unsettled or "down" she would sit quietly for protracted periods and then tell me she is cutting again or will not eat except in the evenings at home or that she has been on the net looking at "proanna" (pro-anorexia) websites and that her friend has an eating disorder, and that she is in fear of becoming too fat. When she was unsettled or overwhelmed, her symptoms all bear the mark of a lack in the symbolic function of the father (Lacan, 1957–1958). There was an inability to produce a symbolically structured symptom, and in its place, there was the symptom in the Imaginary (the rowing rivalries of the schoolyard, and with her mother), and the symptoms in the Real (the cutting, and the attempts at starving).

In the fairy story Rapunzel has a beautiful voice and sings out the window when alone in her tower. This, in due course, attracts the attentions of a prince who waits and watches until he learns how to approach her. Standing beneath the tower he calls out the magic words "Rapunzel Rapunzel let your hair down" (Brothers Grimm, 2014, p. 39). Rapunzel does so, and it is not long before she is enthralled by the Prince who comes to visit, and he with her. He arrives every day to spend time with her. It is only when Rapunzel asks Gothel why her waist is getting thicker, that Gothel realised what was happening: locking her up in a tower had not separated her from the world.

Elva found her own way to "sing out the window", so to speak. It was through social media that she "sang" and spent a lot of her time in her room re-posting, surfing, and chatting to friends. Unfortunately, many of the friends she had were struggling with similar anxieties and the result was a reinforcement of the very things her mother was trying to protect her from: bad eating habits, cutting, depression, and a sense of worthlessness. Freud had identified a "particularly frequent and important case of symptom formation in which the identification leaves any object relation to the person who is being copied entirely out of account" (Freud, 1921c, p. 107). Not finding a stable "identity" in her identifications with girls of a similar age, neither did she find the answer to "who she was" from the plethora of "available Princes"

Figure 2.

she encountered when she was allowed out socially. Although she was attractive to boys and could choose from the various ones who indicated their attraction, this merely increased her anxiety, since liaisons with them did not produce a safe position for her to be in.

The drawing of the hand came out of this period of her treatment with me (Figure 2). The hand on a black background is letting free some birds, so that they can fly away. It is a masculine hand, a strong hand, devoid of shaped or painted nails. Elva didn't notice this until I suggested it as potentially "male". She told me that the tree growing out of the hand is an oak. It was also representative to her of her cutting. I wondered aloud whose hand it was; whose wrist she was slashing, but got no response.

Bruce Fink remarks that "the subject comes into being as a form of attraction towards and defence against a primordial overwhelming experience of jouissance, a pleasure that is excessive" (Fink, 1996, p. xii). Elva was certainly overwhelmed and confused by the experiences which were situated in reality but were also encounters with the Real for her as she rebelled, with alcohol, drugs, and male attention. Just as Rapunzel was banished into the wilderness so Elva felt herself to be unworthy and banished too.

The work with Elva did not have one single major turning point. At the very beginning the only way I could engage her was to ask her what she was reading in school so that I could read it and talk to her about it. I did this, and we had something we could discuss that wasn't "what she was doing or not doing", that didn't put me in the position of another adult specifically concerned by her behaviour. Rather I managed to be an Other specifically concerned about who she was, what she thought, with no judgment, no assessment, no right, no wrong. This began to create a space in which Elva could speak, and resulted in her finding an equivalent space in school in her art classes.

There were a couple of key times when she made complete reversals of her stated position of "wanting it all to stop", or "wanting to die" which allowed her to reposition herself. The first was when she started listening and participating in art class, enjoying the production of work for its own sake. Another major shift was when she cut her hair, not completely short, but half the length it was. It symbolised for her a letting go of childhood and a moving forward to a new and more sophisticated teenage life. She now had a new position with regard to boys: now they could be talked to. She no longer wanted a boy-friend but wanted to understand her male friends and to enjoy them for their interest in sport and film. A shift also occurred in relation to her mother. She was no longer perceived as the "witch" at home: she appeared fairer and often good fun. Though for Elva the need to spend time on her own in her room lessened, it did not dissipate entirely, rather it slowly took on a new form as homework and reading became a greater part of the time she spent alone and time surfing the net diminished.

"But the fairy story's happy ending occurs in fairyland, a country we can only visit in our minds" (Bettelheim, 1995, p. 133). It was initially the re-engagement with reading which allowed Elva to believe in magic again, a possibility for a happy ever after ending. For her the final chapter of her story is firmly out in the future. Her latency period is behind her, and her time in the desolate and isolated wilderness is finishing as she re-engages with everyday concerns such as school and ordinary home life. A passage into the Symbolic took place as she began talking, writing and drawing, while leaving her imagination to flourish; encounters with the Real of her body, the cutting and dieting lessened, resulting in a more secure sense of her own identity and perhaps what Freud would have considered a more ordinary level of unhappiness in Elva's day to day life. In one of the last pictures she showed me, we see a beautiful young girl, sitting in a contemplative manner, possibly sad, but not distraught, with a strong oak tree behind her (Figure 3). She depicts herself in this picture very much as the subject of the drawing, in a position where the strength of the oak tree is behind her but not being leaned upon. She is alone, but individual, a position she had to

Figure 3.

take up. To understand herself as an object for others she had first to become a subject for herself.

Elva's reading of Rapunzel was not a conscious searching out for a structure to understand her own dilemmas. In a roundabout way she came to reread fairy tales and stories from her earlier childhood and formed an identification with Rapunzel in the fairy tale. She did feel locked in her tower with no way out. She was angry because she was not allowed to endlessly go out and hang with her friends. There were never-ending rows about her smoking and she was, at least in her eyes, confined too much to home and treated too much like a child. At the same time for Elva there was no father as a "knight in shining armour" and the boys she knew didn't reach up to the mark. This resulted in an ambivalent relationship with her mother. Elva very much wanted to continue to enjoy her mothering care while simultaneously to be away from it. Her fantasy was to picture herself as a young and beautiful princess "who is kept captive by the selfish, evil female figure and hence unavailable to the male lover" (Bettelheim, 1995, p. 112).

Elva's position has changed, she is no longer trying to make up for what is missing in her father with a succession of boys, she has re-engaged with her younger siblings and is enjoying being with them. She has come through her "desolate land" but without the need of a prince to save her or to define her. Rather she is defined by her re-engagement in school and her focus on achieving good results with the view to applying to university. Her relationship with her mother could be described as un-dramatically "normal". Now the rows no longer lead to overwhelming anxiety and Elva understands that her mum is there trying to look out for her and help her, rather than to imprison, control, or hold her captive. As her life has changed Elva no longer finds in Rapunzel a metaphor for her life (maybe it's time for her to read "The Ugly Duckling"…).

References

Bettelheim, H. (1995). *The Meaning and Importance of Fairy Tales.* London: Penguin.

Fink, B. (1996). *The Lacanian Subject: Between Language and Jouissance.* Princeton: Princeton University Press.

Freud, S. (1905d). *Three Essays on the Theory of Sexuality. S. E., 7*: 123–230. London: Hogarth.

Freud, S. (1921c). *Group Psychology and the Analysis of the Ego. S. E., 18*: 69–143. London: Hogarth.

Grimm, J., & Grimm, W. (2014). *The Original Folk and Fairy Tales of the Brothers Grimm: The Complete First Edition.* J. Zipes (Trans.). Princeton: Princeton University Press.

Lacan, J. (1957–1958). *The Seminar. Book V: The Formations of the Unconscious.* C. Gallagher (Trans.), London: Karnac.

Lacan, Jacques. (2006). Seminar on "The Purloined Letter". In: *Écrits: The first complete edition in English* (pp. 6–48). B. Fink (Trans.). London & New York: Norton & Co.

CHAPTER EIGHT

Pushing the envelope: a skinful of trauma

Marie Walshe

The child is confluence of three desires—the family's, society's, and his own nascent desire (Lacan, 1969). The family as primary paradigmatic social unit constitutes a symbolic matrix of signifiers into which the non-verbal child is inserted and from which the symptom of the child is derived. The child's first position, therefore, is as object of the familial Other, whether oedipal, narcissistic, or real. The analyst's desire to work with the child as a subject and the other's demand to enjoy the child as an object: these are the cornerstones of the analytic discourse to be distinguished in the initial consultation and preliminary sessions, so that the child-analysand might delineate his own particular "relation with a desire that is not anonymous" (Lacan, 1969, p. 8).

A clinic of multiple transferences

In this clinic the analysand arrives almost exclusively on foot of a demand by an other (Rodriguez, 1999). The three imperatives of a psychoanalytic treatment—to bring oneself, to speak freely and to pay for the privilege—are undermined here, hence the analyst must strive to act not as agent of an other but of the child's Other, privileging the child's own speech, the rule of free association and the particularity of his own signifiers.

The analyst's first act is to determine whose symptom requires treatment. The child's symptom is a response to the parental drama and so their narrative is intrinsically relevant to the treatment. The parental dramas and family myths must be interrogated and the parents' signifiers noted for use in interpretations and constructions during the analysis. The adolescent in particular is trapped between discourses; a careful history-taking reveals the underlying myths which position the child as symptomatic of the family (Freud, 1909b; Lacan, 1969), or in an acting-out among his peers (Rodriguez, 1995). Freud discovered to his chagrin the relevance of these dramas (Freud, 1909b; Freud, 1905e), and the imperative of remaining non-collusive with the demands of parents and contemporary social mores (Freud, 1920a) with these analysands. This is a clinic of multiple transferences in which it behoves the clinician to heed Lacan's reproof, "the tree of daily practice hid from my colleague the forest which rises up from Freud's texts" (Lacan, 1979, p. 409). The analyst's own analysis, personal supervision, and regular return to fundamental texts are essential to maintain the requisite clinical neutrality and to withstand the bombardment of projections and demands.

The child's symptom "answer(s) to what is symptomatic in the family structure" (Lacan, 1969, p. 7). However, the symptom of the adolescent desiring to assume a civilised, social position must address what is symptomatic in the social Other. Hence, adolescent symptoms are socially determined, reflecting the politicisation of this emerging subject: body image, belonging and not-belonging, cyber-bullying, sexual promiscuity, etc. The enactments of the adolescent analysand are acting-outs and *passages à l'acte* whose life-altering consequences include pregnancy and death.

The symptoms and signifiers in this clinic constitute a mourning and working through of what Lacan called "the hidden transgressions" of previous generations (Rodriguez, 1996, p. 33) which the child-subject rejects as imposed narratives. New and old myths clash, as the position of big Other oscillates in a traumatic shifting between familial and social Other. Each new narrative—sexuality, subjectivity, identity—in which the child implicates his own desire, develops agency in this social, political, and ethical subject.

Lacan delineated the paradigmatic developmental and social anxieties in three complexes: weaning/separation, intrusion/sibling rivalry, and Oedipus (Lacan, 1938). He stressed the originary traumatic "prematurity of birth" that inserts us as infants into a pre-conceived symbolic matrix of signifiers, a realm of inconceivable fantasies and ill-conceived jouissance (Lacan, 1949, p. 78). Each mourned other, from mother to lover, reawakens the weaning complex (separation anxiety), a nostalgic longing for the lost jouissance of the primordial parent–child union. He called the intrusion complex the paradigm of all social interaction; from transitivism to paranoia, the encounter with the other sets the stage for a lifetime of self-doubt. He isolated three moments of the determinant complex of sexuality, the Oedipus complex: the discovery of sexual difference, the incest prohibition and the promise inherent in one's own sexual awakening.

In my clinic, I have repeatedly observed that adolescence is characterised by regression to these old psychic wounds: the pain of separation, the anguish of intrusion, and the trauma of Oedipus. Today's adolescent must also contend with what I have come to think of as the contemporary complex of enjoyment: the traumatic anxiety of enjoyment without limit, the obscene injunction against castration, to "happiness". The adolescent subject presenting with self-harm, addiction, panic attacks, phobias, and aggressivity cannot be brought to analysis unless the perverse familial demand for a "happy" child, which denies the fundamental lack which underpins the Symbolic, is addressed. The encounter with the Real which generates anxiety, the privileged affect in psychoanalysis, is insupportable otherwise.

Psychoanalysis aims not to produce a perfect solution for the child's symptom but rather a substitution. Its goal is not the production of an ideal object (happy, successful, satisfied or satisfying) calibrated to satisfy a familial or social demand. It perceives such a treatment as an attack on the particularity of the child-as-desiring-subject.

It is the analyst's function to manage the parents' transference to a clinic where meaning rests solely in the analysand—even when this analysand is a child. Managing the conflicting transferences and counter-transferences in this clinic is especially difficult. Parents presenting their child for psychoanalysis demand an act of nomination, a diagnosis whose imaginary labelling is often correlative to their own dismay e.g., "panic disorder", "anxiety disorder", "depression". The scientific discourse has assured them of a solution that restores their child to them as ideal, as object of their gratification. They find it difficult to support a work that does not respond to this demand for knowledge.

The desire of the modern parental couple is also perverted by its insertion into discourses based on knowledge (Verhaeghe, 1995). The "real" of science has replaced the enigma of the sexual non-rapport with an imperative to reproduce and a guarantee of satisfaction. The psychoanalytic clinic addresses the real debt incurred by producing such satisfying objects. One history-taking ended when I asked about the child's conception; the mother could not pronounce the signifier "IVF". Product of the discourse of science, it confronted her with an assumption of knowledge in the Real, a knowledge she could neither articulate nor subsume into her own signifier.

Children must know that they are desired; they must puzzle at the rapport that produced them and struggle to produce their own myth about a conception "of another order than that of life according to the satisfaction of needs" (Lacan, 1969, p. 8). If not given these signifiers, the child's origin remains a locus of real anxiety and he may, as in the example above, act out of the lack of a parent who cannot say "IVF", for example. The parents' history reveals the signifiers lost or inarticulable to the child. The analyst's interrogation of that coalescence of signifiers by which the child-imago was conceived by his parents reveals a history experienced, but not always understood, by the child.

Framing a space in which a psychoanalytic treatment may occur, therefore, requires an ethical vigilance on the part of the analyst and her supervisor. In a treatment where meaning rests only with the analysand, such inter-mixing of narratives must be carefully parsed. Whether the work will survive this initial intervention; whether a symbolic transference can be established and maintained; whether anxiety at the level of desire can be distinguished from anxiety at the level of the Real, depends upon the analyst managing these multiple transferences (Mathelin, 1999; Rodríguez, 1999; Tunnecliffe, 2004).

If a therapeutic alliance cannot be established with the parents, the analysis risks being prematurely ended or even perverted. The analyst must bear in mind that parents who present their child for psychoanalysis confront a narcissistic wounding (Freud, 1914c; Mannoni, 1970). The modern scientific discourses—of "assisted", even imperative, reproduction; of psychiatric models of deficit—amplify this countertransference by identifying the child as object of narcissistic investment and gratification. Outside the session, the parents' transference to the analyst as possessing an assumed expertise must be fostered as an essential therapeutic investment in the work. A separate discourse requires to be mobilised within the symbolic transference with the child whose *desire* to speak, may *speak* of desire. Until these transferences are established, the child remains a no-thing, only the object of the fantasy and jouissance of its familial Other.

Clinical example: Mary

A fourteen-year-old girl was referred for "cutting". As usual, I began by asking for the child's pre-history: her conception, pregnancy, birth, and infancy. Her mother's response to a question about the girl's birth was stunning: "Cut out of me, she was. They couldn't get her out except to cut her out", she announced. "Cut?" I repeated. "So, 'cut' is your mother's word?", I said to her daughter. The work began with this interpretation. Like a joke, condensed with meaning, this moment established a symbolic transference, born of the child's recognition of her symptom as a piece of non-sense, an illicit joke she enjoyed at the expense of her mother's signifier.

Without these signifiers, the pubertal child is in danger of falling into a "hole in the Real" (Lacan, 1974, p. 33). The child must be confronted by and separated from the enigmatic non-rapport of the parental couple that conceived him (the oedipal difference between generations) and the adolescent must be seduced into the desire to make an exogamous other into a parent in his turn. Without this transmission of the prohibition of returning to those who created him and the promise of that which he will become, all others are reduced to the "small other" position. Without Oedipus, there remains only the intrusion complex.

The adolescent's social symptom is a re-working of the infant's *fort–da* game, a regulation of jouissance in a discourse seeking to recapture the lacking object, $<>a (Lacan, 1969–1970). As in the adult clinic, the progression is: symptom (usually an enactment in children)—*nachträglichkeit* (the unconscious associations and signifiers from which the symptom is constructed)—*hilflösigkeit* (the moment of de-idealisation and destitution which confronts the subject with his fantasmatic formula)—*sinthôme* (a knotting of fantasy, drive and desire which transforms the enactment of jouissance into its use or a *savoir faire*). The child's symptom which had been addressed to the family is transformed into an adolescent symptom, a particularity that knots his own signifiers and myths into a *savoir faire* about his own jouissance. In *Seminar XXIII* (Lacan, 1975–1976), Lacan revised his earlier conception of the symptom as a cipher which could be de-constructed in analysis to reveal a sense-value. Borrowing from mathematical topographical models, he re-conceived the symptom as regulating the signifier, affect, and jouissance in a loosely knotted configuration which he called a Borromean knot. He used the neologism "*sinthome*" (p. 27) to describe this knot, a non-analysable sliding of meaning which indicates a unique jouissance-value, or operational instruction for going on as a particular divided subject.

The self-body

From conception, the child accretes what I have come to think of as a "skin" of signifiers which define and delineate his body within the discourse of the Other. These form the basis of the infantile ego-ideal, the signifiers of the Other's desire which offers only a mortifying identification with the family ideal. The adolescent must relinquish this position and, in his separation from the family, assume his own desiring, sexual position. The mutual de-idealisation of child, parents, and analyst acknowledges the fundamental non-rapport of all love relations.

The primary adolescent symptom is an attack on language: either its renunciation or its refusal. In contemporary capitalist discourse, characterised by a foreclosure of castration, the social bond is supplanted by the consumption and exchange of objects of enjoyment (Soler, 2014). Its concretisation of language offers an outcome that is more death-by-signified than the desired birth-by-signifier, what Soler calls "objection" (p. 209). For the adolescent, the result is often a self-harming encryption, a cut at the level of the self-body rather than a cut at the level of the Other-signifier.

Real separation in adolescence is the traumatic sexual re-awakening of puberty. The symptoms of this inarticulable drive are auto-erotic enactments (e.g., bullying, cutting, suicide) in the body, the primary container. These enactments revolve around a holophrase: "cut"/"pain"/"feel", cathected as word instead of as signifier.

Clinical example: John

John's parents feared that their brilliant son would drop out of school. He felt "disconnected", he said. He was socially withdrawn, addicted to internet fora and chatrooms. A suicidal acting out online prompted comprehensive peer group support which included summoning the police. In the ensuing discussion with his parents, he abandoned speech and poured a cup of scalding tea over his head. In the session he described, "writhing on the floor in agony" and calling out, "Why did I do that to myself?" His distracted mother replied as she fetched wet towels, "I have no idea but never do it again!"

He explored the feeling of "disconnectedness" that had provoked such an act. "It was all just a struggle of a feeling of separation between (my)self and all things ..." He regretted his acting-out but he was confounded by his passing to the act. He recalled clearly "looking at his father" while doing it. His associations, and a slip—"withered"—led to an extraordinary subversion of the family signifiers, revealing that his family name derives from the French for "impoverished". This undid the imaginary omnipotent identification to which he had been in thrall for so long.

His associations had produced a series of signifiers ("writhing", "withered", and others) on themes of separation, sexual difference, and powerlessness. This moment of destitution, of *hilflosigkeit,* was pivotal. In the session, John relinquished his omnipotent isolation and acknowledged castration in its sublimation within his peer group. The appeal to the Law, the analyst's interpretation and his own associations, transformed his enactments—a child manifesting his absence in an all-too-real presence in order to effect separation—into a chain of signifiers composed of his own master signifiers and signifying matrix. The consequent mutual de-idealisation of father and son supported a new myth based on a dialectic of difference, not identification.

His mother's immediate prohibition of further assaults on John's body also had an effect. The infant marks the parental couple with an archaic trace of their own desire. This trace is mourned by the parents who discover the child's self-wounding; their investment in a prohibition of further attacks upon the body mobilises the child's own re-cathexis of that body. Each of these moments—mourning, prohibition, cathexis—are moments of separation. The body is ceded to the adolescent in these moments, a construction not contingent on birth but on separation.

In adolescence, the subject is assailed by a body seeking "recognition in its virile function ...", by the anxiety that "he has it only by fluke" (Lacan, 1979, p. 416). The adolescent body incarnates the return of the Real in a series of jouissance-laden ejaculates: sweat, semen, menstrual blood, acne, even "growth-spurts". The adolescent counters this alien invasion by all unconscious means available: identification, splitting, fetishism, projection, even a regression to pre-oedipal absolute enjoyment or its autistic foreclosure. These mechanisms are responses to a fear of falling out of the Symbolic (Winnicott, 1974), provoked by his alienation in a jouissance-laden body not yet circumscribed in language.

I have come to see adolescence as a disorder of namelessness, by which I mean the lack of a *nomination*, a name that is not a diagnosis, a prescription or a disavowal of the sexual non-rapport. It requires a privileged nomination to release the child from his primary non-rapport, to determine his social and sexual identity and grant him the symbolic authority of an ego ideal. The Mirror Stage "Thou art …" gestalt injunction (Lacan, 1949, p. 77) must be superseded in adolescence by Lacan's "Thou wilt follow me …" commandment (Lacan, 1955–1956, p. 301) to assume a position as oedipal procreator in his own turn. The adolescent subject must acknowledge his relation to a drive-object and the consistency of his jouissance in that drive relation. I see this movement as a bridge to the *sinthome*, to the subject becoming the operator of his own jouissance. What is crucial here is that the analysis produces a nomination that generates an "eternal interrogation" of the signifier (Lacan, 1955–1956, p. 305). At this stage, it is possible to have all the words and still not be inserted in language.

The adolescent fort–da *game*

The adolescent's real body and imaginary image must be dialectically inscribed and circumscribed to produce a "civilised" subject whose discontent is regulated by the signifier. The analyst triangulates the tensions in this *fort–da* game (Lacan, 1964), directing the treatment as semblant of the object. As the analysand produces an object of his own and his own chain of signifiers in the analysis, the analyst, like the child's plaything, may be discarded.

The analyst's principal function is to engage a symbolic transference, to bring something into play at the level of interpretation that addresses the failure of the child's symptom and to create a therapeutic space in which the child may produce his own fantasy formulation (Lacan, 1953). Within the transference, each shift posits a new interpretation by the analysand in an enactment, a narrative, a dream. The analyst isolates the key elements: subject, other, satisfaction.

Clinical example: Sarah

Sarah, aged seventeen, began having panic attacks following the death of the woman who had been her child-minder since birth. A history-taking with the parents revealed that this death had been more significant to the girl than to her parents. Her depression did not fit with the parents' demand for a "happy" child; they demanded that she be "sorted out soon" because "the Leaving" loomed. They asserted that their daughter's "happiness" lay in a "good" school and eventually a "good" job. When asked to speak about how they had met, to say more about the original conception of this "happy" child, the parents responded with blank stares and their daughter with surprised interest.

In Ireland, "the Leaving" is the national Leaving Certificate examination on completing second-level education. This powerful signifier crystallises the Irish adolescent's dilemma in a traumatic mourning of an inescapable "Leaving". In painstaking signifiers, Sarah formulated a question: "Why did she *have to* go and die and *leave* me?" (my italics). The imperative "have to" resonated with the imperatives of death and the recent discovery of her own sexuality. Talking of the panic in her body revealed a matrix of signifiers on life, death, sexuality: her body was "lost" in a desperate "fight" for breath that felt like "death".

According to Winnicott, the child's "I am alone" develops from his "I am", an experience of containment while imagining alone-ness and alive-ness, separation and survival (Winnicott, 1958). It should be pointed out here that oedipal time is vertical—marking a progression across generations not developmental stages, from past to future. In the panic attack Sarah registered only the real immediacy of a time fixed in a movement without release. Without the child-minder's holding her in mind to guarantee her ego integrity, her symptom expressed her anxiety at completing that final oedipal movement from sexualised to sexuated subject.

"My parents want me to get six hundred points, I want to get a boyfriend!"; the joke's illicit jouissance resonated at her parents' expense. She recalled time spent with her minder, the "she … who …" shared school gossip, heard about boyfriends, soothed her "Leaving" anxiety.

The analyst's reiteration of "She … who …" produced the first of a signifying chain. "She …" was one "who" could leave and be left; the phoneme "who" interrogated her sexual desire in its homophony with her boyfriend's name; and the master signifier "Leaving" resonated throughout. Together, they inscribed a new relation to the desire of an Other: sexual, social, and subjective.

In session, she makes a slip: "living", not "Leaving". The analyst's interpretation pointed to the disjunction between her embodied jouissance in the panic attack and this signifying articulation. As with many other adolescents in my clinic, the signifiers of her sexuality were interchangeable with those of mortality: "leave"/"live"/"love". Over the course of the treatment, the panic attacks (which I considered to be her *passage à l'acte*) shifted to a signifying acting-out, a tattoo she designed herself. Her parents protested at this "piece of nonsense" which she defended as "*my* non-sense". The symbols in the tattoo represented the phonemes "She" and "who …": "she" for her identification as a woman; and "who" for her identification as Other, as a never-ending question. "It makes me feel connected", she said.

This signifier "connect", and its correlate "dis-connect", are highly significant adolescent signifiers indicating insertion or dis-insertion in the Other of language and social grouping. Separation anxiety is paradigmatic of the adolescent experience, in which the subject's position *vis à vis* the Other shifts and settles in a series of traumatic engagements. Separation anxiety begins with separation from the womb at birth, from the breast in infancy, and punctuates one's life thereafter in serial libidinal investments and losses until the final separation at end of life. In adolescence, the price of imaginary separation is the de-idealisation of one's position in the family and of one's parents, dis-identification with family ideals and the assumption of social ideals.

The infantile subject requires only one parental Other but this Other of the imaginary dyad must be de-completed in adolescence so that the child's desire may emerge in the "between" of their enigmatic *fort–da* movement. An oedipal third term must triangulate the identification of the child with the phallus for his parents and interrogate their desire for each other. The parental couple must be seen to represent something for each other that is beyond the child's capacity to represent; like Freud's Dora (Freud, 1905e), he must realise that *being* the familial phallus does not equal *possessing* it. He must be frustrated in his encounter with this originary sexual relation and thus encouraged to seek his place as either bearer or non-bearer of the phallus within the extra-familial social group.

As the Irish psychoanalyst Cormac Gallagher once commented at a case conference: "A child needs someone to eat for … and someone *not* to eat for." The adolescent must relinquish the familial love relation characterised by preoccupation (Winnicott, 1958) to take up the oedipal sexual relation characterised by procreation. The adolescent and analyst engage in a dialectical exchange to disturb the homeostatic satisfaction of the child situated as phallus for the family. Dora's neurosis was precipitated by her unconscious recognition that the "subtle circulation of precious gifts" between her father, his lover, and Herr K revealed the truth of the sexual non-relation (Freud 1905e; Lacan, 1951, p. 65). Her unconscious acknowledgment that the Other lacked, and her inability to collude with the deception enacted by the adults around her, brought her to Freud's clinic. His inability, in turn, to support the creation of her own myth, provoked her acting-out and departure from the analysis.

As a Lacanian analyst, my practice has been informed by Lacan's Schema L (Lacan, 1955) which maps the intersubjective dialectics—transference, idealisation, identification, and sexuation—in which the analysand is revealed as subject of his own desire or as object for an other. The analyst, operating from "the locus from which the question of (the subject's) existence may arise for him" (Lacan, 1955, p. 459), points to the impossibility of the identifications, seductions, and rivalries by which the child finds himself narcissistically captured. She introduces a third, symbolic element—to castrate, to prohibit, to point to an emergence of something in the Real. Collusion between the analyst and the parental or the social Other, supports these imaginary deceptions and leads to the annihilation of the child as subject. The adolescent does not require the analyst to act from the position of parental or social arbiter; this is not a clinic of compassion or good intentions. Her act must be mobilised only by her desire, interrogating the jouissance of child and his others, in a symbolic castration. Neither is it appropriate to do more for him than the adolescent subject desires. Hence, analysis in this clinic frequently follows a pattern of *fort–da* movements itself, in which the young analysand departs to consolidate what was previously worked through, and returns for a further slice of the psychoanalytic cake when another symptomatic acting-out presents.

For the adolescent trapped in a ferocious enmeshment with the family myth or a family ego-ideal, psychoanalysis offers another proof of life: a symbolic register that is not of the family, the social or of the body. The collusion of family and society Others to create a "happy" child which is a frozen, psychotic subject is inhibited by the analyst's act. This act reveals the subject not as sense but as a "dis-continuity in the Real" (Lacan, 1960, p. 678). In her refusal to be the agent of truth or knowledge, the analyst punctuates this frozen positioning with her act—the cut, silence, punctuation, equivocation, interpretation, invocation or construction. Her function is to cut the real jouissance that binds the child to his symptom, whether the anxious guilt of separation, the aggressive refusal of the intrusion complex, or the sexualised jouissance of the fetish (Lacan, 1969).

If the Other cannot be demonstrated to be lacking, the young person's body, in which both parents and child are libidinally invested, is symptomatically inserted into this gap in a defensive splitting. In the words of one young client: "My body is all that I have and yet at times I turn against my self (body) as though not me."

The social mirror

In "Spring Awakening" Lacan wrote: "A Man becomes a Man when he situates himself as One-among-others, by including himself among his fellows (*semblables*)" (Lacan, 1974, p. 33). The image that the social mirror offers is a gestalt; the body *appears* sexually mature, and socially normative. In his "Mirror Stage" article, Lacan pointed to the "formative effects" of such a gestalt for pigeons and locusts becoming sexed and gregarious by encountering an other, or even the image of an other. These imaginary moments produce a series of "Thou's" for the Other in which the nascent "I" becomes "an object who knows himself to be seen" (Lacan, 1949, p. 77).

In adolescence, the oedipal transformation is a movement towards a subjective organisation of the real of jouissance. A prohibition against leaving the family (being a subject for the family Other) evolves into a prohibition against returning to the family (becoming a subject for the social Other). As Rodríguez puts it, the family unit "incarnates" the big Other by fulfilling the "cultural mandate of procreation and biological continuity" (Rodríguez, 1996, p. 21).

The Other of civilisation intervenes from birth to seduce the child away from his primary carers. When these desires—of family and social Others—are conflated, the child becomes an object of exchange rather than an object of desire. There must be seduction, something traumatic in a *fort–da* movement that points to lack and therefore desire. Failure to distinguish the oedipal Father-function from the social Family-function places the adolescent simply in the position of "happy" subject of the complex of enjoyment. The prohibition eroticises; the promise enlivens. Without these oedipal limits the adolescent is an indentured jouissance-slave.

"Adolescence … directly affects the social bond and cohesion of the group" writes Alain Vanier (Vanier, 2001, p. 584). In psychoanalysis the adolescent encounters a subversive clinic in which rebellion is structurally privileged so that renunciation of the familial bond can be negotiated. Lacan described the difficulties of this separation movement by quoting Hegel's belief that "the individual who does not struggle to be recognised outside the family group goes to his death without having achieved a personality" (Lacan, 1938, p. 22). Those paying the psychoanalyst—parents, schools, hospitals, etc.,—assume that the child's psychoanalysis can be bought like any other treatment. Psychoanalysts understand, however, that a psychoanalysis can never be bought by an other but must be paid for by the analysand. As director of such a treatment, the analyst supposes that the child is the sole agent in the discourse and extracts payment in the form of his signifiers and associations. This supposition by the analyst is the crucial "act of faith" (Lacan, 1979, p. 425) that sustains the analyst as interpreter and symbolic agent of separation for the child-subject within the transference.

In the child and adolescent clinic, the transference of the child to the work is manifested in his supposition of Lacan's *sujet suposé savoir* (Lacan, 1964). As in the adult clinic, the child's symptom is addressed to the Other. This Other—the family, school, law—must be troubled sufficiently to send him for analysis. All too quickly in the child clinic, the symptom gives way to speech—a verbal act—and the parents' delight in a "cure" must be mediated through the analyst's desire for a treatment. The work of working-through must be sustained until a substitutive fantasy formulation has been constructed.

Unfortunately, as Freud discovered, (Freud, 1905e, 1920a) this is a clinic where a mis-handling of the transference can lead to further acting-out or a passing to the act by the analysand, or the parents' pre-emptive narcissistic reclaiming of their "cured" child. Even if not abrupt, termination of the analysis is frequently premature, coming at the behest of the family whose symptom has been rehabilitated.

The psychic skin, the ego, that containing envelope of signifiers which cuts up the subject's jouissance, is a constantly evolving narrative. Traumatic separations and punctuations re-constitute past and future contexts in a revolutionary retroactive movement. The ego is both alienating and familiar, "something that the subject at first experiences as foreign to him but inside him" (Lacan, 1979, p. 423). Anxiety is transformative, challenging the subject to produce new imaginary fictions to serve as his "truths" and mobilising desire. Each new name to call oneself, each new group ideal, treats this anxiety in an evolution of symbolic co-ordinates that mark the subject's assimilation within the social bond. "What is realised in my history is … the future anterior as what I will have been, given what I am in the process of becoming" (Lacan, 1953, p. 247).

The symptoms of this clinic are the determinants of the adult presentations, e.g., attention deficit and addictions; unresolved Oedipus and sexual psychopathology; unbounded narcissism and "personality disorders". In this praxis the subject of knowledge is the child, in all his evolving symptomatic particularity.

The child and adolescent analysands I have encountered are thoroughly comfortable with Freud's clinic. These analysands attend for an initial transformation, presenting their "dis-order", to be "cured" at the demand of their adult others. They return later of their own volition, representing the transmission of the signifiers of psychoanalysis, familiar with the process and its boundaries. They recognise the fundamental fact of their own divided subjectivity and treasure the experience of a discourse that is not predicated on any other's truth or knowledge except their own Other's.

A young man returned after almost a year. School refusal, self-harm, the "Leaving": he had attended regularly if peripatetically over the years. I did not ask what brought him back, trusting that he knew the rules at this stage. Indeed he did; it was my turn to be surprised. Not school refusal, not exam fever, something else. Throwing himself upon the couch, he announced, "I'm here for a shift!"

A "shift" in Irish slang connotes a sexual encounter. In supervision it was pointed out that this was also an unconscious reference to his positive transference to me and the work.

In the session, in that moment, I invited him to speak.

References

Freud, S. (1905e). Fragment of an Analysis of a Case of Hysteria. *S.E., 7*: 1–122. London: Hogarth.
Freud, S. (1909b). Analysis of a Phobia in a Five-Year-Old Boy. *S. E., 10*: 1–150. London: Hogarth.
Freud, S. (1914c). On Narcissism: An Introduction. *S. E., 14*: 67–102. London: Hogarth.
Freud, S. (1920a). The Psychogenesis of a Case of Female Homosexuality. *S. E. 18*: 147–172. London: Hogarth.
Lacan, J. (1938). *Family Complexes in the Formation of the Individual.* (2010) C. Gallagher (Trans.). London: Karnac.
Lacan, J. (1949). The Mirror Stage as Formative of the *I* Function as Revealed in Psychoanalytic Experience. In: *Écrits* (pp. 75–81). B. Fink (Trans.). New York: W. W. Norton, 2006.
Lacan, J. (1951). Intervention on transference. In: J. Mitchell & J. Rose (Eds.). *Feminine Sexuality: Jacques Lacan and the École Freudienne* (pp. 61–73). J. Rose (Trans.). London: W. W. Norton, 1982.
Lacan, J. (1953). The Function and Field of Speech and Language in Psychoanalysis. In: *Écrits* (pp. 197–268). B. Fink (Trans.). New York: W. W. Norton, 2006.
Lacan, J. (1955). On a Question Prior to any Possible Treatment of Psychosis. In: *Écrits* (pp. 445–488). B. Fink (Trans.). New York: W. W. Norton, 2006.
Lacan, J. (1955–1956). *The Psychoses, Book III.* R. Grigg (Trans.). London: Routledge, 2000.
Lacan, J. (1960). The Subversion of the Subject and the Dialectic of Desire in the Freudian Unconscious. In: *Écrits* (pp. 671–702). B. Fink (Trans.). New York: W. W. Norton, 2006.
Lacan, J. (1964). *The Seminar Book XI. The Four Fundamental Concepts of Psychoanalysis.* A. Sheridan (Trans.). London: Penguin, 1977.
Lacan, J. (1969). Note on the Child. *Analysis, 2, 1990*: 7–8.
Lacan, J. (1969–1970). *The Seminar of Jacques Lacan Book XVII: The Other Side of Psychoanalysis.* R. Grigg (Trans.). New York: W. W. Norton, 2007.
Lacan, J. (1974). L'Éveil du Printemps. *Ornicar? 39*: 5–7. *Spring Awakening.* S. Rodríguez (Trans.). *Analysis, 6*: 32–34.
Lacan, J. (1975). Geneva Lecture on the Symptom. *Analysis, 1*: 13.
Lacan, J. (1975–1976). *Seminar XXIII, Joyce and the Sinthome.* C. Gallagher (Trans.). London: Karnac.
Lacan, J. (1979). The Neurotic's Individual Myth. *Psychoanalytic Quarterly, 48*: 405–425.
Mathelin, C. (1999). *Lacanian Psychotherapy with Children: The Broken Piano.* S. Fairfield (Trans.). New York: The Other Press.

Mannoni, M. (1970). *The Child, his "Illness", and the Others.* London: Tavistock.
Rodríguez, L. (1996). The Family and the Subject: a Lacanian Perspective. *Analysis, 7*: 21–33.
Rodríguez, L. (1999). *Psychoanalysis with Children.* London: Free Association Books.
Rodríguez, S. A. (1995). The Public and the Private: The Process of Sexuation in the Boy. *Analysis, 6*: 40–49.
Soler, C. (2014). *Lacan—The Unconscious Reinvented.* E. Faye & S. Schwartz (Trans.). London: Karnac.
Tunnecliffe, D. (2004). Children in Distress: Approaches and Challenges to Psychoanalysis with Children in the School Setting. *The Letter. Lacanian Perspectives on Psychoanalysis, 30*: 62–76.
Vanier, A. (2001). Some Remarks on Adolescence with Particular Reference to Winnicott and Lacan. *Psychoanalytic Quarterly, 70*: 579–597.
Verhaeghe, P. (1995). From Impossibility to Inability: Lacan's Theory on the Four Discourses. *The Letter. Lacanian Perspectives on Psychoanalysis, 3*: 91–108.
Winnicott, D. W. (1958). The Capacity to be Alone. *International Journal of Psycho-Analysis, 39*: 416–420.
Winnicott, D. W. (1974). Fear of Breakdown. *International Journal of Psycho-Analysis, 1*: 103–107.

PART III

SYMPTOMS AND SYSTEMS

CHAPTER NINE

The watershed of the symptom: from Rhine to Rhône with Piaget and Spielrein

Michael Gerard Plastow

"I'm driving my car down to Geneva …"

… sings Nick Cave in "Higgs Boson Blues" (Cave & Ellis, 2013). The Higgs Boson is the smallest particle of matter yet discovered, or rather, created, and it was produced at the Large Hadron Collider near Geneva, many years after it had first been proposed. The search for the smallest particle, the elementary substance, is also a search for a cause, through the hypothesis that if we search far enough we will eventually find the final cause, the cause of the matter. But we can say that this type of thinking is neurotic thinking, in so far as neurosis conflates cause with substance and endeavours to find an irreducible notion of origins. Indeed, Freud first separated cause from substance when he proclaimed, "I no longer believe in my *neurotica*" (Masson, 1985, p. 264). Thus psychoanalysis was born in the very moment when the cause was no longer to be found in history, but rather in the way the subject structures his or her fantasm: a symptomatic formation.

The symptom of the child also provokes such a search for a cause, a search for a substantial meaning in a past time, articulated in an aetiological formulation, whose purpose—if only this cause were able to be found—would then be to explain and relieve the child's suffering.

This modality of *cause as aetiology*, whatever its function in physics—or indeed in psychotherapy—is destined to be futile in psychoanalysis, to end up in the *blues*. Curiously though, the Higgs Boson, this elementary cause, even in physics cannot be found in nature: it must be *produced* by a collision in the sophisticated equipment of the Large Hadron Collider.

> Flame trees lined the streets
> I can't remember anything at all

Nick Cave drives on: here he encounters a fleeting childhood memory, and a failure of memory. There is a limit to what can be explained by reminiscences. Therapists and their patients embark on the pursuit of memories in their *search of lost time* that might, in a Proustian manner, be able to be a *time regained*. Nonetheless, this is a search for a time that never was, a time prior to history, the *pre-historic* to refer to Freud, which can then only be imagined. Thus for the adult this search goes back to childhood, and in the case of a child, to infancy, which is an infancy *in fancy* only: fancied infantile and even fancied intrauterine experiences or traumas. Of course we can evoke external physical events, disturbances, deficiencies, and neglect during the birth or pregnancy which have an effect on the child taken as an objectified entity. This, however, explains nothing for the child as subject. And what can never be explained—the excess or surplus of the symptom—is then referred further upstream to genes, to epigenetics, and DNA, to which the enigma of the symptom is then attributed. The frequency with which the child's symptoms are referred back to some attributed genetic or organic cause is itself testimony to the failure of the explanatory model of psychogenesis.

Perhaps Nick Cave in his drive down to Geneva saw the sign at the side of the freeway that informs the driver that he or she is passing over the watershed from the drainage basin of the Rhine to that of the Rhône. The sense of "shed" here is that of a division: a dividing of the waters. There is a difference of only one letter that produces a division of the flow from one side to another. I am proposing here that this watershed is not at all a metaphor, but that it marks the itinerary of the subject in a manner that is quite real. Thus the subject's progression across a history and a topography produces a singular mapping (*cf.* Deleuze, 1993), which in Nick Cave's song has him driving down a street of his childhood on the way down to Geneva. In a recent publication, I put forward that:

> In such a mapping, the subject that emerges from the child creates a type of mythological topography of his existence. Like with Freud and then Lacan's mapping of little Hans' trajectory through Vienna, the mapping of one's history and its topography effects a type of writing: the topographical becomes topological in the writing of the structure of the subject. (Plastow, 2016, p. 2)

If I write here of different watersheds, they are ultimately all one: the watershed of the division of the subject and of his or her separation.

In this chapter I would like to examine the division in the approach of the developmental psychologist Jean Piaget, and that of psychoanalyst Sabina Spielrein. Each went down to Geneva in the early 1920s to work in the J.-J. Rousseau Institute, established for the scientific study of the child and the training of teachers. Piaget had analysis with Spielrein over the time that they worked together but saw this as a "learning experience" in which he was "glad to be a guinea-pig" (Vidal, 2003, p. 273). Thus he approached psychoanalysis as he would any objectified experiment. I would put forward that his previous scientific work with molluscs, and ongoing objectified scientific method with children, had hardened his shell to free association and the unconscious. There was talk of a joint project, a book to be written together by Spielrein and Piaget. But the watershed between the psychoanalyst and the burgeoning child psychologist was far too starkly demarcated to make possible such a collaboration. This watershed here is primarily that of the conceptualisation of the place of language in relation to the symptom of the child: for Piaget language is a means of communication; for Spielrein, on the other hand, language is the means by which the transference is articulated, privileging the unconscious and the emergence of the symptom. I will come to propose that Piaget, unlike Spielrein, was never able to traverse the Alps: he remained on the lee side, unable to effect the crossing, not risking the undermining of communication by the unconscious.

What is a symptom?

Firstly though, I would like to consider the way in which there is also a watershed between the notion of the symptom in psychoanalysis, and that of psychiatry or psychology. What some common psychiatric symptoms of children have in common is a loss, and more particularly a loss from the body. For psychology also, the symptom can be reduced to a deviation from the norms of development, that is, they are deficits or deficiencies in regard to what the Other expects of the child. In this sense we can also consider them, like in psychiatry, as fundamentally conveying a loss.

Such a symptom can take the form of losses from the orifices of the body, as in enuresis or encopresis. There may be a failure to take in adequate food or fluid, and indeed a regurgitation of what is ingested, whether it be through the reflux of the infant, or the vomiting and weight loss in the anorexic teen. The parents complain of a loss of sight and hearing, the teen "can't see our point of view", the child "doesn't listen to me". There can be a loss of hair in trichotillomania, or a loss of the integrity of the body when it is cut, or through repeated piercings. These means by which an object may fall from the body are what I would like to designate as the *taps* of the body—the privileged places where the inside becomes continuous with the outside, in which a bodily fluid flows or is arrested. And at puberty certain of these taps are literally turned on, through the menses and other secretions of the young woman, or the nocturnal and diurnal emissions of the young man. Even in this crude way, the symptoms of the child pertain to the orifices of the body and their productions. The leaks from these taps, as for any other tap, occur under pressure: in this case the pressure of the drive.

Freud's definition of the symptom is the following, "the symptom is a sign of, and a substitute for, an instinctual [drive] satisfaction which has remained in abeyance" (1926d, p. 90). There is a loss, in this case the loss of the satisfaction of the drive. The satisfaction is lacking and is substituted by suffering, or what we might call the jouissance of the symptom. Already in Freud's definition, the suffering of the symptom is part and parcel of the substitution for the loss of anticipated satisfaction. But there is another element to Freud's definition, which is that the symptom is also "a sign of" the drive satisfaction remaining in abeyance. Thus on the one hand we have the substitution for a loss, but on the other the symptom functions as a sign of the drive satisfaction, that is, an excess or surplus elsewhere that remains in abeyance.

Freud's notion of the symptom for psychoanalysis is something that goes well beyond the description of a behaviour, a malfunction, or a failure to meet developmental norms or milestones. And with Lacan the symptom conveys, or is "a sign of", an enigmatic jouissance. In my recent book, *What Is a Child?* (Plastow, 2015a), I utilised a formulation of the symptom by the author José Saramago. I would like to draw upon it again here as it very simply and eloquently conveys the essence of a symptom. I will later connect this to Spielrein's elaboration of the notion of the symptom.

In Saramago's novel *The Year of the Death of Ricardo Reis*, the principal protagonist Ricardo Reis, who happens to be a doctor, speaks with a teenage girl by the name of Marcenda. She tells him about her paralysed arm, a loss of function of the limb that followed her mother's death. She had been taken by her father to consult many medical specialists, but none have been able to properly diagnose let alone treat her. At best—or worst—she was told that her paralysed arm was the consequence of heart disease. Ricardo Reis responds to her in the following way:

> As far as I can judge, Marcenda, if you are suffering from heart disease, you are suffering from yourself [...]. We are all ill, with one malaise or another, a deep-rooted malaise that is inseparable from what we are and that somehow makes us what we are, you might even say that each one of us is his own illness, we are so little because of it, and yet we succeed in being so much because of it. (1984, pp. 106–107)

Here what is referred to as an illness or a malaise is specifically what can be called, from psychoanalysis, the symptom. The symptom, regardless of how much sense we can derive from it, remains as enigmatic and incurable as it is the most intimate part of our being. This symptom is tied as much to our suffering as it is to our specific modes of enjoyment. In this formulation we can read the two sides of Spielrein's notion of the drive in the following manner: the *destruction* that makes us "so little" and causes us to suffer, and the corresponding *becoming* that allows us to "succeed in being so much" if only we might be able to make use of it (Spielrein, 1912a).

Lacan, following Saussure, proposes that there is no difference between literal and figurative expressions (Lacan, 1962–1963, p. 216). Thus the diagnosis of heart disease no doubt carries a value of truth in so far as Marcenda could be considered to suffer from a *broken heart*. There is a loss of function of the body, not just the loss of function of the arm, but also the rupture and loss of Marcenda's relationship with her mother that leaves her heartbroken. Saramago proposes that if we succeed in being so much, it is precisely because of this malaise or symptom. He emphasises both the suffering and hence destructiveness conveyed by the symptom, as well as the jouissance of *becoming* which may be formed out of the suffering.

Marcenda's doctors, despite not knowing what ails her, have told her that she is suffering from heart disease. However absurd this may be, it remains the prevailing practice in clinical disciplines to propose an aetiological formulation and diagnosis in order to explain the suffering of the patient. Both for the clinician and the patient, the attribution of cause attempts to put an end to the constant slippage regarding this question of causality, or an end to the child's persistent question: *Why*? The symptom, moreover, presents itself as something enigmatic, as something that suggests to the individual that it has a cause. And what provokes anguish in the subject is precisely the enigma regarding the question of cause.

The symptom presents the subject with a fundamental question regarding whether a tap, or an orifice, has been left dripping or not (*cf.* Lacan, 1963–1964, p. 280): a question of the relation of the subject to his or her objects. There is a watershed—again—always the same watershed of division and separation—between the child as object for the parent: the infant who breaks the mother's waters during the act of birth, for instance; and the child or teenager who produces his or her own waters, in the form of tears, saliva, milk, urine, faeces, blood, menses, and any other ejaculations emitted from the body. The symptom bears upon the carnal relation of the child to the turning on or off of these taps of the body.

Language, Piaget, and the symptom

Ferdinand de Saussure, a native of Geneva, initially followed the nineteenth-century philological model in his own studies in the then new discipline of linguistics. This field of study first endeavoured to explain language by tracing it back to a postulated language source, a supposed original Indo-European, in the model of Sanskrit: an origin or cause of language. However, in later pursuing his own structural study of language, he had the following to say about this question of origins:

> The question of the origin of languages does not have the importance given to it. The question does not even exist. Question of the

> *source* of the Rhône: puerile! The moment of genesis is not in itself able to be grasped: it cannot be seen. (Cited in: Arrivé 2007, p. 20, translated for this edition)

So for Saussure, the pursuit of origins, at least in regard to language, is puerile, or infantile.

The infant or child in psychoanalysis may pursue the cause of the symptom through play, but ultimately the child's demand must be articulated in language, via the very notion of the signifier introduced by Saussure. Hence the play of the symptom must be articulated through the play of the signifier (*cf.* Plastow, 2015a, pp. 34–35). However for the analyst to pursue the cause of childhood suffering in infancy, or even the foetus or embryo, is infantile: the *source* of the symptom cannot be seen.

For psychoanalysis, furthermore, what can never be seen by the subject is the primal scene, the moment of one's parents' enjoyment in which one's origins lie, but from which one is necessarily excluded. This is a fundamental lack at the heart of the symptom, a lost time, an exquisite moment of jouissance that is fundamentally lacking for the subject. It is this lack that is at the heart of the symptom that promotes an always failing search for this missing moment in which one was created (Plastow, 2015b, p. 5).

By contrast, in his book *The Language and Thought of the Child*, first published in 1923, Jean Piaget returns to this question of the origin of language by questioning its function: "What are the needs which the child tends to satisfy when he talks?" (p. 1). If Saussure the linguist turned away from the question of origins in linguistics, Piaget the psychologist effected a retrogressive movement back towards the idea of the source of language. He posited that primitive language exists, "in the case of defective persons, primitive races and young children" (p. 2). These are precisely the three reference points studied by nineteenth-century philological linguistics, in the presumption that it was in such instances that one would find primitive forms of language: Piaget specifically refers to "primitive child language" (p. 4). Since he puts forward the notion that language exists in order to communicate, his experiments are designed to demonstrate the nominal failures of communication that are part of what he construes as this primitive language. From the outset, in the study outlined in this book, Piaget defines the monologue that he hears in the younger child as, "simply a side-tracking of the original function of language", noting that the child's words in this instance "have no social function" (p. 16). This social function is narrowly defined as an adult-type speech that is directed to another imaginary being. In defining the language of the child in this way, Piaget inevitably finds that the child differs from the adult, referring to the speech of the child as "egocentric language" (p. 35).

In the part of Piaget's book commented upon by Lacan, Piaget is interested in what he supposes to be the loss of knowledge in the transmission from one child to another. This experiment involves the examiner, Piaget, giving the child a diagram of a tube with a tap in its lower part. However, what we can discern is that the child, *contra Piaget*, articulates the function of the tap as *cause*. Cause for psychoanalysis is something that specifically pertains to the body, and the desires of the subject. What the experiment demonstrates is that the child, far from being the imperfect exponent of language that Piaget sets out to prove, is caught up in language, subject to its ebb and flow, just as he or she is caught up in the high and low tides of the fluids of the body. The child is able to articulate his own notion of the tap, the fact that it excites him, perhaps not only makes him want to pass water, but also to pass on his singular account to the other child (Lacan, 1963–1964a, p. 280). The child produces an account that has the same structure as Lacan's *passe*. And whether it is to produce a flow of speech, or emission from his or her body, this production is also the formation of the child's symptom. This is what Piaget misses in his efforts to find deficits in the child's speech.

In reference to little Hans, Lacan alludes to the plumber who might be able to come and fix the leaking tap. In Freud's case history, this is little Hans' final fantasy: "The plumber came; and first he took away my behind with a pair of pincers, and then gave me another, and then the same with my widdler [*Wiwimacher*]" (Freud, 1909b, p. 98). We give the German here because little Hans refers specifically to his *wee-wee maker*, an organ that *makes* an object, the wee-wee in this case, that falls from his body. This wee-wee maker—which Lacan says is the principle of his phobia, his symptom—is the carnal cause of his desire. It is his little pound of flesh that, in his fantasy, can also be shed from his body. Thus little Hans gives voice to a type of intervention, which involves his body and its taps, by virtue of which he is able to position himself in the symptom that he has elaborated in his fantasies.

Spielrein's apprehension of language and the symptom

In 1912, Sabina Spielrein had published a paper entitled, "Destruction as cause of becoming" (1912a). Although it is not explicitly articulated as such, in this paper Spielrein elaborates a theory of language based on making use of that which—with Saussure and then Lacan—we can refer to as the *signifier*. This is in stark contrast to Piaget's instrumental and teleological grasp of language. She draws, for instance, upon Freud's paper, "The Antithetical Meaning of Primal Words" (1910e), and from Stekel, as well as her own clinical experience, to play with the signifier. For instance, in following the thesis of her paper, she remarks that "The woman [*Frau*] is bored through [*durchbohrt*] in the sexual act", but that there is an homophony between "to bore and be born [*bohren und begoren sein*]" (1912a, pp. 103–104). I read Spielrein as saying—through Nietzsche—that it is precisely through the destruction of the image (*das Bild*) (p. 107), that something is created: something that we can call the signifier. In this way Spielrein is able to articulate, through her use of the signifier, her explicit thesis that it is only through an act of destruction that there is a corresponding act of creation or formation: from the destruction of a *Bild* (image) to a *Bildung* (formation).

Spielrein's paper is said to have influenced Freud in his development of the death drive. Launer, for instance, remarks that, "Freud acknowledged her as the original source of his 'death instinct', and she has been credited with originating this idea ever since" (2014, p. 247). Freud makes reference to it in *Beyond the Pleasure Principle*, although in a rather ambiguous manner. He writes in a footnote to the paper that: "A considerable portion of the speculations have been anticipated by Sabina Spielrein [...] in an instructive and interesting paper which, however, is unfortunately not entirely clear to me" (Freud, 1920g, p. 55). However, what I would like to put forward here, is that in this attribution, the originality of Spielrein's notion of the death drive is lost. In particular, what is overlooked are the two other terms of Spielrein's paper, that is, *cause* and *becoming*. In any case, Spielrein's death drive is clearly different to Freud's as she views it as part of the sexual drive—the libido—and not opposed to it. In this sense we could propose that Spielrein's death drive is closer to Lacan's, as, for the latter, the drive is ineluctably also a death drive: the drive is always destructive in its excess (*cf*. Lacan, 1960–1961, p. 212).

But if for Spielrein the drive leads to a becoming, it is in so far as what is imaginarily missing by virtue of destruction, or symbolically lacking by virtue of death, in turn functions as real cause: the cause of becoming. So we can then read this *cause* to which Spielrein refers as a positivised instance of this imaginary loss, or symbolic lack at the heart of death. In this sense it is not so far from Lacan's invention of the object *a* cause of desire: an object of pure presence. In German, the word for cause utilised by Spielrein is *Ursache*, which etymologically, is *Ur-Sache*, literally the *primal thing*.

For Spielrein, it is specifically by virtue of the destructive surplus of the drive that this destruction can be the cause of a potential coming into being, or formation. So although Spielrein still contrasts destruction with becoming, nonetheless becoming is produced by the *causative effect* of destruction. Thus the destructiveness of the symptom can ultimately be harnessed into a becoming or formation.

She elucidates that the death drive tends to be overlooked in the libido and elaborates upon this in the passage cited below. With Lacan's linguistic formulation of the unconscious, we must read what is translated here as "images"—*Vorstellungen* or *presentations* in the original German—as *signifiers*:

> Under normal conditions the becoming-images [*Werdevorstellungen*] must predominate somewhat, particularly since becoming is the result of destruction, is occasioned by destruction; and, of course, it is much easier to think about the end results instead of always seeking the *cause* [*Ursache*]. However, it does not take much to give preponderance to the destruction-images [*Destruktionsvorstellungen*], especially with children and emotional people. The destruction component predominates in neurosis and expresses itself in all the *symptoms* [*Symptomen*] of resistance against life and natural fate. (Spielrein, 1912a, p. 101, my italics)

In this passage it is a question of how the jouissance of the subject's symptom in neurosis might be able to swing from the destruction side of the drive, to the becoming or formative side. And we note that she cites children, in particular, as being vulnerable to the destruction side of the drive. The direction of the treatment then, for Spielrein, would be to allow the subject to utilise the symptom in its formative rather than its destructive capacity.

With Lacan we come to see that the question of a cause or genesis *per se*—including ascribing the child's difficulties to genetics—is not only a false path, it serves to deliberately obscure the manner in which the symptom functions and dispenses with the very knowledge that it conveys. As Lacan said in his seminar on *The Psychoses*, "The great secret of psychoanalysis is that there is no psychogenesis" (Lacan, 1955–1956, p. 7). Any number of infant observations—which have remained a central aspect of training in many forms of psychoanalysis and psychotherapy—is effectively infantile, or puerile to utilise Saussure's word. This failure of psychogenesis belongs to the drainage basin of developmental psychology. Here we need to divide those waters from the question of the appropriation of the suffering, or jouissance, of the symptom. There is an enigma at the heart of the symptom, which can be an *effective cause* that the subject puts to use in the transformation of becoming. Hence Spielrein states the following:

> Every mental image [*Vorstellung*] reaches its maximum life when it waits most intensively for its transformation into reality; with such realization it is destroyed at once. [...] This actual *event* [*Ereignis*] produces ever new differentiation products, which are psychically transformed, now in the form of abreaction [*Abreagierens*], now as artwork. (Spielrein, 1912a, p. 101, my italics)

Here we see that with Spielrein, the maximum life—becoming—is produced in the very event of becoming, not in the products of this formation. Here what she calls *event* is the effective cause, the cause effects a becoming out of destruction. Spielrein has differentiated out this event, as cause, from any substance. It is also a cause that moves forwards towards a formation, rather than a retrogressive and infantile notion of cause.

We understand that Spielrein here uses the term "artwork" (*Kunstwerk*) with a much broader scope than is implied by the term used in English as some creative act or production. It is here that we can discern the manner in which Spielrein's proposition is co-extensive with Saramago's account of the symptom: "each one of us is his own illness, we are so little because of it, and yet we succeed in being so much because of it". We are so little by virtue of the destruction inherent in the symptom, but through the cause as effective— or as productive—we can succeed in becoming so much.

Therefore, for Spielrein, it is the moment of formation—the *event* of something being produced—that is of the greatest value. Any stasis is already a destruction, or a succumbing to the death drive, and it is only the active movement in which the subject is caught up, which allows this transitory moment of becoming. Becoming, then—whether it is the coming into being of the subject, or the formation of the analyst—is never achieved once and for all, but is a transient effect produced through an act of formation.

Conclusion: the symptom between destruction and becoming

I'm driving my car down to Geneva
Ah let the day break
Rainy days always make me sad
[...]
I can't remember anything at all. (Cave & Ellis, 2013)

Little Hans remembered nothing of the events that were described in the case history written up by Freud. We might say that the ability to forget, to forget what it is that ails us, is a product of the analysis.

Lacan also went down to Geneva in 1975, where he gave a lecture on the symptom and spoke at length about Little Hans (Lacan, 1975). He also spoke of Freud's *soll Ich werden*, questioning the signification of this *werden*, or becoming. He remarks that it is very difficult to translate this word, but that it denotes a going toward something, but is also a type of destitution (*dénuement*). But the *Wo Es war, soll Ich werden* is limited in its scope in so far as Freud proposes that the id, or the *it*, can be colonised by the ego, or *I*. He proposes that, "It is a work of culture—not unlike the draining of the Zuider Zee" (1933a, p. 80). But whilst the Zuider Zee may be able to be completely drained, the transformation of the symptom is always a work in progress, effected by an act or event in any one moment, in which there is always a surplus that remains.

On the other hand, if we consider Spielrein's prior "Destruction as cause of becoming", or *"Die Destruktion als Ursache des Werdens"* (Spielrein 1912b), then we have a *Werden* (here as a noun) that is tied to an act of destruction: it is bound to the death drive through the function of cause. Spielrein's *Werden* requires an act—an intervention in the Real—that is able to make suffering into another formation. It has to be enacted by the subject in the particular moment that Spielrein denotes as an *event*, which we could link to what Freud calls the "accidental factors" (1905d, p. 131) of history. To encounter the Higgs Boson, a *collision* must also be produced. An event as proposed by Spielrein, is then a cause without substance: it is a cause that is *a posteriori* and not *a priori*. This is precisely how the symptom is able to be taken up in psychoanalysis following both Spielrein and Lacan. Through the flow of the transference there is a forward movement of becoming and formation, in contrast to the retrogressive movement towards the imagined *lost time* that occurs in psychology and psychiatry as we have seen, but also in most forms of psychotherapy in psychoanalysis.

Spielrein's *becoming* is also the notion of the formation—no longer a *Bild,* or even a *Bildung,* but an *Ausbildung* (training)—of the analyst, first of all Spielrein herself as analyst, a formation that for her occurred through her own encounter with destruction, lack, and destitution. In accordance with Spielrein, we can also propose that in psychoanalysis, the formation of the psychoanalyst is something that is never definitively accomplished, but always needs to be demonstrated.

Spielrein was able to traverse the watershed of the Rhine and the Rhône: she moved from Zürich to Geneva via Vienna, from Jung to Freud, and from psychiatry to psychoanalysis. But Jean Piaget, even though he went down to Geneva, studying molluscs in the Alps along the way, was not able to move from objectified science to psychoanalysis: he studied children as he did invertebrates.

It was in Geneva that Spielrein wrote her paper "Some analogies between the thought of the child, that of the aphasic and subconscious thought". In this paper she maintains her emphasis on the place of language at the forefront: "Thought does not exist for us in any way other than its expression" (Spielrein 1923, p. 297, translated for this edition). In her work with the child, it is a question of the ability to create original ideas, ideas that spring from the unconscious. She finishes this paper with the following paragraph, using her own terminology which derives from both Freud and Jung: "It is only the collaboration of subconscious thought with conscious thought that can engender a creative work in this world: conscious thought must grasp what it is that the subconscious thought offers up to us, and utilise it" (p. 309).

Spielrein articulated for psychoanalysis—via the experience of her own analysis—something akin to what Lacan called a *savoir-y-faire,* a knowing what to do with the symptom. We see that is not at all a question of removing a symptom, but rather of being able to utilise it in order to succeed in being so much. In such a case we can no longer speak of a baby, a child, or a teenager, but rather of the *subject* that is realised through the symptom in an *event*. The subject here is able to effect an event that may transform a suffering into an abreaction—that is, into the act of speech or writing—or into another creative act. The young person inhabits a very particular point in this structure, a point that might be that of destruction, but which might be utilised for the causative effect of a becoming, of a formation.

References

Arrivé, M. (2007). *À la Recherche de Ferdinand de Saussure*. Paris: Presses Universitaires de France.

Cave, N. & Ellis, W. (2013). Higgs Boson Blues. In: Nick Cave and the Bad Seeds. *Push the Sky Away*. London: Mute Song.

Deleuze, G. (1993) What Children Say. In: *Essays Critical and Clinical* (pp. 61–7). Minnesota: University of Minnesota Press, 1997.

Freud, S. (1905d). Three Essays on the Theory of Sexuality. *S. E., 7*: 123–246. London: Hogarth.

Freud, S. (1909b). Analysis of a Phobia in a Five-Year-Old Boy. *S. E., 10*: 1–150. London: Hogarth.

Freud, S. (1920g). *Beyond the Pleasure Principle*. *S. E., 18*. London: Hogarth.

Freud, S. (1926d). *Inhibitions, Symptoms and Anxiety*. *S. E., 20*: 75–176. London: Hogarth.

Freud, S. (1933a). The Dissection of the Psychical Personality. Lecture XXXI. *New Introductory Lectures on Psycho-Analysis and Other Works*. *S. E., 22*: 57–80. London: Hogarth.

Lacan, J. (1955–1956). *The Seminar of Jacques Lacan. Book III: The Psychoses 1955–1956*. R. Grigg (Trans.). London: Routledge, 1993.

Lacan, J. (1962–1963). *Anxiety: The Seminar of Jacques Lacan, Book X*. A. R. Price (Trans.). Cambridge UK & Malden MA: Polity, 2014.

Lacan, J. (1975). Geneva Lecture on the Symptom. *Analysis, 1* (1989): 7–26.

Launer, J. (2015). *Sex Vs. Survival. Life and Ideas of Sabina Spielrein*. London: Overlook Duckworth.

Masson, J. M. (Ed. & Trans.) (1985). *The Complete Letters of Sigmund Freud to Wilhelm Fliess: 1887–1904*. Cambridge, MA: Belknap.

Piaget, J. (1923). *The Language and Thought of the Child* (*3rd edn*). M. Gabain (Trans.). London: Routledge & Kegan Paul, 1959.

Plastow, M. G. (2015a). *What is a Child? Childhood, Psychoanalysis, and Discourse*. London: Karnac.

Plastow, M. G. (2015b). The Ages of the Child. *Écritique 10*. Available at: http://www.fsom.org.au/ecritique2015cover.html

Plastow, M. G. (2016). The Kangaroo Rat Man. *Papers of the Freudian School of Melbourne 25*: 181–190.

Saramago, J. (1984). *The Year of the Death of Ricardo Reis*. G. Pontiero (Trans.). Orlando, FL: Harcourt Brace, 1991.

Spielrein, S. (1912a). Destruction as Cause of Becoming. S. Witt (Trans.). *Psychoanalysis and Contemporary Thought, 18*: 85–118.

Spielrein, S. (1912b). Die Destruktion als Ursache des Werdens. *Jahrbuch für psychoanalytische und psychopathologische Forschungen, IV*: 465–503.

Spielrein, S. (1923). Quelques Analogies Entre la Pensée de l'Enfant, Celle de l'Aphasique et la Pensée Subconsciente. In: Sprielrein, S. *Sämtliche Schriften*. Geißen: Psychosozial-Verlag, 2002.

Vidal, F. (2003). Sabina Spielrein, Jean Piaget—Going their own ways. In: Covington, C. & Wharton, B. (Eds.). *Sabina Spielrein: Forgotten Pioneer of Psychoanalysis* (pp. 271–285). Hove: Routledge.

CHAPTER TEN

Transference today and the necessity of invention—notes on working with adolescence

Kate Briggs

Working with young people has the particularity of requiring the agreement and participation of parents and carers in order to arrive at preliminary interviews and support ongoing work. The different positions given to knowledge in analytic, educative, and medical practices often need to be made explicit in introducing the idea that analytic work is a subjective construction on the part of the analysand, where the analyst is not applying a method or technique but engaging in a nuanced response to what is emerging. As a response to the dominant discourses of behavioural modification and control, where demand can't be refused, the body is often used instead. While this is often the case in adolescence, it is exacerbated for young people in situations where the function of a limit is not operating effectively either for themselves or within the family or institutional setting in which they are placed. This chapter takes up the question of transference in relation to the moments of invention that may mark a case or be turning points within it. While finding reference to such moments in analytic literature regarding autistic and schizophrenic children, it will be suggested that such moments of invention are also called for in other cases, of neurosis and phobia. That while illustrated in working with the phenomenon of psychoses, invention is coming into clearer focus as a key aspect of analytic work in the twenty-first century where the Real is having more pervasive and disordered affects (Miller, 2003, 2013).

The demand carried with a request for consultation made by a carer or parent carries a transference to the possibility of something being known. Maud Mannoni wrote of situations where the mother of the child in therapy believes that "only her own presence can help the child" (1972, p. 48), which is understandable from the aspect of the parent or carer's intimate engagement with the child and may nevertheless carry a further claim, the conviction of being the only one who knows what the child needs. Working with what the child represents for the parent or carer may not be possible from the perspective of the parents, and a first and necessary condition of working with the child is to listen to the child's own position, as distinct from and in so far as it is a response to the parents or primary Others. This is not to suggest they be seen as the singular cause of the child's suffering, but to recognise that whatever the child presents, through and beyond the particular experiences they may have, is also a response to the Others with whom they are and have been engaged. The term "subject" in Lacan's work is based on this dimension of the right to respond, and indeed is reduced to it: the subject is a response (Miller, 1988, p. 75). Psychoanalysis aims to effect the subject, not through an educative or pedagogical approach where what is good for the subject might be assumed and imposed upon them.

Subjectifying experience

Sometimes asking a young person about their life or asking them to describe things they have experienced in the day meets with a particular kind of silence, marking not a reticence to engage or to speak but an anomaly regarding their place as a speaking subject. Where a young person struggles to knot together her body, her self and her own history as lived, this lived experience remains somewhat remote (Pereira, 1999, p. 60); it is not subjectivised in terms of desire, which turns around the registration of an absence or lack, but presents by way of the imperatives of jouissance. Theodoridis (2013) describes a fifteen-year-old girl who presents at an outpatient clinic after an impulsive suicide attempt following an argument with her father who had forbade her going out: "She is smiling, dressed in a provocative way, excessively made up, with piercings and tattoos on her body. Her discourse is quite poor. She has not subjectified her attempt. She is indifferent, as if it had nothing to do with her psychical reality" (p. 64). Her pursuit of immediate satisfaction involves trying any kind of drug and new boyfriends every week. Oscillating between absolute boredom and intense experiences, he describes her as:

> [...] a disorientated subject, with no formations of the unconscious or manifestations of desire, who becomes satisfied from the surplus jouissance offered abundantly by our era. Confronted with her subjective void she tries to hold on to her image and the various fashionable practices of jouissance. This young woman with drive deregulation, without presenting a delirium or being delusional, is a paradigm of a great percentage of adolescents in our Geek era who, in a world with no Name-of-the-Father, take on this unlimited, compulsive jouissance. (Theodoridis, 2013, p. 64)

For some young people a connection between the Imaginary and Symbolic appears not to have occurred to integrate experience as lived, making it accessible in speech. Early in his work Lacan noted there "is a connection between the imaginary dimension and the symbolic system, so long as the history of the subject is inscribed in it—not the *Entwicklung*, the development, but the *Geshischte*, that is that within which the subject recognises himself, correlatively in the past and in the future" (Lacan, 1953–1954, p. 157). The juncture of the Imaginary with a symbolic system is particularly at stake in adolescence, a time of transition when the physical changes of puberty converge with symbolic systems that can be in flux. This fluidity, exacerbated by the imaginary worlds of online games, social media sites, and devices, can bring the task of being able to recognise oneself "correlatively in the past and in the future" into varying degrees of crisis played out across the body via cutting or suicidal acts, the idea of perfection or the demand to change gender.

Subjective crises are dramatised across the junction of the Imaginary and Real and the specular image takes on a particular significance, with the relation to the other reduced to a purely specular relation where the function of the father is not operating or to the extent that it is foreclosed. Desire is originally located and recognised through the intermediary, "not only of his own image, but of the body of his fellow being" (Lacan, 1953–1954, p. 147): recognising her desire in the body of the other allows her to recognise herself as a body. Hence the import of the peer in adolescence, a time of transition that involves relocating oneself subjectively with regard to a changing physical body, masculine or feminine identifications, the specular image, and the Other sex. This involves encountering the absence of a sexual relation, that is, that there is no one way of understanding or accounting for the Real of sex or a harmony between the sexes. The question of desire faces off against the impossible Real, which for some erupts as an impossible void subsumed by the other's address.

Some adolescents present with a body image that may be contentious and cause suffering in various ways, with the question, for example, of whether or what an other finds attractive or interesting in them. For others, the body may not be there in a way that is supported by a symbolic identification that allows it to be. We see young people trying to create a body, one that she might master to perfection or one that is constituted under the gaze of an Other. This is the case for each subject insofar as the ego ideal as the place from which the child might see herself as worthy of love, is related to the position of observer, as the gaze from this place in some way ratifies the child's association with its specular image. For these young people, however, the work is to introduce the Symbolic, that is speech, with the possibility of some vacillation into the certainty marked with regard to the Real. One young person presents with the complaint of disturbing thoughts of a sexual nature; another describes aggressive behaviours that disturb her; anxiety overwhelming on occasions when they find themselves alone or without a routine. The agitation experienced in their bodies might point to their role as an object that circulates, addressed to the jouissance of an Other. Cutting and restrictive control of food are different strategies in responding to excess; one uses the body to mark an ineffable tension that pervades her, to mark a cut; the other raising the question of what has to be controlled so tightly. For whom does the child seek to embody the idea of perfection in a staging where anxiety does not take the form of a question? The idea that she should be doing something induces panic as do intrusive thoughts that disrupt the demand she places upon herself to appear perfect. Analysis might allow her to find another response, to open her self to imperfection, to being one among others rather than the one all alone. Analysis might allow for the loosening of this identification with being the only one, so there would be less panic around being.

Borderline phenomena

In contemporary cultural conditions where the Other rather than providing a regulatory function tends to demand or incite enjoyment, the Imaginary is used to sustain identity, but it is fragile as Kohut (1977, 1984) made explicit in his work on self object relations. Recourse to using the body rather than speech is particularly evident with young people who are described as having or developing borderline personality disorders, into which category the fifteen-year-old girl mentioned above would probably fall. Borderline personality disorder (BPD) is defined as a "pervasive pattern of instability of interpersonal relationships, self-image, and affects, and marked impulsivity, beginning by early adulthood" (APA, 2013, p. 663). While the prevalence of early trauma in the experience of people diagnosed with BPD is widely recognised, they are considered notoriously difficult to treat, and the diagnosis often gives rise to negative stereotyping given the perception that BPD is both a lifespan developmental disorder yet also indicative of poor "choices" (NHMRC *Clinical Practice Guideline for the Management of Borderline Personality Disorder*, p. 22).

Fiona is an eleven-year-old Indonesian girl with a complex trauma history, living with her mother's sister and her husband and experiencing difficulties in school and at home. She self-harms by way of cutting and has suicidal ideation at times when she is elevated. Diagnosed with developing borderline personality disorder by more than one consulting psychiatrist, she has had a series of short admissions at an adolescent mental health unit and been discharged each time on the basis that "it is a behavioural rather than mental health issue". It is in this gap between psychiatric classification and the management of behavioural issues that psychoanalysis has a particular role to play. Fiona had significant exposure to family violence, coming into care at an early age after being abandoned and then separated from siblings who went into unsupervised care. Visits with her birth mother had recently recommenced after years of no contact; they were referred to as "monthly visits" but were sporadic and unreliable as her mother, who has a diagnosis of BPD with drug and alcohol dependency, might turn up weeks late or not at all. Her father had a diagnosis of schizophrenia, his whereabouts unknown. Being the child who is abandoned or rejected has therefore insisted in the reality of this young person. When

I received the referral from her case manager who as it happened was leaving, Fiona was described as lashing out of control.

Being at the centre of revolving teams of uncoordinated care from teachers, teaching aids, school psychologists, other health professionals, changing child protection and caseworkers, this young person can recite bits of behavioural plans and the rules of various settings. It takes time to establish that I am responding to her from a different place, that I am not telling her what to do or giving her more behavioural routines. While she is eager to engage, she is also hyper vigilant. If I asked about something, like an argument she had just had with her uncle who would bring her to the sessions, she would routinely state that she did not want to talk about it. I am careful not to insist or ask too many questions that she couldn't answer, indeed from the first session I comment on how words may not be able to say everything but they can have an effect. Whatever she is doing, whether painting or drawing or catching a ball, she says to me "watch this", often testing boundaries and commenting that I am still someone she has just met. The end of each session was an issue, as she would ignore statements that it was time to end for today, marking the impossibility of extracting herself from the field of the Other. After a few sessions Fiona said she would like to live with me. This way of attaching herself to another too quickly was also evident at school where she wasn't able to remain in class for full days and when triggered would be physically abusive. She said her friends were scared of her though she didn't know why. In sessions I noticed a pattern of physical proximity and elevation, and whenever she started to escalate in excitement, I would quietly move away. If for example, she insisted on doing something I asked her not to do, I would move away; if she ran off and hid at the end of a session, I might gently hum as I walked away. One day she brought to the session a girl she had met that day, and while it would not be common practice, I felt it would be helpful to see them together. As they talked and drew, it appeared that the imaginary identification between them was immediate and adhesive as if Fiona had found someone to speak for her, who she could be, assuming this other as her own image, in an intensity that could only end in rupture. This form of imaginary compensation by way of imitation, by "latching on" to a counterpart (Lacan, 1955–1956, p. 192) makes the other something from which she had to separate with an actual attack on herself or another. This, it appeared, was her only way of making a space for herself. Her use of the body was directed to gathering the attention of others, drawing people into a proximity that then became impossible and had to be expelled which was enacted in the Real.

Where there is a call to the signifier that is not available, there is in varying degrees a hole in signification that "produces traumatism in the sense in which there really is a hole in the Real, which for the child cannot be filled" (Laurent, 1999, p. 190). Situations that confront the young person with a jouissance they have no way of symbolising can trigger a crisis: when, for example, a child protection worker scheduled to pick Fiona up from a half day at school didn't show up without phoning and simply left her waiting. It seemed that each time, as the object literally abandoned, Fiona responded with acts of elevated and uncontrollable behaviour. Faced with a sense of the impossibility of a semblance of peer acceptance, her self-harm and suicidal ideation increased. Repeatedly suspended from school in consequence of violating behaviour plans, it became apparent that a more therapeutic educational setting was needed, along with further support for her carers who might inadvertently reinforce Fiona's sense of persecution, as she was responding to their comments such as "you didn't think that through" with "I'm stupid". Introjecting such comments as negative injunctions further eroded the place she did not have, marked as it was by the jouissance without limit of an Other that could not be contained. In this situation, Fiona began doing intricate cut outs using origami paper squares within the sessions, and was very calm, cutting along lines printed on the sheets rather than her body. While it is too soon to say that Fiona has stopped cutting her body, small though significant statements mark a shift: nominating herself as a child who was born drug effected, noting that a child cannot say "no" to that, and how in the moment of assaulting the other, her counterpart, some thing overtakes her. She has spoken to this effect and is beginning to note the effects of speech. Engaging in sensory and play activities had a calming effect and it was within that effect that a cut between the Other and jouissance could begin to be made. By marking and confirming a loss she could symbolise, Fiona began to de-complete the Other of jouissance, which would be the work of analysis.

To support this de-completion requires keeping a proximity that is close without "coming to represent a persecutory threat" (Tendlarz, 2003, p. 129). It involves taking up the position of an *intervenant*, someone who comes between the subject and the Other, to manage the jouissance which invades the subject and encourage that which supports her place as a subject in the field of an Other that does not presume or insist on knowing. This is a position that has been well articulated in the work of *Le Courtil*, an institution in Belgium catering for children in difficulty on a day care or residential basis regardless of their diagnosis. Before elaborating on the conditions enabling that position to be held, let us consider some further examples.

Making oneself a body

Mathelin (1999) describes a seven-year-old girl, Alice, who had tantrums in which she would scream, bite, and hit her head, to the extent that, as her father remarked, it stopped them having "the same life as everybody else" (p. 109). In one session when Alice "went crazy", Mathelin was holding her hands, trying to calm her down, thinking that:

> She was finally hearing me, that a word had passed between us, and that what I said had enabled her to come back to herself, I realized that this was not the case. I noticed that her eyes were fixed on my lips, and that the movement of my lips was rocking her as if in a cradle, just as had happened with her mother in the first session. [...] Alice had indeed quieted down, not because of what I had been saying to her, as I had hoped, but because of the movement of my lips: she had not come back to herself but glued herself back together. (pp. 110–111)

Holding herself together with something borrowed in this way may allow a child to be "a presence among others" yet it is fragile (Otero & Brémond, p. 72). For six months Alice alternated between violent outbursts and sitting transfixed and immobile, oblivious to the analyst who considered that her "constant reference" to Alice's experience and history allowed an overwhelming anxiety to subside. Alice began speaking in a less robotic way, "as though a world in which ideas could exist were gradually coming to replace one in which everything happened through the body" (p. 114). During the fifth year in which she began drawing more intently, she included a black hole, "a flash of emptiness", in each picture, and this, Mathelin considered enabled her to draw what she was unable to say: devouring monsters, the gaze of people who spoke inside her head and then finally she began to include drawing herself. Mathelin notes that knowing what she was afraid of, a phobic mechanism, seemed to make it possible for Alice to exist by circumscribing her fear (p. 121). Along similar lines, Koehler presented the case of a twelve-year-old girl with schizophrenia who felt persecuted by a swarm of bees until she began collecting coloured plastic boxes for the bees to be contained in (cited in Tendlarz, 2003, p. 124). There are similar examples in narrative therapy work with children using boxes to catch nightmares while they sleep (Marner, 2000). Attention to these moments when a child finds ways to support themselves via the imaginary need to be considered with reference to the associated signifying effects of these constructions. There are dramatic examples of how a subject position is accessed via experiences of jouissance articulating a void in the body (Yankelevich, 1995) or a rim on the body (Maleval, 2012), that is, where experiences of the body begin to articulate a signifying dimension.

Virginio Baio (2002) describes how incessant repetition of activities or words that involve a signifying opposition (an alternation of presence and absence), can indicate an attempt to decomplete "the absolute knowledge of the crazy Other" in children who do not otherwise speak. Autistic children often appear not to hear what is said to them, in order to keep the Other at a distance, yet as Lacan (1989) noted, something can indeed be said to them. Many analysts describe the activity of giving words to the song an autistic child is humming or entering into the child's repetition of words such as "yes-no" by adding the "no" when the child says "yes". When the child responds with interest to this voice and presence of another, it allows her to leave the initial construction behind and find a place in an Other that is regulated "because it is held at the level of the subject" (Baio, 2002). The therapist can then be associated with the realisation of the child's construction, for the child considers the analyst as "a regulated place, an Other in which she can verify her construction" (Baio, 2002). Being inscribed in the Imaginary, these constructions are fragile, yet may give rise to a kind of metaphoric knotting and can be realised for the subject on the condition that it is "taken inside a field regulated" by an Other who indicates desire, which is to say, appears as lacking. Tendlarz (1995) notes that where a child himself has become an object gaze that is offered to the Other, the analyst aims to intervene by introducing "a gap between him and the object [...] he incarnates" (p. 69), a gap which facilitates a signifying alienation and the child's choice to start talking (Maleval, 2012). Such instances might be recognised in a variety of cases (such as Klein, 1986, discussed in Briggs, 2007; Mannoni, 1972, 1999; Mathelin, 1999; Lefort, 1994) and while there may be debate regarding the type of structure, each indicate the work of circumscribing the Real at the heart of an emerging symptom that can, rather than being eliminated, form the basis of a position from which there is the possibility of some kind of social bond.

When the impasses a child faces are considered only behavioural or developmental issues, whether as a result of trauma or disability and treated only according to an educative or behavioural approach of conditioning, the impossibility they are reacting to finds no name, no point of address. Where the child's difficulties are located only with the child, rather than seen as his or her response to the Other, development is considered with implicit reference to normative terms. While the discourse of the parents and carers, the relations between them, the fantasy of the mother contribute to the Imaginary and Symbolic world into which the child is born or received, a problem arises when the impasse he or she faces is continually referred to those points, "maintaining the child as child" rather than as a subject in his or her own right (Periera, 1999, p. 68).

The language and therapeutic aim of invention is integral to considering the subject in structural rather than developmental terms, for a structure carries an unsayable, a point of impossibility. An encounter with the enigma of the Real is a "decisive moment in the subject's inscription of their history" (Pereira, p. 67), and the child builds a structure around it, starting from the particular and idiosyncratic elements to which they respond. Focusing on and responding to the singularity of each subject necessarily brings us to recognise the original invention each person arrives at or demonstrates. As "the accidental, the trauma, the hitches of history" fall away in the process of analysis, it is, Lacan says, "being which then comes to be constituted" (1953–1954, p. 232). In later work, Lacan underlines that the Real as impossible "makes effective the historical connection by knotting the Symbolic and Imaginary. An analysand, in order to recognise themselves in their history as lived experience, also must construct that which is remote, logically, to their history" (Pereira, p. 69). Recognising oneself in one's history as lived thus relies on what "is exterior or remote to that experience, that which is not demonstrable", an impossible which "subverts the categories of child-adult in favour of a different logic", the structure of the subject position (Pereira, p. 69).

To focus on the singularity of each subject, regardless of the diagnosis they may present with, is to move away from attempts to inscribe each case within diagnostic categories which tend in the direction of, or can be linked to the ideal of treatments defined and administered according to the category of groups such as eating disorders or borderline patients and the evidence-based practices considered to treat them. It is, however, worth noting similarities between the Australian National Health and Medical Research Council (NHMRC) *Clinical Practice Guideline for the Management of Borderline Personality Disorder* and the practice developed at *Le Courtil*, a singular use of "psychoanalysis applied to therapeutics" (Otero & Brémond, 2014, p. 83), that articulates guidelines we can take into practice.

Constructive care teams

For adolescents younger than fourteen with features of BPD, the NHMRC *Clinical Practice Guideline* recommends a stepped care approach, "through a range of services, as appropriate to the individual's current clinical presentation" (p. 26), including psychological therapies, psycho-education, family therapy, and/or group sessions as appropriate. The *Guideline* recommends therapies that are manual-based, standardised, and structured, noting that Linehan's (1993) model of Dialectical Behavioural Therapy (DBT) has been evaluated in more randomised controlled clinical trials than other structured psychological therapies (p. 56). Lack of particular kinds of evidence does not of course equate with lack of effectiveness (Fonagy et al., 2002, p. 3), and there is a growing evidence base for transference-focused therapies (Kernberg, et al, 2008; Normandin et al, 2015; Levy et al, 2006; Madsen Clausen et al, 2012; Gaskin, 2012, 2014). *Le Courtil* provides a structured approach that is not manual based, it is rather oriented by a discourse developed in the substantial time allowed for staff seminars and studies, with supervision and team meetings to carry and inform the anxiety of practitioners, providing a framework for the child that might reduce what could otherwise become a persecutory aspect in transference. Effective structured therapies are considered to share the characteristics of being "based on an explicit and integrated theoretical approach, to which the therapist (and other members of the treatment team, if applicable) adheres", with suitable support and supervision, focus on relationship and at least one session a week considered generally necessary, sometimes for several years or longer (NHMRC, p. 56). At *Le Courtil*, transference is distributed across a number of intervenants, who regardless of particular training, such as psychology or speech therapy, work in similar ways in a practice shared and sustained by a focus on what each child is developing. Rather than seeking to have the child attain particular things, the work is to step back enough to allow their own inventions to develop. An instructive example of the role of supervision relates how a young intern was frustrated in being unable to get a young girl to shower without registering that for this girl with no perception of her body, being alone in the shower caused great anguish. Seeing it this way, the intern began singing outside the shower door, enabling the girl to wash herself, for "singing behind the door allowed the girl to take on consistency" (Otero & Brémond, p. 91).

In complex casework practitioners and carers need the context of a team that meet regularly to debrief and follow what is happening, to identify moments of invention. Risk regulatory practices may become part of the problem yet recent studies focus on building collaborative teamwork where the management of risk is shared in order to sustain demanding work (Miller, 2007; Brett, Moran, & Green, 2009; NHMRC Guidelines, 2012). The requirement to make incident reports to various agencies and departments can lead carers to feel they are not supported but are rather under surveillance, which can become a negative cycle as their frustration with "the system" is relayed to the young person whose sense of not being contained is thus escalated. As Robyn Miller (2009) points out, there is a danger the family or carers are labelled "resistant" or "non-complaint", and to counter this, a strengths-based approach that sidesteps blame by seeking to understand the constraints for carers and child is needed (p. 117). The *Children, Youth and Families Act 2005*, as Miller (2007) notes, requires a "shift from the common practice of compartmentalised engagement around current risk, to practice that is mindful of the impact of cumulative harm" (p. iii). Meetings with family or carers are needed to "attend to the relationships and feedback between family members, various professionals, and the parts of the service system" (Miller, 2007, p. 16). Robin Clark (2000) similarly noted the importance of "well organised program management which supports, mentors and creates a coherent culture based on trust and respect" (cited by Miller, 2007, p. 17). This might reduce the young person's presentations to emergency room and inpatient settings that while sometimes necessary, can also contribute to a cycle of readmission (NHMRC, p. 20).

Just as a child responds to what is symptomatic in the family structure (Lacan, 1969, p. 7), a child responds to what is symptomatic in a care team and the systems within which they are engaged. Someone incarnating the Other as the locus of the law can have catastrophic effects and when carers are pulled in to implement statutory processes it can be disastrous for the young person, whose Others can appear to merge with a persecutory system. To avoid this, case planning and engagement must be "adaptive, dynamic and evolving"; "we need to be exquisitely tuned into the impact of our practice on outcomes for children" (Miller, 2007, pp. 39, 42). Reflecting on his position as director at *Le Courtil*, Bernard Seynhaeve commented that it's "always a matter of guaranteeing the framework in which solutions can be found" without taking up a position of mastery (Otero & Brémond, 2014, p. 86). This involves a flexible structure in the place of an imperative, where carers, parents, and practitioners are recruited to contribute to a framework in which the work of construction or invention might occur. Creating a space for invention involves listening to the suffering that lies behind difficult or extreme conduct and paying attention to what they as subjects are reacting to and producing. It involves working from a place of desire, not a demand for something specific from the young person, which would tend to reduce them again to incarnating an object for the Other. To sustain this position requires constant work, as desire is not constant, it appears and disappears, ebbs and flows. As Mannoni (1999) noted of another setting, "everything has to be reinvented continually" and this "process of putting oneself in question in relation to the other is the context of the analyst's work and must not be lost sight of" (p. 131). Otero & Brémond (2014) provide a precious transmission of how this work appears, organised as it is by a transference to knowledge that sustains and informs a practice of addressing what is unknown and developing, taking each child as a riddle in their own right.

References

American Psychiatric Association. (2013). *Diagnostic and Statistical Manual of Mental Disorders (5th ed.)*. Washington, DC: Author.

Baio, V. (2002). Cito Tute Iucunde: A Clinic with an Autistic Subject. *Courtil Papers*. Available at: www.ch-freudien-be.org/Papers/.

Brett, J. Anthony Moran, A. & Green, D. (2009). *Managing Risk in Community Services. A Preliminary Study of the Impacts of Risk Management on Victorian Services and Clients*. An ARC Linkage Project 2006–2009. Melbourne: La Trobe University School of Social Sciences, School of Social Work, School of Social Policy.

Briggs, K. (2007). Symptom Formation: From Klein to Lacan. *Analysis, 13*: 45–62.

Fonagy, P., Target, M., Cottrell, D., Phillips, J., & Kurtz, Z. (2002). *What Works for Whom. A Critical Review of Treatments for Children and Adolescents*. New York: The Guildford Press.

Gaskin, C. (2012). *The Effectiveness of Psychodynamic Psychotherapy: A Systematic Review of Recent International and Australian Research*. Melbourne: PACFA.

Gaskin, C. (2014). *The Effectiveness of Psychoanalysis and Psychoanalytic Psychotherapy: A Literature Review of Recent International and Australian Research*. Melbourne: PACFA.

Kernberg, O. F., Yeomans, F. E., Clarkin, J. F., & Levy K. N. (2008). Transference Focused Psychotherapy: Overview and Update. *International Journal of Psychoanalysis, 89(3)*: 601–620.

Klein, M. (1986). *The Selected Melanie Klein*. J. Mitchell (Ed.). Middlesex: Penguin.

Kohut, H. (1984). *How Does Analysis Cure?* A. Goldberg & P. E. Stepansky (Eds.). Chicago: The University of Chicago Press.

Kohut, H. (1977) *The Restoration of the Self*. Chicago: The University of Chicago Press, 2009.

Lacan, J. (1953–1954). *The Seminar of Jacques Lacan. Book I: Freud's Papers on Technique 1953–1954*. J. -A. Miller (Ed.) & J. Forrester (Trans.). NY: Norton, 1988.

Lacan, J. (1955–1956). *The Seminar of Jacques Lacan. Book III: The Psychoses, 1955–1956*. J. -A. Miller (Ed.) & R. Grigg (Trans.). New York: W. W. Norton, 1993.

Lacan, J. (1969). Note on the Child. *Psychoanalytical Notebooks, 20*: 7–8, 2010.

Lacan (1989) Geneva Lecture on the Symptom. *Analysis 1*: 7–26.

Laurent, E. (1999). Rethinking Kleinian interpretation: What Difference does it Make? In: *The Klein-Lacan Dialogues*. B. Burgoyne & M. Sullivan (Eds.). New York: Other Press.

Lefort, R. & Lefort, R. (1994). *Birth of the Other*. M. Du Ray, L. Watson, & L. Rodríguez (Trans.). Urbana: University of Illinois Press.

Levy, K., Clarkin, J. F., & Yeomans, F. E., Scott, L. N., Wasserman R. H., & Kernberg, O. F. (2006). The Mechanisms of Change in the Treatment of Borderline Personality Disorder with Transference Focused Psychotherapy, *Journal of Clinical Psychology 62(4)*: 481–501.

Linehan, M. M. (1993). *Cognitive-Behavioural Treatment of Borderline Personality Disorder.* New York: Guilford Press.

Madsen Clausen J., Ruff S. C., Von Wiederhold, W. & Heineman, T. V. (2012). For as Long as it Takes: Relationship-Based Play Therapy for Children in Foster Care, *Psychoanalytic Social Work, 19(1–2)*: 43–53.

Maleval, J -C. (2012). Why the Hypothesis of an Autistic Structure? *Psychoanalytical Notebooks, 25*: 27–49.

Marner, T. (2000). *Letters to Children in Family Therapy.* London UK: Jessica Kingsley.

Mathelin, C. (1999). *Lacanian Psychotherapy with Children: The Broken Piano.* S. Fairfield (Trans.). New York: The Other Press.

Mannoni, M. (1972). *The Backward Child and his Mother. A Psychoanalytic Study.* A. M. Sheridan Smith (Trans.). New York: Pantheon Books.

Mannoni, M. (1999). *Separation and Creativity. Refinding the Lost Language of Childhood.* S. Fairfield (Trans.), New York: The Other Press.

Miller, J -A. (1988). Mental Health and Public Order. *Psychoanalytic Notebooks, 23*: 73–84, 2011.

Miller, J -A. (2003). Milanese Intuitions 2. *Mental Online, 12*: 7–16.

Miller, J -A. (2013). The Real in the 21st Century. *Hurly-Burly 9*: 199–206.

Miller, R. (2007). *Best Interests Principles: a Conceptual Overview.* Melbourne: Victorian Government Department of Human Services.

Miller, R. (2009). Engagement with Families Involved in the Statutory System. In: J. Maidement & R. Egan. (Eds.). *Practice Skills in Social Work and Welfare* (pp. 114–131). Sydney: Allen and Unwin.

National Health and Medical Research Council. (2012). *Clinical Practice Guideline for the Management of Borderline Personality Disorder.* Melbourne: National Health and Medical Research Council.

Normandin, L., Ensink, K., & Kernberg O. F. (2015). Transference-Focused Psychotherapy for Borderline Adolescents: A Neurobiologically Informed Psychodynamic Psychotherapy. *Journal of Infant, Child, and Adolescent Psychotherapy, 14(1)*: 98–110.

Otero, M. & Brémond, M. (2014). *Like An Open Sky, Interviews. Le Courtil, Invention From Day To Day.* A. R. Price (Trans.). Paris, France: Buddy Movies.

Pereira, D. (1999). The Infans and the (K)not of History. *Papers of the Freudian School of Melbourne, 20*: 59–71.

Tendlarz, S. E. (1995). Object and Image in Autistic Children. *Journal of the Centre for Freudian Analysis and Research,* 6: 63–71.

Tendlarz, S. E. (2003). *Childhood Psychosis. A Lacanian Perspective.* London: Karnac Books.

Theodoridis, E. (2013). Adolescents in the Geek Era. *Hurly-Burly, 10*: 61–65.

Yankelevich, H. (1995). Jerome's Laughter: A Case of Autism. *Clinical Studies: International Journal of Psychoanalysis,* 1 (1): 109–19.

CHAPTER ELEVEN

The symptom and the system: notes on the foster child

Kristen Hennessy

Introduction

In Lacan's "Note on the Child", he states: "[T]he child's symptom is found to be in a position of answering to what is symptomatic in the family structure" (1969, p. 7). What are the implications for children who spend significant portions of their childhood in foster care? What happens to the symptom when a child is raised in the system?

Unlike separations arranged for by the parents, children in foster care are separated from their parents due to an intervention of the "real" law, the written law of a jurisdiction. It is no simple matter to determine if biological parents wanted the law to intervene and to invoke a separation from the child, particularly given the influence of the unconscious. It is certainly the case that the parent's demand is not the only player, and the law as enforced by judges, child protection workers, and police, is also in effect. These children rarely know what will happen to them next, by whom they will be raised, and their symptoms are developed in the context of this uncertainty. This chapter explores some of the implications of this for the symptom and in the clinic.

The foster care system

In Pennsylvania, where I have treated children and adolescents in the foster care system for the past seven years, a child's entry into the foster care system begins with a mandated reporter contacting the state agency designated for the reporting of suspected child abuse or neglect. Adults in Pennsylvania who have regular contact with children are mandated to report suspected child abuse and can, according to the Pennsylvania Child Protective Services Law, face criminal charges if they fail to do so. If the allegation is indeed one of abuse or neglect, the agency notifies the local county, and a Children and Youth Services intake worker assesses the situation to determine if there is sufficient evidence that the child has been abused or neglected according to the standard of state law. When the county agency determines that the treatment of the child has violated state law, a hearing is held requesting that the child be found "dependent". If the judge grants the request, legal custody of the child is given to the county Children and Youth Services Agency. The child's case is reviewed periodically in court to determine whether or not the parents have rectified the situation leading to the child's placement. Unless there is a compelling reason that visitation is not in the child's best interest, supervised visitation is arranged between the child and the biological parents.

The most recent report from the U.S. Department of Health and Human Services indicates that, on the day selected to gain a snapshot of the foster care system, 415,129 children were in foster care in the United States (2015, p. 1). Of those children, twenty-eight per cent had been in foster care for more than two years, with seven per cent remaining in foster care for a duration of more than five years (p. 2). Fifty-two per cent of children who have been identified as awaiting adoption had been waiting for a family for more than two years (p. 1). These statistics account for a single stay in foster care and do not account for those children whose childhoods are spent in a revolving door of foster care, or children who are so-called "failed adoptions", children who are adopted but whose parents seek to "dissolve" the adoption.

The majority of my cases involved children who have been in the foster care system for many years. I have worked with many adolescents who have been in the foster care system for more than eleven years, who ultimately "aged out" meaning that they turned eighteen years old and left the foster care system without ever having been placed with a parent or guardian.

What is clear, and is of particular interest for this chapter, is that a subset of children exist who are raised in the foster care system, leaving us with questions regarding symptoms when the child is raised in the system. Lacanian treatment honours the child as a speaking subject, and children who are "in the system" are often in particularly dire need of such recognition. The situation of the foster child has implications throughout the treatment, implications that will be explored below.

A note on abuse and neglect

Working with children in foster care means, by definition, working with children who have experienced abuse and neglect. From Freud's shifting stance from his seduction theory on, psychoanalysis has had a fraught relationship around questions of childhood trauma, particularly childhood sexual abuse.

Freud's rejection of his seduction theory has received much attention. I argue that Freud does not deny that sexual abuse sometimes occurs or that it harms children when it does occur. In his September 21st, 1897 letter, Freud writes to Fliess: "I no longer believe in my *neurotica.*" In accounting for this shift, he states: "[...] there are no indications of reality in the unconscious, so that one cannot distinguish between truth and fiction that has been cathected with affect." This letter marks a shift in his understanding of the etiology of hysteria. In other words, Freud is now realising that it is not *always* the case that the hysteric has experienced sexual abuse, which is a far cry from saying that the hysteric has *never* experienced sexual abuse. Along with this realisation came an increased respect for the function of the unconscious, and a growing realisation that a successful analysis must go beyond the recounting of traumatic events.

I find that some analytic practitioners minimise the significance of profound abuse and neglect in the name of the child as subject, while others see the experience of abuse as causal and abandon the unconscious entirely. Michael Plastow (2012) cautions analysts against a "culture of blame of the Other for one's suffering" (p. 74). He is, perhaps, speaking to analysts such as Valerie Sinason (2011) who is quoted in The Guardian as follows:

> I'm an analytic therapist. The idea of that is someone showing, through their behaviour, that all sorts of things might have

> happened to them. Signs that a patient has suffered satanically include flinching at green or purple objects, the colours of the high priest and priestess's robes. And if someone shudders when they enter a room, you know it's not ordinary incest.

Plastow does a great service to remind analysts that there is no set of symptoms that means that a child has been abused, not to mention the reaction a particular colour! Nevertheless, he does not fully account for the stance of children whose symptoms are developing within the context of severe abuse and/or neglect.

Plastow (2012) argues that each psychoanalysis must follow the path of moving from the seduction theory to its abandonment, from blaming the Other for one's suffering to accepting responsibility for one's symptom: "It is also to take on the fact that one's history is not able to fully account for one's suffering. In this way, we encounter the limits of seduction and of history as a causal hypothesis. This is what we refer to as castration" (p. 76). This is true, as even the child in the most extreme of circumstances is implicated in his choice of reaction and symptoms. Plastow states: "We could summarise the position of the patient presenting for analysis in the following way: 'If only I'd had a decent mother and father, if only they had treated me and loved me as I imagine I should have been, and not how they did, then I would never have turned out like this'" (p. 75). This is not, in my experience, anything like the most common presentations of children who have been profoundly abused and neglected. Such children, in my experience, come to therapy seeing themselves as the cause of abuse, via some kind of profound, innate badness. "Of course they tied me to a chair and tasered me! They had to!" These children must first come to the seduction hypothesis before it can be rejected.

The solution in the clinic is simple: one must listen at the level of the unconscious. The clinician must allow the unconscious to serve as guide, without preconceived notions. As Catherine Vanier (Mathelin, 1999) reminds us: "[T]he analyst, following Freud's recommendation, is without prejudice and without preconceived ideas, available, open to the other and the unconscious. If theory guides us, it is only so that we may better listen to our analysands" (p. 18). Psychoanalytic principles do not change simply because one is discussing child abuse.

The challenge is to allow the child to find freedom despite his or her history, to play with/in the signifier in a way that allows for something new to emerge. Suzanne Hommel recounts one such powerful moment from her analysis with Lacan in the 2011 film *Rendez-vous chez Lacan*. Associating to a recurring nightmare, Hommel recounts that she awakens at five a.m. each morning, the time that the Gestapo came for the Jews, and which resonated for her because of her history as a child growing up in occupied France. Lacan intervened by caressing her face, transforming "Gestapo" into "*geste à peau*"' which, by Hommel's account, "didn't diminish the pain but made it something else". Hewitson (2012) states: "[T]he effect on his analysand was to turn the nightmare she recounted, and the painful associations of the Nazi occupation that followed from it, into a quite literal gesture of kindness: from 'Gestapo' to '*geste à peau*'." This then, is the challenge of work with children who have been abused and neglected, working with the signifier to make it [the pain] into something else.

Parental stance regarding the law

Children in the foster care system are children whose parents have been accused of breaking laws regarding their care. Although it is very occasionally the case that a child is placed in foster care after a single incident that violates the law, it is far more often my experience that the violation of the law goes undetected for a period of time, and that the child develops symptoms in the context of the violation of the law. Parents present their abuse and neglect to their children in many different ways. The child's particular plight varies based on the parent's manner of handling the law in its transgression. This is in the background of the child's choice of symptom prior to foster care.

Some parents who abuse or neglect acknowledge to the child that the parent is violating the law. This parent, who is, in my clinical experience, almost always neurotically structured, nods to the law when breaking the law, such as the father committing incest who admonished his child that she mustn't tell or he would go to jail. Their children are typically neurotics who enter foster care plagued by guilt, seeing themselves as complicit in the violation of the law, even as they also feel guilty for their role in the discovery of the violation.

Other parents who abuse or neglect their child communicate to the child that there are no limits, that might prevails, and the parent is bigger and will do whatever she or he wants to the child. If the police or other authority figures are referenced, they are referenced without an appeal to the law itself. Their children are frequently structurally psychotic and they enter foster care utterly uncontained by any set of internalised rules. For example, one adolescent could not get over his outrage that his father was incarcerated for committing a murder, not proclaiming his father's innocence, but rather wondering why everyone was so concerned about this murder. This same adolescent was perplexed with the intensity with which others reacted to his own acts of violence.

In perhaps the most complex of cases, the child is in the process of being ushered into a perverse law, a law that is in direct contradiction with the law of the land. One such child had been taught that good little boys "help" their mothers by "kissing" their mother's genitals, and his father threatened him with punishment if he failed to engage sexually with the mother. Stephanie Swales (2012) provides a thorough accounting of the conditions under which a child comes to adopt a perverse structure (pp. 54–67). It is not unusual to encounter cases of perversion in which the father or lawgiving Other failed to prohibit incestuous contact with the mother in a convincing way or in which the child is difficult to persuade. The situation for the child I am describing is different in that the law giving Other is forceful—perhaps brutally so—in forbidding separation from the mother, leaving the child in the position of accepting the law giving Other through the very act of sexual contact with the mOther. This situation is quite different from many we see in the literature. Freud's "Little Hans" suffered precisely from a father who did not want to assert his authority (Freud, 1909b). Fink's case of W involved a mother who verbally undermined the father (Fink, 2003). Swales' case history includes a father who is at the bidding of the mother and only disciplines the children at the mother's behest, and even then, laughably so (Swales, 2012). And, in Tostain's case of "Little Jean", the father was selected due to his suspected inability to father a child (1993, p. 251). In these cases, incest is in the background, obviously hinted at and yet absent. The mother of Fink's W case puts her hand on her son's erect penis and leaves the room without a word, and the mother of Tostain's case of Little Jean inserts thermometers and enemas into the child's rectum, but only when he shows signs of illness (p. 250). She requests help with the buttons of her dress but does not request overtly incestuous contact (Tostain, 1993, p. 253). Swales' "Ray" was kept home with mother instead of attending sleepovers due to enuresis. In all of these cases, the father failing to sufficiently intervene and separate the child from the mother. Freud's Little Hans had a mother who resisted his separation from her and engaged in rather excessive physical care after his baths (1909b, p. 19) but did not engage in overtly sexual activity with her son. This is quite a different situation from the father who threatens the child with violence should the child fail to engage in incest with the mother.

The parent's presentation of the law to the child has great implications for the way in which the child will take up the secrets in the family system. The manner in which parental transgression is taken up by the parent is the context in which the child takes up the symptom of the family system.

Symptoms and the foster care system

Lacan's 1969 note that "the child's symptom is found to be in a position of answering what is symptomatic in the family structure" (p. 7) does not mean that the child is passively responding to that structure. Michael Plastow (2015) claims: "[T]hus we need to differentiate between the child who *is* a symptom of the family structure from the child who *has* a symptom in response to what is problematic or fails in that structure" (p. 99). The symptom is where the child can go beyond the place provided by the parent. Plastow argues that: "[T]he symptom is the means by which the child is able to accede to his or her truth, through an experience that exceeds the place reserved for the child by the mother and father" (p. 101). The child analyst must always work at the intersection of these categories. This is succinctly put by Catherine Vanier (Mathelin, 1999): "[T]he symptom belongs both to the child and to the parents, and it is in this middle ground that we have to work" (p. 15). Thus, the child's symptom comes from the child even as it responds to the family system.

Prior to entry

What is unique in the situation of the child who ultimately ends up in foster care is that the secrets of the family system are in violation of the real law, and the child's symptom, speech, and silence are in dialogue with this knowledge. At times, it is the child's symptom that leads to the intervention of the law, such as seven-year-old Amanda whose open masturbation and provocative sucking of doorknobs in her classroom ultimately led to the discovery of longstanding father/daughter incest. Amanda's father cautioned her against telling, explaining to the child that he would go to jail and she would not see him again. She adored her father, her sole caregiver, and did not want to lose him, yet found certain aspects of sexual abuse to be repulsive and physically painful. She was wracked with guilt, feeling that she was complicit in breaking society's law by having sexual contact with her father but feeling that the only alternative was to do something wrong by breaking her father's rules. Amanda's symptom became a way of *telling without telling*, of following her father's rules while also ensuring that her secret was discovered. As her case progressed, questions of telling without telling surfaced repeatedly. In cases like Amanda's, the child is acutely aware of the power (and perhaps responsibility) to have one's parent incarcerated. In all such cases, the child is navigating the violation of the law which may have an impact on the choice of symptom.

Symptoms during foster care

A popular book for children in foster care by Jennifer Wilgoicki (2002) is entitled *Maybe Days* pointing to the uncertainty of the life of the foster child. Maybe she will return to the care of her biological parents. Maybe she will be adopted. Maybe she will move to another foster home. Decisions will be made by a Judge and only after each side presents evidence, leaving children to be told "the Judge will decide". Some children find that their cases resolve relatively quickly. Others find that their case languishes in the system as the court battle rages. Still others never find parents who are willing to raise them, and they bounce between foster homes and residential treatment facilities without ever having a clear sense of what comes next.

A question about the symptom arises for children in the midst of *Maybe Days*. We know that the child's symptom speaks to what is unspeakable in the family. But, when a child has been in the foster care system for half of his life, to whom or where are these symptoms addressed? How does the situation change if a child is in multiple "placements" as opposed to when a child is in a single foster home?

Symptoms with multiple placements

Certain children, including those who have symptoms that foster parents find to be difficult to bear end up in multiple placements. Some children go through a few transitions after a long period of time. Others get used to moving every few weeks and are constantly trying to conform to the demands of new families. All children face the question: What do my parents want from me? Children who are cycling through multiple foster care placements face this question regarding each new set of parents. These children often craft an identity that appeals to the foster parent of their fantasies. They market themselves to this fantasised ideal parent on websites designed to attract potential parents, creating commercials of which they are the product, aimed to entice the fantasised good parent (such as can be found on the US State-wide Adoption and Permanency Network's website at www.adoptpakids.org).

Some children conform to whatever demand is placed on them, working desperately to become precisely what each family wants from them even as they are simultaneously compelled to thwart the same. A child I had known only to wear camouflage sweatpants with uncombed hair moved homes and arrived for her next session in a pleated skirt and sweater with her hair contained in a tidy French braid. Once she was again removed (this time into a family that values modesty) she surfaced for session in an ankle-length skirt and loose cotton shirt with sleeves extending to her wrists. The foster parents seem to remake the child in their own image or the image of the child of their fantasies with the child as compliant blank slate, and the startling contrasts in the child's appearance point to the powerful forces with which the child contends as she moves from home to home. As I watch my patient's body being written and rewritten in the imaginary realm, I wonder what is happening in the symbolic realm. At times, this willingness to be rewritten itself becomes the symptom.

Of course, the child may choose to accept or resist these demands, to conform or not, as well as where to conform and where to resist. Observing the child's stance is of import, with the stance I initially described (passively allowing oneself to be remade) correlating to hysteria and certain forms of psychosis. Many such children, while studiously sniffing out and adopting the desire of the latest parental figure, are equally compelled to undermine what those new parents want. I find that these children are experts at becoming what the parents want while also finding precisely the one thing that will make the family request the child to move, thus indicating something of their desire and its metonymy.

Children who continuously move often adopt symptoms that are an answer to this situation. For example, the "rewritten" child above developed the symptom of urinating on her clothing piled by her bed. She was, in a sense, marking them with her scent, imbuing them with something of her own while also causing her scent to slowly leak through the floor, invading and taking over the foster home, until it dripped into the living room, and led to her removal. On the surface, she conformed and allowed herself to be rewritten, and yet she leaked, reminiscent of Plastow's (2015) "leaking tap". Plastow says, of the leaking tap:

> The symptom is the means by which the child is able to accede to his or her own truth, through an experience that exceeds the place reserved for the child by the mother and the father. This is an aspect of the symptom that is concerned at the same time with a leakage and with a surplus: a leakage at one point produces a surplus at another. (p. 101)

This was also a manner of resistance and showing allegiance to her biological mother, a woman who often reeked of urine. Thus, with this urinary unary trait, she sought yet repelled foster families, her unspoken allegiance to her biological mother dripping from the ceiling.

The symptom in a long-term placement

Those children with a foster family that is a potential adoptive resource are in a position of choosing, consciously and unconsciously, between their biological parents and their foster parents. Unlike the children in the previous section who were desperately seeking whilst repelling families, these are children who are deeply torn between families.

Children with a consistent foster family must find a way to differentiate their biological parents from the foster parents. Some children refer to their foster parents by their first names and refer to their biological parents as "mom and dad". Other children call one set of parents "mom and dad" while referring to the other set of parents as "mom Sally and dad Bob". Other children adopt specific phrasing for their sets of parents, such as "the hitting mom", "jailbird dad", "mean daddy", or "safe mom and safe dad". I find that names often shift suddenly when something new has been articulated.

Some children aim their symptoms at what cannot be spoken within the biological family, others shift their symptoms to suit the foster care situation or the demands of the foster family. This is a place where the brilliance of the unconscious truly shines with symptoms that speak to more than one family system at a time. These children adopt symptoms that speak, for example, to the biological family and to the system, or to both the biological family and the foster family. The child's solution lurks within the symptom.

For example, Jeb entered foster care with his body covered in small wounds that he had inflicted. His symptom was complex, having to do, so it emerged, with maintaining his mother's attention while also maintaining some control over her all-consuming attention and spreading it over his body, away from her focused attention on his penis. Jeb, as it so happened, was placed with a man who went by the name Mark. Jeb continued to pick his flesh throughout his stay in foster care with Mark. At some point, his pick marks evolved into a kind of *picking Mark*, with Jeb picking a great wound that scarred him, allowing his body to be *Marked* permanently prior to this symptom disappearing for good. Jeb maintained a symptom that spoke both to his mother's engulfing attention while also allowing him to identify with the foster father at the level of an inscription, and abandon the mother.

The Judge as the father

In both types of cases, the Judge takes on the role of the Name-of-the-Father, but with everyone involved in the child's care as subject to the authority of the Judge. This does afford the psychotic child who is young enough to transition into neurosis ample opportunity to see the functioning of the law and to understand that everyone is subject to the law. Nevertheless, the child does not feel loved by the Judge, and the child often hears about conflicts presented by adults to the Judge in a manner that often makes it sound as though the Judge is making decisions based on whim rather than the law. Another unfortunate side effect is that, at times, the authority of the foster parents is diminished in the eyes of the child. This is helpful when it serves to help the child understand that even those caring for the child are subject to the law, but is not helpful when the foster parent is attempting to instil the law and the child views the Judge's authority as undermining that of the parents.

Challenges working with the child in foster care

There are several unique challenges of working with children in the foster care system which will be briefly explored here. The child must take up the situation of the changing caregiving system and the interaction with the law but the analyst must also navigate this in the work with the child.

Contact with the legal system

Clinicians working with children in foster care are also encountering the "real" law, often in uncomfortable ways. The referral often comes from a Judge or county caseworker, frequently from someone the child does not even know. There are demands coming from many, sometimes invisible, locations, and finding a way for the treatment to *belong* to the child is no simple task. Catherine Vanier (Mathelin, 1999) asks, regarding child analysis in general: "[W]ho is demanding what? How, in this labyrinth, can we find the red thread that will finally enable the child to become subject?" (p. 28). This is all the more the case when the child is in the legal custody of Children and Youth Services, with a labyrinth that involves a tremendous cast of characters with competing agendas. Sometimes the child is referred in order to "prove" that what happened to the child was detrimental, with the county agency wanting therapy for the child and the biological parents viewing it as unnecessary. At other times, the referral is initiated in a last-ditch effort to prevent a child from being removed from the foster home. Frequently, children are told that they are coming to me to "talk about what happened" and I must work hard to insist that the child is the one to decide what is the trouble.

Children in foster care are frequently involved in forensic investigations and have undergone repeated interviews with professionals whose job it is to uncover the legal truth about specific events. It is often initially difficult to help a child to see the clinical space as one that is different. One must work hard to express an interest in the child and her unconscious as opposed to matters of forensic concern. Such children sometimes express tremendous relief when they are invited to talk and play about dreams and fantasies. I have often been told, when I ask children to tell me their dreams: "I haven't had any nightmares." These children are sometimes in an environment that is so focused on their traumas that they are surprised to learn that the clinician is interested in their "good dreams" as much as in nightmares. I find that certain children understand quickly the different kind of space that is being offered to them, while others need concerted, sustained effort to differentiate this space from other spaces.

Complete confidentiality can never be promised to a child, as those working with children in the United States are mandated reporters and the analytic situation should never be used as an excuse to permit children to be harmed. Catherine Vanier (1999), in speaking of a child whose symptoms functioned as a distress signal pointing to her experiences of sexual abuse: "What concept, what theory, justifies us in withholding the minimum respect owed to a child who, like Samira, asks to speak of the horror of her background and be protected from it" (p. 48). The clinician must find ways to report that which is necessary to protect the child while also protecting the confidentiality of the child's communications to the greatest extent possible.

Staying in the role of the analyst

Given the high turnover in the child protective services field and the number of children who change foster homes (as well as schools and physicians), the clinician sometimes becomes the person the child has known the longest in her life. One child, who attended her first session with me the day after she was placed in foster care, is now on her fifth foster home, third school, third case worker, and second *Guardian ad Litem*. In certain such cases, I have found that the child comes to see me as the person who "already knows". This is certainly different from the "subject-supposed-to-know" that is desired in psychoanalysis, and it can take sustained effort to keep the child talking and playing. The clinician must repeatedly shift to be facilitating the child viewing the clinician as the subject-supposed-to-know regarding the child's unconscious, as opposed to the subject who knows details of, for example, the child's educational history. All clinicians must work to stay in the role of the analyst, but this is particularly true for analysts working with children in the foster care system who do not have other longstanding attachment figures.

The answer to the question: "What happens to the symptom in the system?" is as varied as the answer to any other clinical question. This chapter outlines a few of the complications faced by children in foster care as they navigate the challenges of ever-changing family systems, uncertainty about the future, and complex interactions between the Real and Symbolic law. The clinic does well to make a space for these children to speak and play about what troubles them as they grow up in the system.

References

Fink, B. (2003). The Use of Lacanian Psychoanalysis in a Case of Fetishism. *Clinical Case Studies, 2(1)*, 50–69.

Freud, S. (1909b). Analysis of a Phobia in a Five-Year-Old Boy. *S.E., 10*: 3–149. London: Hogarth Press.

Freud, S., Masson, J. M., & Fliess, W. (1985). *The Complete Letters of Sigmund Freud to Wilhelm Fliess. 1887–1904.* Cambridge, Mass: Belknap Press of Harvard University Press.

Hewitson, O. (2012, August 12th). A story from Lacan's practice. Available at: www.lacanonline.com/index/2012/08/a-story-from-lacans-practice/.

Lacan, J. (1969). Note on the Child. R. Grigg (Trans.). *Analysis, 1990, 2*: 7–8.

Masson, J. (1998). *The Assault on Truth: Freud's Suppression of the Seduction Theory.* New York: Pocket, 1984.

Mathelin, C. (1999). *Lacanian Psychotherapy with Children: The Broken Piano.* S. Fairfield (Trans.). New York: The Other Press.

Miller, G. (2011). *Rendez-vouz chez Lacan.* (Motion Picture). France: Éditions Montparnasse. O. Hewiston (Trans.).

Plastow, M. (2012). The Child and Seduction. In: L. Clifton (Ed.). *Invention in the Real.* (pp. 71–77). London: Karnac.

Plastow, M. (2015). *What is a Child? Childhood, Psychoanalysis, and Discourse.* London: Karnac.

Storr, W. (2011, December 10th). The Mystery of Carole Myers. *The Guardian.* Available at: www.theguardian.com/society/2011/dec/11/carole-myers-satanic-child-abuse.

Swales, S. (2012). *Perversion: A Lacanian Approach to the Subject.* New York: Routledge.

Tostain, R. (1993). Fetishization of a Phobic Object. In: S. Schneiderman (Ed.). *How Lacan's Ideas are Used in Clinical Practice* (pp. 247–260). Northvale NJ: Jason Aronson.

U.S. Department of Health and Human Services, Administration for Children and Families, Administration on Children, Youth and Families, Children's Bureau. (2015). *AFCARS Report #22.* Available at: www.acf.hhs.gov/programs/cb/resource/afcars-report-22.

Wilgocki, J. & Wright, M. (2002). *Maybe Days: A Book for Children in Foster Care.* Washington DC: Magination Press.

CHAPTER TWELVE

Sex and terror: psychoanalysis with adolescents in an Irish sexual health service

Donna Redmond

Adolescence and sexual health

Within the last twenty years, there has been an affirmation of a worldwide commitment to adolescent and youth health. The framework for this initiative is the World Health Organisation's definition of health as a state of complete physical, mental and social well-being, and not merely the absence of disease or infirmity (WHO, 1948). Arising from this framework, a unique service was established in Ireland, which focused on sexual health. Funded by the Irish health service, the service provides a free sexual health service to young people aged thirteen to twenty-three years. Teams of doctors and nurses offer consultations, treatment, and advice about sexually transmitted infections, contraception, pregnancy, and post termination care. Professionals offer education about sexual development, and guidance to young people regarding their sexual health.

I was employed by the service to provide counselling and support. Young people could self-refer, as well as being referred by general practitioners, social workers, or family members. With the young, questions about sexuality are always central, but were more so in the sexual health setting. Some came to speak about an unplanned pregnancy, and the decisions they were considering to deal with it. Some came to speak about their sexual identity, grappling with issues regarding gender and sexual preferences, and their difficulty in expressing themselves confidently within their familial and peer groups. The theme of "terror", dominated the speech of many individuals and was conveyed through the use of signifiers such as "terrified" and "horrified". My work as a psychoanalyst was to provide a space where those who came to speak, could question their subjective positions with respect to questions of relationships and love.

The most frequently attended clinic dealt with the treatment of sexually transmitted infections. While the sexual act is always tainted by the silent kiss of death, the reality of contracting an infection confronts the subject with the Real of death. A young person may develop a range of sexually transmitted infections following a single sexual encounter. Although this type of infection is treatable, what remains is a continuous effect in the Real. The individual may always need to use barrier contraception, even in long-term relationships, and for a woman, the infection may threaten any future pregnancies.

Despite the extensive educational work, and the provision of free barrier contraception, these clinics remained busy, with ever-increasing waiting lists.

This raised a question; why were young women, engaging in potentially risky sexual behaviour despite the widespread availability of education and medical resources? Colette Soler has recognised a change in cultural norms since Freud's era (Soler, 2005, p. 590). With less pressure to marry (and I would include the availability of contraception), Soler contends that the woman "gets off" like the man. The woman in this position is also being used by the man, the man "gets off" as a result of her availability. The woman therefore inhabits a passive *and* an active position. In taking up the active role, she is effectively taking up the male position that Freud discussed in his paper on debasement in the sphere of love (Freud, 1912d). The tendency towards debasement therefore emerges as a relevant concept, which could shed light on the so-called "dark continent" of female sexuality. Drawing upon clinical examples I will explore how the concept is linked to childhood sexuality and emerges as frigidity in various forms.

The libido blows its lid

Pascal Quignard (2014) claims that the animal is not something alien within us. We are born animals. There is, he argues, a sort of brutishness, within the subject, from which humanity cannot emancipate itself. This brutishness can become evident during adolescence when puberty begins and the sexual instincts in the body become heightened. Within the animal kingdom only puberty exists, and animals, driven by instinct, mature and reproduce—a relatively straightforward process. For the human subject however, adolescence is distinct from puberty; a time of socialisation when the subject definitively takes up a gendered position as either a man or a woman. The desire to form relationships with others gains significance, and the young person can become consumed with figuring out, not only who they are, but also, how others view them. The young person is, as Freud puts it, engaged in a re-finding of a love object from childhood (Freud, 1905d, p. 221).

This re-negotiating of relationships with others is not a straightforward task. As Quignard describes, "each of us will never know the sexual position, bodily life, and mental behaviour, that possession of the other sex would induce" (Quignard, 2014, p. 30). The curiosity this arouses, may perplex, confuse, and confound the subject. The divided subject faces the other, not at the level of gender, but at the level of the unconscious, as a phantasm, and will always be confronted with the knowledge that there is no such thing as a sexual relationship (Lacan, 1975).

Aligned with these tasks, the re-awakening of the sexual during adolescence results in the Real of the body breaking through, and this can be disconcerting for the young person. Psychoanalytic concepts illuminate what is at stake for the adolescent, particularly the female, during the time when "sexual energy goes on the rampage" or, as Dolto once remarked, "the libido blows its lid" (Vanier, 2001, p. 580).

The Real, which underpins the reality of the body and sexuality, is of profound importance for the adolescent renegotiating the quagmire of the drives. Lacan describes the Real as the unthinkable; that which causes us to stumble, psychically speaking, and as Lacan explains, these stumblings are dealt with through the creation of symptoms. Equipped with a transformed body, the adolescent can now potentially enact repressed infantile desires. In Lacan's observations, concerning Freud's description of Little Hans, a boy's first erections represent a kind of breaking and entering of the reality of jouissance (Vanier, 2001, p. 593). This experience of the Real is re-experienced in adolescence when changes occur in the developing body, and through the first experience of arousal and orgasm.

In his text on debasement, Freud (1912d) explains that it is necessary for affectionate and sensual currents to combine, to ensure, what he terms, a normal attitude in love. The affectionate current is the older of the two. It originates in childhood and is directed towards members of the family and those who care for the child. It is effectively an incestuous love and an amalgamation of the life drive and the sexual drives.

The diphasic nature of human sexuality, means that the sensual current appears at adolescence, but is thwarted in its aim for satisfaction, due to the prohibition against incest. Within the terms of the classical oedipal myth, the situation is resolved by choosing another object, which unites the sensual and affectionate currents. However, at a psychical level, a young man's sensuality can remain tied to the incestuous object in the unconscious, resulting in impotence. As Freud states:

> Where they love they do not desire and where they desire they cannot love. They seek objects, which they do not need to love, in order to keep their sensuality away from the objects they love. (Freud, 1912d, p. 182)

The psychical debasement of the loved object is a protective mechanism against impotence. Freud speaks about men, but does say that frigidity in women is the corollary of impotence in men; "the condition of forbidden-ness in the erotic life of women is comparable to the need on the part of men to debase their sexual object" (Freud, 1912d, p. 185). Women may prefer to experience their erotic life in terms of fantasy rather than reality. Freud claims that if and when a woman has the opportunity to engage in a sexual act with a man, she may be unable to undo the connection between the sensual activity and the prohibition, and prove to be psychically impotent, that is, frigid. This retreat into fantasy therefore maintains the desire to have access to the forbidden. This certainly reflects the fascination for romance and intrigue in literature and films widely consumed by women, from the earliest novels, including Jane Austen's work, to countless contemporary books and movies.

Secrets and lies

Freud's discussion of the forbidden in female sexuality, can be seen as connected to the idea of "secret keeping". (Freud, 1912d, p. 185). The over-valuation of something being "forbidden" is illustrated in the enjoyment women experience through creating and maintaining secrets, including secret love affairs, and in the predilection for keeping diaries in which adolescent girls often delight. A famous diary is that of Anne Frank containing her writings about her love for Peter Schiff.

Freud illustrates in the case history of "Dora" (Freud, 1905e) how colluding in secrets and lies can in essence be an indication of a woman's desire. The secret that Dora keeps involves her in her father's sexual life and is an indication of her identification with him and her desire for Frau K. What Freud does not attend to in the case history is Dora's secret love for her mother depicted in Dora's first dream when her mother tries to save her jewel case demonstrating her longed for female allegiance with her mother (Balsam, 2015, p. 47).

In "Two Lies Told by Children", Freud illustrates how a child's witnessing of a secret love affair is the basis for difficulties in her adult sexual relationships (Freud, 1913g, pp. 303–308). When the child was three and a half, a nursemaid of whom she was extremely fond, was involved in a secret love affair with a doctor, whose surgery she visited with the child. The child witnessed various sexual proceedings and was given money by the nursemaid to ensure her silence. To take money therefore became linked to the idea of an erotic relation. She disclosed the secret by overtly playing with the money exemplifying Freud's observation in the case history of Dora that "chattering fingers" betray the unconscious (Freud, 1905e, p. 77).

When the child was seven, her father lied to her and this had caused her to doubt his love for her, and unconsciously evoked the earlier memory. The child's lie to her father was in relation to some money she had appropriated and when discovered, her father asked her mother to punish her. The chastisement caused the girl great anguish, which appeared disproportionate, pointing to a displacement of affect. This affect had initially been displaced onto her much-loved nursemaid. The girl manifestly was upset because she had fallen from her father's favour however her distress was latently attached to her now repressed erotic bond to her mother. This moment reflects Freud's observation that: "We cannot understand women unless we appreciate this phase of their pre-oedipal attachment to their mother" (Freud, 1933a, p. 119). This first erotic relationship is the basis for all future relationships for both men and women.

A young woman, Lena, requested an appointment with me at the sexual health service to discuss her sexual orientation. The woman had a boyfriend but had embarked on a secret relationship with a woman. She felt that being with a woman was something forbidden but something she wished to experience. When the affair came to light, the man angrily ended the relationship. The woman was heart-broken and ended her relationship with the woman, because she no longer felt attracted to her.

The vignette indicates that the expression of feminine desire is problematic. Lacan (1960) specifically explains feminine desire in relation to feminine homosexuality, by arguing that femininity is the primary interest for the female homosexual. For Soler, if a female homosexual competes as a subject with a man, it is "with the intention of exalting femininity, with the proviso that she locates femininity in her partner" (Soler, 2002, p. 106). The woman's affair is not necessarily a homosexual act, but could be a heterosexual one serving a dual function; to be the object that serves as cause of desire for the man and to exult femininity. Soler argues that "perhaps we see thereby the doorway that leads from feminine sexuality to desire itself" (Soler, 2002, p. 106).

Boy crazy

Karen Horney distinguished various types of changes in adolescent girls, which coincide broadly with the onset of menses (puberty). They all relate to a turning away from the erotic sphere, or frigidity (Horney, 1935, pp. 19–26). Horney designates four broad categories; the girl who becomes absorbed in intense mental activity, academics, art and sport; the girl who becomes emotionally detached and cannot put energy into anything; and the girl who develops homosexual tendencies.

The fourth position is what Horney calls "boy crazy". These girls compulsively fall in love with one boy after another, without really caring for any of them. They will either break off the relationship or provoke the boy into breaking up with her. Such girls are generally, according to Horney, clever and ambitious but suffer from feelings of apprehensiveness in relation to themselves and their abilities. They suffer, what she calls, a free-floating anxiety, and the strategy to ward this off is to cling to men. Their insatiable thirst for the admiration of men eclipses their need for sexual gratification. A relationship with a man functions as a reassurance against anxiety, insecurity, and loneliness. Horney links this need for reassurance to the girl's fear of not being normal, which is, she argues, an outcome of the fear of being damaged by masturbation. She claims that the symptom is created as a defence against fear and guilt linked to fantasies associated with masturbation. The excess of fear and guilt connected with sexuality precludes the girl establishing a satisfactory relationship with a boy.

Within the family constellation, it often becomes evident that there may have been childhood rivalries between the girl and her mother, or older sister. This may appear as an aversion to competitiveness in adult life. Various factors can intensify the natural competition between mothers and daughters, such as premature sexual arousal, an invalidating environment, marital conflicts between parents (where the child was forced to divide loyalties), open or disguised rejection on the part of the mother, or an overly eroticised relationship with a father. As Horney observes, for the girls who are "boy crazy" only the ever-renewed conquest of men may service the purpose of reassurance (Horney, 1934, pp. 605–638).

Colette, a young woman of seventeen, was attending the service to receive treatment for a sexually transmitted infection. The nurses suggested that she speak to me and she initially spoke about feeling anger towards herself. She admitted that she actively courted boys and sought sex from them, but found that during the sexual act she often experienced a feeling of being disconnected from her own body, and lost interest in, and enjoyment of, the experience. The young woman worried that she was developing "a bad name" amongst her male and female friends and spoke about being confused by her behaviour. She courted attention from boys and commented that "she enjoyed sex" but that she often felt "empty" and "disappointed" following the encounters.

Over the weeks, Colette spoke often about her mother, and the ambivalence she felt her mother directed towards her. She described how five years previously (just as she was entering puberty), her mother had suffered a serious illness and the young woman had fastidiously cared for her, believing that she was the only caretaker available. During this time, she felt a harmonious relationship between them that she had not previously experienced. Caring for her mother's body was, in her words—"like when I was little and my mum minded me all the time". Following her mother's recovery, she began to feel overlooked and abandoned, and that her sister replaced her in her mother's affections. She experienced great anger in her mother's company, and spent more time outside the house in the company of young men.

We can hypothesise that the girl's experience of an ambivalent mother was a displacement of her own intense pre-oedipal love. Cut off from this early erotic relationship, she temporarily re-experienced it when nursing her mother, and subsequently re-experienced the cessation of this erotic bond when her mother appeared to replace her with her sister. Her numerous sexual encounters with boys can be perceived as attempts to again find the close relationship she had with her mother, together with a repetition of her experience of feeling empty and disappointed. The aggression projected onto her mother, and subsequently towards herself abated as the work continued.

Figures of women

Lacan (1958) supports Freud's thesis that there is a split between phallic jouissance and desire for men and for women. He observes that for the man to find satisfaction for his demand for love in his relations with the woman, there may well be a divergence towards "another woman" who may signify the phallus in various ways, either as "a virgin or a prostitute" (Lacan, 1958, p. 583). For the woman, a division exists between the object of love and desire, the first is hidden by the second, or in other words, love and desire converge on the same object. For Lacan, "one can observe that a lack in the satisfaction proper to sexual need, in other words, frigidity, is relatively well tolerated in women (in contrast to men), whereas repression inherent in desire is less present in women than in men" (Lacan, 1958, p. 583). The idea that, for the woman, love and desire converge on the same object, stresses a fundamental distinction between feminine and masculine sexuality. It also evokes an important clinical question. What are the implications for the woman who positions herself as the debased object?

A seventeen-year-old girl whom I will call Maria, requested an appointment to speak to me at the health centre because she was suffering from panic attacks. At first, she spoke about her debilitating anxiety, which had taken the form of an agoraphobia; she could not go alone anywhere outside the home. She also found it difficult to speak to people she did not know well. She explained that it was impossible to concentrate in school because she was experiencing paranoid and anxious thoughts, and this had resulted in a mediocre academic result, which would jeopardise her chances of entering college. She worried about what people thought about her, particularly with regard to her various relationships.

Maria sighed resignedly that she was used to doing "everything" for others and "getting nothing in return except abuse". These words effectively positioned her as the self-sacrificing and debased woman, to whom everything was owed and nothing ever given. Rather than supporting and motivating her ego, Maria's narcissism could be viewed as a destructive force, which she directed towards herself.

In this first session, Maria spoke about an ex-boyfriend, with a reputation for pursuing lots of girls. She believed she still loved him. When the relationship ended, Maria had begun to experience panic attacks and an exacerbation of her agoraphobia.

Maria's mother accompanied her to the following appointment. Her mother explained that she allowed her daughter to stay overnight with her boyfriends but found it impossible to address the question of sexual activity. She hoped Maria was "taking care of herself". She often reprimanded the girl for returning "too late", and displaced her anxiety about the girl's activities onto arguments about the completion of household chores. I silently wondered whether the signifier "late" referred to a period being late, indicating a pregnancy.

Maria's mother's anxiety increased as she spoke about wanting her daughter to have a contraception device inserted within her arm. When I asked Maria what she wanted, she only expressed the manifest desire to satisfy her mother's demand. I asked Maria's mother why it was so important that her daughter have this form of contraception and was told that she conceived her daughter when she was seventeen. Her intense wish that her daughter did not become pregnant at seventeen as she did, resulted in her intrusion upon her daughter's body and reproductive life.

It should also be stressed that within the mother's desire for contraception for her daughter, is a wish to conceal the enigma of her daughter's desire, and by default her own. The mother is reluctant to relinquish her own desire for a child to effectively "plug up" her own lack. The child can function as a precious object in the imaginary of the mother, the object which plugs up the subjective experience of "not-all" for the woman. For Lacan, it is vital to recall that "it is not about hiding the object, but hiding the lack of object" (Lacan, 1956, p. 166). The mother keeps a metaphorical veil over the illusion of her daughter as being her phallus. In acknowledging her daughter's sexuality, she also acknowledges her daughter is a woman, like her. As Freud states: "Thus she becomes a woman who is unapproachable and repels all sexual desire since she displays the terrifying genitals of her mother" (Freud, 1940c, pp. 273–274). For Maria's mother, the sexual is utterly unthinkable. Her wish to retain her daughter as a non-reproductive being is in effect a wish that her daughter does not grow up, because, if she does, she will be able to separate from her, and then effectively become her rival.

Rassial argues that the period of adolescence is ordered by repetition, reproduction, and invention. There is a repetition of a primal scene, but, this repetition is not a real one, and thus the adolescent is forced to merely repeat the repetition (Rassial, 1990, p. 589). Rassial emphasises that the adolescent phase of life is when reproduction becomes possible, and often appears as an alternative to repetition. This is partly why some adolescents rush into parenthood, illustrating why the availability of contraception is not sufficient safeguard against unplanned pregnancy.

Maria declined the invasive contraceptive measure demanded by her mother, instead choosing an oral contraceptive. There is a passive display in Maria's partial acquiescence to her mother's demand. As Salecl notes, Lacan considers that the fundamental dissatisfaction involved in the structure of desire in a woman is "pre-castrational" and suggests that a woman "knows that in the Oedipus complex what is involved is not to be stronger or more desirable than her mother [...] but to have the object" (Salecl, 2002, p. 94). At the following appointment, Maria said that she no longer needed to be accompanied by anyone to appointments.

As time went on, Maria embarked on a clandestine relationship with one of her ex-boyfriend's best friends, who had little interest in sexual intimacy and was sometimes impotent because of the amount of cannabis he smoked. This alliance was attractive to Maria because she manifestly always had a companion, and latently succeeded in continuing to betray her old boyfriend.

Maria's previous simultaneous relationships with a boy and a girl, resembles the male position in the classic form of debasement in the sphere of love, namely she may desire but does not love. In the relationship with the boy who was effectively impotent, Maria moved to the feminine corollary, frigidity. She could love without sexual desire. Lacan describes frigidity as that which "hides behind the veil" (Lacan, 1960, p. 617) and establishes that this apparent unity maintains a real duplicity of the subject, which cannot be reduced to the conservation of the oedipal link to the father. Frigidity as a symptom therefore functions to sustain a lack of satisfaction. This reference to a veiling of female sexuality emphasises the problematic structure of femininity with regard to castration.

> Why not admit, in fact, that if there is no virility that castration does not consecrate, it is a castrated lover or a dead man (or the two in one) who, for the woman, hides behind the veil in order to call her adoration to it—that is, [he calls] from the same locus beyond the maternal semblable from which the threat came to her of a castration that does not really concern her. Thus it is because of this ideal incubus that an embrace-like receptivity must be displaced in a sheath-like sensitivity onto the penis. (Lacan, 1960, p. 617)

Lacan argues, that within the woman's unconscious mind, there exists the phantasy of a secret lover, or "ideal incubus" whom the woman adores and who adores her in return. The woman's jouissance arises from the embrace of the incubus, which is transferred, like a sheath, onto her lover's penis. Lacan's reference to the mythic concept of an incubus alerts us to an ever-pervasive quotient of anxiety aligned with subjectivity.

According to legend, an incubus is a demon who seduces women in the dead of night. The inclusion of this detail reminds us of the unwished for dimension of jouissance, beyond the pleasure principle. Ernest Jones, made the original connection between the incubus and incestuous desire (Jones, 1931). He describes the incubus as a lewd demon who has carnal knowledge of a woman while in the shape of a man. The presence of the demon accounts for phenomena such as arousal dreams, and nocturnal emissions, and are most assuredly sexual.

Within Maria's multiple relationships, there exists, what Salecl designates as, a redoubling of partners:

> Women redouble their partners because they can be never be sure what kind of an object they are in the Other's desire. Thus for a woman it is better to fantasize that there is more than one man who is emotionally interested in her. (Salecl, 2002, p. 96)

What can be said about the two young men Maria chose to be in relationship with? They appear to be quite different from each other; one aspires to being a lothario, and the other is shy, and often impotent. Perhaps we can see a redoubling at play?

In his seminar *On Anxiety*, Lacan underscores the essentially feminine fantasy of Don Juan (Lacan, 1962). This fantasy reassures the woman that there is at least one man, who never loses himself in a relationship. The uncertainty regarding his desire allows the woman to have access to jouissance. As Salecl explains "this fantasy proves that there is at least one man who has it from the outset, who always has it, and cannot lose it, meaning that no woman can take it from him" (Salecl, 2002, p. 97). This fantasy is not at all anxiety provoking for the woman since it provides a veil which shields her from becoming the object of desire. In the same way, the woman gets the most reassurance about her own value as *objet a*, in fantasising about a man who never actually desires her in the first place. Is this what is at play within Maria's relationship with the two boys?

Maria's anxiety escalated when the first relationship ended; the veil was torn, unmasking her desire. She described feeling calmer and more in control of herself while in the second relationship. The relationship continued and towards the end of a year of weekly meetings, Maria ended our sessions because she had a university place.

Lacan's teachings remind us that the psychoanalyst must focus on listening out for traces of unconscious desire so that the analysand can assume the repressed unconscious knowledge to which their speech bears witness. Also, crucially, the analyst evokes a desire within the analysand to interrogate their own desire. The contemporary psychoanalyst maintains the centrality of *objet a*, to propel this evocation of what constitutes desire for an individual. This is what is at stake in any psychoanalytic intervention. This was central to the work in the sexual health setting with Maria, who like a modern-day Salome, created her own dance of the seven veils.

References

Balsam, R. (2015). Eyes, Ears, Lips, Fingertips, Secrets: Dora, Psychoanalysis and the Body. *The Psychoanalytic Review 102(1)*: 33–58.

Barnard, S. & Fink. B. (Eds.) (2002). *Reading Seminar XX Lacan's major work on Love, Knowledge and Feminine Sexuality*. New York: State University.

Freud, S. (1905d). *Three Essays on the Theory of Sexuality*. *S.E., 7*: 123–246. London: Hogarth.

Freud, S. (1905e). Fragment of an Analysis of a Case of Hysteria. *S.E., 7*: 1–122. London: Hogarth.

Freud, S. (1912d). On the Universal Tendency to Debasement in the Sphere of Love (Contributions to the Psychology of Love II). *S.E., 11*: 177–190. London: Hogarth.

Freud, S. (1913g). Two Lies Told by Children. *S.E., 12*: 303–310. London: Hogarth.

Freud, S. (1933a). Femininity Lecture XXXIII, *New Introductory Lectures on Psychoanalysis and Other Works. S.E., 22*: 112–135. London: Hogarth.

Freud, S. (1940c). Medusa's Head. *S.E., 18*: 273–274. London: Hogarth.

Horney, K. (1934). The Overvaluation of Love: A study of a common present day feminine type. *Psychoanalytic Quarterly, 3*: 605–638.

Horney, K. (1935). Personality Changes in Female Adolescents. *The American Journal of Orthopsychiatry, 5*: 19–26.

Jones, E. (1931). *On the Nightmare*. London: Hogarth Press.

Lacan, J. (1956). *La Relation d'object*. L. V. A. Roche (Trans.). Unpublished.

Lacan, J. (1958). The Signification of the Phallus. In: *Écrits* (pp. 575–584). B. Fink (Trans.). New York: W. W. Norton, 2002.

Lacan, J. (1960). Guiding Remarks for a Convention on Feminine Sexuality. In: *Écrits* (pp. 610–620). B. Fink (Trans.). New York: W. W. Norton, 2002.

Lacan, J. (1962). *The Seminar of Jacques Lacan Book X On Anxiety*. C. Gallagher (Trans.). Karnac: London.

Lacan, J. (1974–1975). *The Seminar of Jacques Lacan Book XXII R.S.I.* C. Gallagher (Trans.). Karnac: London.

Lacan, J. (1975). *Encore: The Seminar of Jacques Lacan XX. On Feminine Sexuality, The Limits of Love and Knowledge, 1972–1973*. B. Fink (Trans.). Norton, New York & London, 1999.

Quignard, P. (2014). *The Sexual Night*. C. Turner (Trans.). London: Seagull Books.

Rassial, J. J. (1990). *L'Adolescent et La Psychanalyste*. Paris: Rivages.

Salecl, R. (2002). Love Anxieties. In *Reading Seminar XX. Lacan's Major Work on Love, Knowledge and Sexuality* (pp. 93–98). S. Barnard & B. Fink (Eds.). New York: New York Press.

Soler, C. (2002). What Does the Unconscious Know About Women? In: *Reading Seminar XX. Lacan's Major Work on Love, Knowledge and Sexuality* (pp. 99–108). S. Barnard & B. Fink (Eds.). New York: New York Press.

Soler, C. & Holland, J. (2005). New Figures of Women. *Psychoanalytic Review, 92*: 581–593.

Vanier, A. (2001). Some Remarks on Adolescence with Particular Reference to Winnicott and Lacan. *Psychoanalytic Quarterly, 70*: 579–597.

PART IV

"FATHER": INVENTIONS AND REINVENTIONS

CHAPTER THIRTEEN

To invent a father ...

Megan Williams

Lacan at one point states of Freud: "[...] the entire Freudian interrogation is summed up in this—*what is it to be a father?*" (Lacan, 1956–1957, session of 6th March, p. 233). Hyperbole, no doubt, yet there is something evoked by his words of the *Vatersehnsucht* or father-longing that Freud considered universal (Freud, 1923b, p. 37; 1927c, p. 18; 1930a, p. 72; 1939a, pp. 109, 148). How does it come about that a speaking being has such a longing and what can be done with it? In this chapter I will discuss these questions and propose the notion of a fictional answer, requiring something of invention.

A child of six enters the consulting room. Amongst the first exchanges which occur he asserts that he is a boy and then announces sadly, "there's no Daddy". Recognised as a boy by the formal agencies of society, he nevertheless complains that his mother tries to make him look like a girl and asserts that, at school, he has no friends except one girl, whose name is the feminine version of his. He adds: "I don't have anything to give her", indicating his notion that one of the insignia of masculinity is to have something to give. A first thesis, then: that for him to properly be a boy, a Daddy is necessary. An implied premise: that his own father is not a Daddy. With tears, he elaborates the ways in which this father fails to provide what he regards as the insignia of masculinity: strength, power, and the capacity to win. These insignia are enacted in ferocious and interminable play fights between superheroes, in which the loser always comes back from defeat to take up the battle again. The battles are unable to reach a conclusion in which a title would be awarded. It would seem that he has the body of a boy but not the semblance; the biology but not the title; that he is lacking the deeds to future manhood in his pocket, to paraphrase Lacan—and that he would need to receive such deeds from a Daddy (Lacan, 1957–1958, session of 15th January, pp. 10–11).

Two questions come to mind: what makes a Daddy? and what makes this child know that a Daddy is what is lacking to him?

Daddy as metaphor

In regard to the second, we might consider the words of Robert Lévy, who writes that the idea of "'some father' is already there before the metaphor is effectuated"—already there in the discourse surrounding the child (Lévy, 1998, p. 75, my translation). The metaphor he speaks of is Lacan's paternal metaphor, which gives a central place and operational efficacy to a particular signifier, the Name-of-the-Father. It gives rise to the title of *Daddy*, though we will come to see that there is no living person who is equal to it. Note Lévy's comment that, prior to the metaphor taking effect, there is already an idea of this Daddy, which is what Lacan says—a father is something which is already there in the game—and the analysand says: that he has the idea that there ought to be a Daddy, and yet there isn't one (Lacan, 1956–1957, session of 6th March, p. 239).

The paternal metaphor is Lacan's account of what is essential in the Freudian Oedipus complex, and gives a first response to the question of what is operational in a father. Lacan first proposed that the coming-to-be of a subject necessitates castration as a symbolic operation, in which the essence of "father" is to be a signifier, the Name-of-the-Father (Lacan, 1957–1958, session of 15th January, p. 14; 2002, pp. 464–465). Castration is here a linguistic operation of metaphor, in which this signifier substitutes for, and sends into repression, some other signifier with which the subject represents the desire of the mother. The effects are to bar the child from taking up a place as object of the mother's desire, to institute the unconscious as condition of this separate subjectivity, and to institute a new signification of lack and desire: the phallus. The theory holds that the metaphor removes the child from the menace of two unknown desires: the demand of his sexual organ, which doesn't participate in and obey his ego and is therefore, Lacan writes, "not at all auto-erotic ... the most hetero thing there is" (Lacan, 2009, p. 15); and the unspoken demand issuing from his mother, related to the place that the child holds in her fantasm, which the child wishes to satisfy in order to retain the recognition necessary to him. Lacan emphasises the opacity of these demands in the form of two subjective questions: "what does it want, here inside?" and "*Che vuoi*?/what do you want?" (Lacan, 1960–1961, session of 19th April, p. 8). The Name-of-the-Father places them both under an interdiction signified as universal: a law in place of the caprice of a mother and an organ. The Real for which the child had no representation is assigned a signified place as excluded, forbidden, im-proper, giving rise to the universal signification of lack such that any desire and any object that is desired come under its rubric, including the boy's penis. The Phallus as signifier of this lack of jouissance and of the desire for it, is imagined as the ultimate instrument of desire and attributed to the father *insofar as* he appears to the child to have that which can satisfy the mother—that is, insofar as he is a Daddy. Thus the child subject moves from *being* the imaginary phallus of his mother to *having* the Phallus, signifier of desire (Lacan, 2002, p. 582). However, this is not without the emergence of another kind of *being*: being a Daddy-to-come, we could say, since for both Freud and Lacan, this constitution of a subject is founded on an introjection of the father as ego ideal (Freud, 1923b, pp. 28–39; Lacan, 1957–1958, session of 22nd January, p. 15).

"The scary thing"

The analysand discussed here began his first session by constituting an analytic space composed of a time different to the historical time of everyday—"Can I stay here forever?"—and a subject-supposed-to-know. The latter is witnessed by his question, "Why does that happen?", asked of masturbation. He revealed his fears, first among which was the wolf that accompanied him to the analytic space and was now hidden in the chimney. Then, happily, as if relieved of anxiety, he said that he would draw "the scary thing"—the outline of a very round human figure—and then "the really scary thing": a child (specified as a girl) inside the figure's belly and a line of thought bubbles joining this inside-figure to the head of the containing figure. This would suggest that the really scary thing is the mother's desire, and that his anxiety finds some relief in being able to give it a representation as desire for a girl child—a pregnancy, even if it is one that makes him fearful. Similarly, it and his anxiety in the face of the unsayable activity of his penis are given representation in a known and feared object, the wolf.

Evidently, then, there is no effective function which is able to separate him from these demands that provoke both anxiety and irresistible attraction. Normatively, as we have seen above, the paternal function introduces a prohibition here. However, a paternal metaphor attains its operational force from a mother's desire for the father and in this case the link is weak. This mother revealed in a preliminary interview that she is "just waiting to be rid of" the boy's father, when economic circumstances should permit. That her lack of desire for the father is transmitted to the child is evidenced by the absence of any such representation in his play. It is not that there is no paternal function at all. The child makes appeals for prohibition and he obeys his father—this is clear from both observation and the mother's speech. It is likely that this presence of a forbidding authority is transmitted to the child by the mother's speech about her own father, whom she represents as strict and authoritarian (another man she "couldn't wait to get away from"). The problem is rather at the level of desire: his own desire *for* the mother, which he tries to resist, receives no help from it being represented to him that her desire is turned away from him, towards a man. Thus his obedience is more a manifestation of his attempt to *make* his father function, than a result of his identification with a paternal ideal.

That there is a partial prohibition of masturbation is evident in the analysand's report that he had said to Mummy that he mustn't touch his penis and that she had agreed but then added that she herself had a small penis. That is, he has some representation of what it is his mother desires—a girl child, the jouissance of a small penis—but no articulation of her desire with a represented lack (since the objects which Mummy desires, she is able to have). He is drawn to being the object of her desire: both complaining of and enjoying her painting his nails and adorning him with jewellery, and reportedly behaving "hyperactively", such that his mother says of him that she "can't leave him alone for a second". It is pertinent to note here that the matter which concerns psychoanalysis is not his adaptation to a masculine social norm, nor a morally required renunciation of masturbation, but his own speech. He speaks of a conflict in which the enjoyment of satisfying a certain image he detects in the mother's "eye" is found to be incompatible with his stated being as a boy.

Over a number of sessions, he repeatedly hid himself entirely inside a chest, closing the lid and naming it as a place to be buried, only to throw open the lid and jump up again. Later this cavity became the place inside the mother of his drawing and from which, once inside, he attached himself to the outside world by means of a cord which was sometimes a telephone through which he spoke to the analyst from his enclosure. Naming this cord "the connector bit", he repeatedly asked for it to be cut, only to show how it always re-attached itself, all on its own. He then cut off the connector bit and threw it up the chimney for Mr. Wolf to eat. In a later session and a further development of this theme, he took a toy figure and drew a line down the middle of it, saying: "That's what I need: a line between Mummy and me." Thus his own play manifests an appeal for some instance (normatively, a prohibition) to separate him from his attachment to Mummy's desire.

Some of these elements are drawn from his lived experience of his father. To go into detail here is not possible, but the family history as recounted by the mother and a social service make clear that signifiers of death have been evoked. His play shows his entrapment in his attachment to her desire and his attempts to get out, to separate from the un-named desire that jumps up suddenly in the uncanny space of penis and Mummy: his entrapment by his jouissance. Several hypotheses are possible here in relation to the theory under discussion. His play can be seen as his own writing of the relation between his father and his mother: a relation which is "dead" or without effective link; that is, no link whose representation can take discursive charge of the Real of a jouissance which jumps up startlingly. The relation represented is also one in which his father is "inside" the mother, in the place of another child. (Similarly, the superhero play presents the father as an alter ego and a rival, rather than as an instance outside this series). The "inside" of the mother is represented as the place from which life emerges and to which it goes after death; a totality of significations that subsumes the paternal function (in its imaginary extension to God) within itself and fails to inscribe a lack. Finally, the play tries to make a limit or prohibition between the subject and his mother, calling on Mr Wolf to abolish their connection and incidentally, confirming Lacan's observation that a phobic object functions as a signifier standing in for the absent Name-of-the-Father (Lacan, 1956–1957, session of 13th March, pp. 263, 333).

Lacan makes the latter comment in relation to Freud's case of Little Hans, and this analysand is in a similar position, such that we can apply to him Lacan's observation about Little Hans: enclosed within the mother's universe of significations, he is caught in the anguish of finding himself nothing more than a metonymy of her desire for the phallus; loved not for what he has to give, but for what he represents in his entirety (Lacan, 1956–1957, session of 20th March, pp. 256–261, 281–284, 305–306). The analysand discussed here is faced with a choice between being that which his mother desires by "looking like a girl" or being the boy he recognises himself as, yet nothing in her desire; between being loved for what he *is* and having nothing, or *having* what a boy has and not being loved.

What to do with what jumps up?

The question this analysand poses is what to do with the jouissance that jumps up; how to knot it to a being signified as having, a boy—and still retain a place in his mother's desire. Another way of putting this is how much of that jouissance can be sexualised by the phallic signification of a desire of his own.

The presence of an incipient paternal function in the play has been noted. It can, in theory, be attributed to the presence in the mother's speech of an interdictor of jouissance in the shape of her own father. However, this calls to some extent on a sociological approach. David Pereira has argued persuasively that the logic of an analysis requires that the impossible-to-say which is at play in any analysis must be taken up with reference only to the impasses of the analysand's own speech (or play) and not to an outside (such as the parents' discourse); that to do the latter returns an impossibility to the subject as impotence (Pereira, 1999, p. 68). In addition, the theory of the paternal metaphor is a theoretical framework, not a normative prescription. It is important that the discourse of psychoanalysis not be distorted by analysts attempting to supply with their speech the function held to be absent; that is, to imposing the law. An analyst cannot be a Daddy. Such a stance would conflate the paternal function with that of the subject-supposed-to-know—a problem which has been discussed in detail by Porge (2012) and Norregaard Arroyo and Plastow (2012).

Is this analysand simply left in the lurch then, given the failure of his mother's speech to accord his father the status of a Daddy? I would propose that the analytic question concerns, not solely what is present or not in the discourse of his parents—though certainly his presenting symptom can be taken, in Lacan's terms, as "represent[ing] the truth of the family couple" (Lacan, 1969, p. 7)—but what he can fabricate of a paternal function; even what kind of father he can be.

Father, where art thou?

In the period after the theory of the Name-of-the-Father, Lacan noted and decried the neuroticising tendency of the paternal metaphor and the effects of idealisation of the father, which he called the imaginary father. Up till then, the theory had rested on the notion of identification with the father *as ideal*. From Freud's *The Ego and the Id* to Lacan's paternal metaphor, the key of the paternal function was conceptualised as the attribution of the phallus to the father (Freud, 1923b; Lacan, 1956–1957, sessions of 10th April, pp. 334, 352, 5th June, 427–432; 1957–1958, session of 22nd January, p. 14). Symbolically, this should indicate that the father, too, is castrated and subject to desire for that which he lacks. However, the attribution also confers on the father the imaginary phallus; the phallus conceived not as signifier of lack but as a positive instrument of potency which gives him alone access to a jouissance of the mother that is prohibited for the child, thus inscribing the father as exception, or the One who is outside the series of fathers and sons—a kind of primal horde father of Freud's myth (Freud, 1912–1913). This image of the father is what makes him loved/hated and idealised and then, because of this elevation, introjected such that the subject, in his ego ideal, *is* this father, at least by aspiration (a masculine position) or aims to *have* such a father-man (a feminine one). Two problems attach to this theorisation: one is that it rests on the *person* of the father and we can see from the present case that the familial father may be an obstacle to the attainment of the paternal function rather than its source. The other problem concerns the neuroticising effects of the ideal of *The* Father.

In *Seminar VII*, Lacan characterised these effects as giving rise to religion (the idealisation of the father as God) and to the superego, understood as a reproach to God for prohibiting all jouissance, turned against the subject's self via a melancholic identification (Lacan, 1992, pp. 307–308). That is, the subject lives the impossibility of being *The* Father, the all-potent, as his own, personal impotence, and blames both his actual father, the impotent family guy who screwed him up, and God, for reneging on his promise to make the subject such a One. But because the subject still hopes to attain the promise, he turns his blame and hatred on himself, mistaking an impossibility for his own impotence. The superego conceptualised in this way is consonant with the effects that Freud elaborated as the "bedrock" of the castration complex: anxiety at exercising one's own desire without a father's permission, or depression at a lack of having, since it is only the father-exception who has the phallus, and he prohibits it to all others (Freud, 1937c, p. 252). The analysand discussed here evidences the latter, hysteric position. Moustapha Safouan has similarly observed that the deleterious effect of an idealisation of the father is that All is interdicted, not only the mother (Safouan, 1974, p. 45). The move that Lacan makes in *Seminar VII* is the same one that Freud made in "Analysis Terminable and Interminable": namely, to understand that these neurotic effects are not confined to cases where something went wrong, but are a universal tendency of the paternal function: "The perpetual reproach ... remains fundamental in the structure of the subject" (Lacan, 1992, p. 308). Analysis is then understood as the opportunity to undo these effects by re-encountering the fundamental helplessness that *The* Father protected against, and doing something else with it—a something else that he would later conceptualise as the fabrication of a *sinthome*.

A function of naming

In *Seminar XVII*, Lacan critiques and re-conceptualises his previous theory. He moves emphasis from the Name-of-the-Father (symbolic) and the father as beloved and introjected image (imaginary), to the "real father" as agent of castration (Lacan, 2007, pp. 123–129). The real father is no living being but a pure effect of language, the name given to the intervention of the master signifier (as opposed to master-Father) to mark an event of jouissance and thus, represent a subject (Lacan, 2007, p. 89). In this he implicitly references the early Freud of the years prior to his invention of the Oedipus complex, when he theorised how a subject of the unconscious comes to be born, not from a mother and a father, as a child is, but from the inscription in memory of the representation of a moment of arousal or jouissance—born, that is, from entering language (Freud, 1950a, pp. 233–239). Freud writes of how an intolerable arousal, against which the subject is helpless, is represented in memory by a "boundary idea" which has no sense but can be repeated indefinitely while its object, the real experience, is lost by virtue of being represented (Freud, 1950a, pp. 220–228). The boundary idea becomes organised with other ideas, producing meaning which includes at its heart something of fiction or lie (*proton pseudos*), in that it misses its true cause (Freud, 1950a, pp. 352–356). Lacan's theoretical move from the father considered as a *person* draws from this Freudian heritage. He states that identification is not to be seen in terms of being as One but of "Being, marked one"—identification not *with* the father but *by* the trait, a unary memorial of an instant of jouissance which persists in the unconscious (Lacan, 2007, p. 154). This unary trait links with others to become the master signifier: *agent of castration* in that it makes impossible a re-finding of the real jouissance which is sought; *master* in that it commands the repetitive seeking of the symptom: the automaton of signifiers interminably yielding a missed encounter with that jouissance lost to representation (Lacan, 1979, pp. 53–64). That which is lost is imagined as what Freud called "the prehistoric, unforgettable other" and we could add, as *The* Father (Freud, 1950a, p. 239).

This theoretical shift sets the groundwork for the father to become, as he does in Lacan's later work, not the Name-of-the-Father but the father of naming, a father who names (Lacan, 1974–1975, session of 11th March, pp. 1–6). The function of a name is to be what Saul Kripke called a rigid designator: the deictic function Lacan gives to the unary trait of designating a "one" without assigning it any meaning, bringing to birth the symbolic order (Kripke, p. 1972). Gustavo Etkin emphasises that the psychoanalysis of children calls for this *designative*, as opposed to *explicative*, naming in order to produce the Real as non-sense, separated from the sense of the discourse (Etkin, 1995, pp. 72–73). This Real is that which is lost to the naming; Freud's lost object; what Le Gaufey has called the hole of the true cause (Le Gaufey, Text 2). Le Gaufey straddles the different theories of the father by proposing that the move from the imaginary father of the primal horde to the symbolic father, who is no more than a dead function to be utilised, is made by the subject encountering that hole where the father as cause is not represented. This involves a lived moment of missed encounter with a father, where a child is disappointed in his anticipation that the person of his father will in some way measure up to "fatherness"; to being father *qua* father. Le Gaufey conceptualises this moment of failed encounter as necessary, and as synonymous with the mythic murder of the (imaginary) father of the primal horde. The analysand discussed here circles around the possibility of such a moment: he experiences his own father as failing without, as yet, finding the way for such an experience to take effect as the encounter with an impossibility, a hole, designated as such.

Invention

If the Real of the paternal function is to name an instant of jouissance such that its jumping up is localised to the same place, designated relative to the automaton of unconscious signifiers, then it introduces the function of the symptom. This is where Lacan took the function of the father in *RSI*. Here the father is conceived of as the model of a symptom, and the symptom as the never-ceasing writing of a "one" of jouissance (Lacan, 1982, p. 166). No longer he who possesses the mother (of the child), the father becomes he who confronts her *as a woman*, and elects her to that causal "one" which is empty of sense, thus making her the cause of his desire (Lacan, 1982, p. 167). Here Lacan retains the essential function of the father as prohibiting, since, as Benjamin Domb points out, if the father approaches the mother as a woman and she consents to his desire, he not only takes her from the child, but renders her no longer all-mother, able to plug her lack with thoughts and belly full of child (Domb, 1997, pp. 153–155). This father-symptom does not offer himself to idealisation as the One exception to castration who possesses the jouissance prohibited to the child. On the contrary, this father who, in the face of an unknown desire of a woman, makes a symptom of an unsayable trait of jouissance, is necessarily subject to castration. What he models is not potent possession but a knowing how to do with his unconscious. He doesn't know this trait of jouissance beyond his ego, but allows his desire to knot it to that woman chosen unconsciously, bringing her to the place of his designated "one". His symptom thus knots jouissance (Real) with desire (Symbolic) and an ego image (Imaginary). Lacan proposed this as a *savoir-y-faire* or knowing-how-to-do-there that he named *sinthome*, a new kind of symptom which, in knotting the Real, Symbolic and Imaginary registers of experience, is equivalent to the Name-of-the-Father: a father as *sinthome* (Lacan, 1974–1975, session of 18th November, p. 13).

Thus Lacan puts forward a way beyond the effects of the castration complex, which are the effects of the imaginarisation of the father, that Freud considered interminable. The termination—conceived earlier as the subject taking up and doing something with his or her helplessness in front of the hole of the cause or the non-sense of jouissance—consists of the subject making do with this Real by making a *sinthome*. Drawing on this period of Lacan's work, Etkin discusses designative naming as including a new conception of the symptom which he considers to be "a Symbolic in Act, pure signifier, saying, difference in Act, enunciation: the Name-of-the-Father in function" (Etkin, 1995, p. 72). Similarly,

Roberto Harari considers this function as a naming that opens the possibility of inventing new signifiers (Harari, 2002, p. 55). That which is necessary of the paternal function is thus essentialised to this: the naming required to designate and make ex-timate the Real of a jouissance which is thereby made accessible to the symptom function that may knot this passion to the subject's recognition of his self and his desires.

The analysand discussed here works at fabricating a paternal function out of what he has to hand and what was transmitted to him in discourse. From the anguishing oral enjoyment that connects him to his mother's body, he designates some trait (a bite) thence available to an invented paternal function ("Mr Wolf") to cut his boy-self from the sucking exerted by his desire for the mother and her desire for ... a girl. In this he uses his power of enunciation to command; to make what is merely a representation *function*. Evidently it does not yet function entirely. Nevertheless, in this cut, and in the play which shows a designated jouissance jump up repeatedly but always from the same place (he is never hyperactive in the session and jumps up only from the chest), he is on the way to constructing a new symptom by making do with what he has, once his designation (so far by gesture) achieves naming with a signifier. Whether this symptom can be knotted to a phallic desire that would take him towards a woman as object is yet to be seen. When he spoke of the girl to which he had nothing to give, the response he received in the analytic session was "you could give her your words; speak to her", to which suggestion he replied "I don't know what to say". The response was a mistake along the lines discussed above. A solution that knots the impossible of jouissance to desire cannot be suggested to a child from an analyst-who-knows (an analyst-father) because castration means that no subject knows: if the impossible is not to be returned to him as impotence, it can only be dealt with contingently, by an invention of the unconscious.

Thus a symptom requires the alterity of an unconscious: that the child no longer be dealing with the immediate, outside-presence of the discourse of the parents, but with the non-sense that comes from elsewhere, as if from a pre-historic time. Le Gaufey locates the murder of the father in a necessary discordance (which the murder effectuates) between mythic time and historical time; "necessary" because no living father knows consciously know-how-to-do-there, with the unconscious, any more than any other speaking being: "the father *qua* father [is] no conscious being" (Lacan, 1977, p. 59). The father-symptom is possible precisely because that "father" does not exist in this time and place; he is not the father of everyday but an invention of the unconscious. It is in this sense that he is an exception. Lévy speaks of an evolution over time in the progress or maturation of the paternal metaphor, leading to its culmination in complete repression, which he considers as necessarily co-efficient with the functions of metaphor and memory (Lévy, 1998, p. 76). Similarly, Pereira asserts that, if the Real as impossible is required to knot the Symbolic and Imaginary, then an analysand, to recognise himself, must also construct that which is logically remote to the discourse within which he recognises himself, an alterity in which an Other time is designated to contain that impossible-to-say (Pereira, 1999, pp. 68–70). He adds that this inexistent impossible-to-say is then able to appear contingently, under the sign of negation, which for Freud was the sign of the unconscious (Freud, 1925h, 235–239).

We find such a negation in the thesis proposed at the start of the analysis: "There's no Daddy". It would, I propose, be a mistake to assume from this statement that a necessary and invariant course, that of the development of the paternal metaphor, has come to grief in the failure of the child's actual father to be a Daddy. For what does a survey of Lacan's developments regarding the paternal function indicate if not that there is no Daddy, in the sense of the One imagined to bear, and to be able to give, the insignia of masculinity? In fact Lacan opined that Freud's myth of the primal horde father was driven by Freud's desire to find the father, given that He is nowhere (Lacan, 1956–1957, session of 6th March, p. 240). The analysand is suffering from that same affect of *Vatersehnsucht* or father-longing which Lacan attributed to Freud, and Freud, to all speaking subjects. To take the analysand's thesis not as the manifestation of an impasse within his own discourse, but rather as the sign of a problem in his environment, would be to return him to the impotence of his familiarly signified place as his mother's object.

The analysand's work begins to mark out the place of a remoteness or alterity, albeit as yet marked in space rather than time—the place before birth and after death; of the chimney and the chest; of a designated impossible. The question is of knotting the impasse he brings about what he has, to the impossible-to-say that jumps up from this space, to his own recognition of himself (as a boy), and to the law located with Mr Wolf in the remote place of the dead father (already co-located with the impossible)—three rings waiting to be knotted. I would say that the analytic work with which the analysand is engaged is the invention of a father; not the *person* of a father, but a necessary function. The function is that of *sinthome*: an intrication of real and contingent jouissance, symbolic desire and self-image such that it knots the registers of the subject's experience in a stable way. Such invention could be thought in Le Gaufey's terms as a killing of the imaginary father: if the subject can make a new act of saying which brings into function the name of a father newly dead and detached from any living instance, then not only is this father an invention of the unconscious, but, in a sense, the subject *is* this father. This would be to mask the empty place of cause with a necessary *proton pseudos* or fiction. Such might be called *identifiction of* a father, as opposed to the neuroticising tendency of identification *with* the person of a father. It is in this sense that I take Lacan's comment that psychoanalysis, if it succeeds, proves that one can do without the Name-of-the-Father, providing one make use of it (Lacan, 1975–1976, session of 13th April, p. 11). The Name-of-the-Father is nothing other than the knot itself (Lacan, 1974–1975, session of 3rd November, p. 59).

References

Domb, B. (1997). A Practice of the Real: The End of Analysis. *Papers of the Freudian School of Melbourne 18*: 149–156.

Etkin, G. (1995). Nothing Returns from the Real: The Structure of Psychosis. *Papers of the Freudian School of Melbourne 16*: 61–75.

Freud, S. (1950a). Draft K. The Neuroses of Defence (A Christmas Fairy Tale) In: Extracts from the Fliess Papers (1950a [1892–1899]). *S.E., I*: 220–229. London: Hogarth.

Freud, S. (1950a) Letter 52. In: Extracts from the Fliess Papers (1950a [1892–1899]). *S.E., I*: 233–239. London: Hogarth.

Freud, S. (1950a). Project for a Scientific Psychology. *S.E., I*: 281–392. London: Hogarth.

Freud, S. (1923b). *The Ego and the Id. S.E., XIX:* 1–66. London: Hogarth.

Freud, S. (1927c). *The Future of an Illusion. S.E., XXI:* 1–56. London: Hogarth.

Freud, S. (1930a). *Civilisation and its Discontents. S.E., XXI:* 57–146. London: Hogarth.

Freud, S. (1937c). Analysis Terminable and Interminable. *S.E., XXIII*: 209–254. London: Hogarth.

Freud, S. (1939a). *Moses and Monotheism: Three Essays. S.E., XXIII*: 1–138. London: Hogarth.

Harari, R. (2002). *The Sinthome*: Turbulence and Dissipation. In: L. Thurston (Ed.). *Re-Inventing the Symptom. Essays on the Final Lacan* (pp. 45–57). New York: Other Press.

Kripke, S. A. (1972). *Naming and Necessity*. Cambridge, Massachusetts: Harvard University Press.

Lacan, J. (1956–1957). *The Seminar of Jacques Lacan Book IV. The Object Relation 1956–1957*. J. -A. Miller (Ed.), L. V. A. Roche (Trans.). Unpublished Manuscript.

Lacan, J. (1957–1958). *The Seminar of Jacques Lacan Book V. The Formations of the Unconscious 1957–1958*. C. Gallagher (Trans.). London: Karnac.

Lacan, J. (1960–1961). *The Seminar of Jacques Lacan Book VIII. Transference 1960–1961*. C. Gallagher (Trans.). London: Karnac.

Lacan, J. (1969). Note on the Child. *Analysis, 1990, 2*: 7–8.

Lacan, J. (1974–1975). *The Seminar of Jacques Lacan Book XXII. R. S. I. 1974–1975*. J. Stone (Trans.). Unpublished Manuscript.

Lacan, J. (1975–1976). *The Seminar of Jacques Lacan Book XXIII. Joyce and the Sinthome 1975–1976*. C. Gallagher (Trans.). Unpublished Manuscript.

Lacan, J. (1979). *The Four Fundamental Concepts of Psycho-Analysis*. J. -A. Miller (Ed.), A. Sheridan (Trans.). London: Penguin Books.

Lacan, J. (1982). Seminar of 21st January 1975. In: J. Mitchell & J. Rose (Eds.). *Feminine Sexuality. Jacques Lacan & the École Freudienne* (pp. 162–171). London: MacMillan Press.

Lacan, J. (1989). Geneva Lecture on the Symptom. *Analysis, 1*: 7–26.

Lacan, J. (1992). *The Ethics of Psychoanalysis 1959–1960. The Seminar of Jacques Lacan Book VII*. J. -A. Miller (Ed.), D. Porter (Trans.). London: Routledge.

Lacan, J. (2002). *Écrits. The First Complete Edition in English*. B. Fink (Trans.). New York: W. W. Norton & Co.

Lacan, J. (2007). *The Other Side of Psychoanalysis. The Seminar of Jacques Lacan Book XVII*. New York: W. W. Norton & Co.

Le Gaufey, G. (Text 1). On Fatherness. Available at: www.legaufey.fr/Textes/Attention_files/40.rtf.

Le Gaufey, G. (Text 2). *Père, ne voit-tu pas donc que tu brûles?* Available at: www.legaufey.fr/Textes/Attention_files/27.rtf.

Lévy, R. (1998). *L'Infantile en Psychanalyse*. Paris: érès.

Norregaard Arroyo, T., & Plastow, M. (2012). Psychoanalysis and the Child. In: L. Clifton (Ed.). *Invention in the Real. Papers of the Freudian School of Melbourne Volume 24* (pp. 99–104). London: Karnac.

Pereira, D. (1999). The *Infans* and the (K) not of History. *Papers of the Freudian School of Melbourne 20*: 59–71.

Porge, E. (2012). Some Cases of "Name of the Father Subject Supposed of Knowledge". In: L. Clifton (Ed.). *Invention in the Real. Papers of the Freudian School of Melbourne Volume 24* (pp. 117–123). London: Karnac.

Safouan, M. (1974). *Études sur L'Oedipe. Introduction à une Théorie du Sujet*. Paris: Éditions du Seuil.

CHAPTER FOURTEEN

The Father of the Name: a child's analysis through the last teachings of Lacan

Annie G. Rogers

Guiding framework

In this chapter I revisit a child analysis across four years, focusing on the last teachings of Lacan through the "Father of the Name" and the "Real unconscious". My aim is to recalibrate the compass of a Lacanian field of psychoanalysis with children. I explore the position of the analyst in that field, and the invitation to the child to discover a space for the Real in the work of play. From my session notes I extricate a trajectory of the analysis from a symptom through primal scene fantasy and family intervention—to show how the child makes use of an unrepresented family legacy. What is crucial in this case is the child's use of the Real of his body—in physical responses that configure what cannot be said, and the "Father of the Name"—the analyst's act of making a space for naming the unrepresented. These two pivots foreground the child's singular experience of analysis and make a new path for his life.

In setting a new compass for a child's analysis through the last Lacan, however, I do not wish to elide the Name-of-the-Father—a lynchpin in the child's entry into the symbolic use of language and his capacity to follow his own desire. For the child who is neurotic, he is already of a symptom of the Oedipus, already living under the signifier of the

Name-of-the-Father, which has come to occupy the place in which the child has encountered the desire of the mother. With a child of six years, he has met his mother's desire as an enigma and has solved it in his particular way. Where once he could make no sense of his mother's acts, and the Other that recognised him was the Other of omniscient knowledge and whim, he offered himself as the object of her unconscious fantasy. He carries this legacy, since he used his body, his very being, to become the embodiment of the mother's unconscious desire. Theoretically, the child represses his fantasy of being the object of the mother, but even so, something in this process can go awry, and we see it in the clinic with many children.

Lacan spoke of his own children in the following excerpt from a lecture he gave in Geneva in 1975:

> I have observed a number of small children closely, even if they were only my own. The fact that a child says, *perhaps, not yet,* before he is able to construct a sentence properly, proves that there is something in him through which everything is sieved, whereby the water of language happens to leave something behind as it passes, some detritus which he will play with, indeed which he will be forced to cope with. This is what all this non- reflected activity leaves him with -debris- to which, later on, because he is premature, there will be added problems that will frighten him. (Lacan, 1989, p. 10)

This is one of the most eloquent notes on *lalangue* (language as a dimension of jouissance, of sound-play) by Lacan. Of his children, he says: "The water of language happens to leave something behind as it passes, some detritus which he will play with ..." These are bits of language linked with the Real, with the body enjoying, and the body afraid. How the child plays with this problematic forms *what he or she will become.* This is a particularly apt quote as we now consider a space for the Real in a child's analysis. What is this space, and what are its conditions?

In "Note on the Child" (1969) Lacan remarked that the child's symptom testifies to something transmitted across the generations through the parental couple, something the child does not recognise as a truth. The aim of the analysis is to offer a space for the child to re-configure what has been transmitted (as a lie, as guilt, as a fetish, etc.). This work not only frees the child from the burden of previous generations, it also opens something quite new to the child. The effective analyst for the child at this precise juncture, in my view, takes the position of what Lacan called the "Father of the Name" (Lacan, 1975–1976). The analyst makes a place for the child to name what was once both overwhelmingly enigmatic and also registered on the body. The "Father of the Name" is not in the desire or discourse of the Other. Rather, the position is a matter of naming, saying the Real, where saying is an act (Soler, 2014). The Symbolic makes a hole, an irreducible hole (or lack) and signifiers circle around it—these are the signifiers of the desire of the Other. But names are not signifiers in this sense. "Names come from the true hole of the unconscious, the Real, the void. This hole, Lacan says, spits out the Names of the Father" (Soler, 2014, p. 156).

If we recognise that the analyst's position as the "Father of the Name" functions to safeguard a space for the Real, this position has an effect on the child. It makes it possible for her or him to speak from the Real—bringing elements of impossibility, moments outside of time/space/reality—into a naming that the analyst enquires into and supports. The child then not only responds to a truth in his or family (a half-saying of truth), but also enters the unknown. The "Father of the Name" makes a space for the child to play with the detritus of language. And the effect is to knit the child's speech and play to the Real in a social link. Then it becomes possible to name what one has never been able to say or know.

Tyge[1]: a child's analysis

Tyge is six years old when I first meet him. He comes into my office, sits on the floor, and draws a train, an engine, and four cars in hot pink crayon. Black smoke flies from an inverted triangle across the page. "Your train has four cars," I remark. "My locomotive," he clarifies. "Locomotive", I repeat, so that he knows I've heard his correction. He bends over the crayons again. This time he draws four figures in blue, two big ones and two little ones, no ground under them, identical except for their sizes. "Your family?" I ask. He identifies each one: "My dad, his name is Mark, and my mum, Michelle, and my brother, he's Mark too, and this is me." "There are two Marks in your family," I say. He is quiet and stops playing. "Are you named for someone?" I ask. "Yes," he says, "my Grandfather is Thomas Tyge Guntheir. I have two of his names." He picks up his drawings as he leaves. He doesn't look at me or speak to me, but he has already shown me a sketch of his family and his ancestry.

I learn later in a family meeting that Tyge's mother and father have separated, and his father (and the two boys) live with his mother and father, Tyge's grandparents. Tyge is not allowed to see his mother, a crack addict, who lives in a motel room.

During the first three years of analysis, Tyge uses small animal figures to fight. His animals fight to the death, when one flies and falls. Session after session, this is what he does, showing me again and again that it is unbearable to lose a fight. Tyge plays out a phobia of losing. He lives this enactment almost daily as well. As he plays, he refers to his fighting as "locking on" to "a target". He picks fights at school, as if he is fighting for his life. At the end of the second year of Tyge's analysis, this fighting moves toward a crisis. I meet with Mark, the father, and learn that he has gone to visit Tyge's school. Three boys have "ganged up" against Tyge. All these boys are bigger, and the teacher is worried that real harm might come to Tyge. Mark wonders if he should enrol him in a karate class. I ask him about his fear for Tyge, and this remedy. "A boy's world is cruel," he says, "If you are weak, you get pounded." Mark, as it turns out, builds "defence communication systems" for the Air Force. He says, "All my work is behind the scenes, so to speak." He then tells me that Tyge's grandmother (with whom they are still living), keeps offering Tyge a "special treat" every time he comes in from school and has not fought. With a grim grin, Mark adds, "So far, Tyge has not earned a single treat."

What is being passed on from Father to son? Does it have anything to do with his Father's chosen work: to fight defensively? Mark's grin, though grim, also *revels in Tyge's fighting* despite the lure of "special treats". Is Tyge the fighter, while his father creates defences behind the scenes? What of Tyge's name? I look it up, wondering about his connection to his grandfather, the original Tyge. Tyge comes from the Greek name *Τυχων* (*Tychon*) meaning "hitting the mark". This takes my breath away. Tyge hits when he fights other children, and his play is primarily about hitting a living target: "Lock on". What is he locking on *to* from his father, named Mark? He does not hit his little brother, also named Mark (a child who is autistic), but Tyge is surely hitting, and his hitting may be over-determined.

* * *

After the meeting with his father, Tyge brings one of his own toys. His toy is a Spiderman figure with a detachable shield and sword. Tyge says: "He's on the blue team. And guess what? He has a button, he presses it and he disappears, does it again and he can reappear." "He can disappear and come back," I comment. "He's going to fight the bears and bats. The bats can snatch you away; the bears can claw you to death. But I have a whole blue team. You can't see them, but I can see them." "A team you can see and I can't see?" He nods and takes the shield off the little figure. It drops to the floor and blinks off and on. I laugh. He looks up and smiles. "I wore this on Halloween, because kids can get run over in the dark, but my Dad he gave me this shield, so I was safe." He runs around the little room and comes to sit at my feet, looking at the rug. He says softly: "I'm going to kill the leader, kill the mother." I repeat: "Kill the leader, kill the mother." He gets up and stands, attacking the air with his little figure, the swords flashing. "I'm killing the red leader. He is losing gravity and falling. I'm the winner, the blue wins!" He dances his little man in the air. He kneels and looks under the rocker. "The mother is in there," he says. I say: "You killed the leader, but not the mother. She's there." He gets up and takes the shield and swords off the Spiderman figure and puts them into his pocket. He goes to the door to leave, but turns back. "I don't want to kill the mother," he says, "She can stay in here?" "Yes, she can stay," I say, without understanding this request.

I am following the permutations in Tyge's play and speech. He has chosen a toy that has detachable parts—both shield and swords come off and can be put back on the figure. This may be Tyge's way of playing with the idea that the penis can be given up, taken off, and put back. In fact, the whole man can disappear and come back again! Moreover, his father gives him a shield that acts protectively in the dark. Tyge plays out a fantasy then: kill the leader and the mother. He can kill the leader, and in doing so makes a space to take his father's place, as we see so often in myths. But he can't kill the mother. I see that he uses no figure to represent her; she is simply "there". And what is there in its place unrepresented is the Real: something of his experience with his mother that is un-representable.

* * *

Tyge sits beside all the toys he has spread on the rug and makes a new sound, "ch, ch, ch, ch". He picks out the cheetah and kangaroo figures. "This cheetah is a motorcycle. This is me" (the kangaroo). He puts the kangaroo on a bird and flies it around the room. "Remember lock on?" he asks. "Target," I say, his word for this kind of fight. He smiles. He makes two lines of trees with small plastic trees. "These are traps, hidden tree traps," he says. I nod. "And here is the volcano jump," he says, picking up a small plastic volcano. He picks up the kangaroo, who "speaks" in a threatening tone, "I'm not here to get your autograph." He laughs. The kangaroo and cheetah fight, retreat, fight, retreat. He says of his kangaroo: "He's getting smaller and smaller." "Smaller," I repeat. Tyge says nothing. The motorcycle cheetah "races" around the room, and Tyge makes sounds: "RRRRRR!" and "EEEEEE!" He drops the toy from his highest reach. "He's falling," he says, and leaves the cheetah on its side. He picks up the kangaroo. "He's hurt. He can't fly." He reaches for a bag of building blocks, swiftly dumps out the blocks. The bag approaches the kangaroo, covers him, and Tyge pulls the drawstring on the bag. "The mouth, it's eaten him alive, and he will never, ever, get out." Tyge walks to the window. "I couldn't kill the mother, and see what happened?" He turns to me, and I simply nod, "I see, smaller and smaller, then eaten alive." "Bye Annie," he says as he goes out to his father in the waiting room.

It was here, as he tried to find acts and words for the unrepresented Real that Tyge entered our work most daringly. He is not remembering, but constructing what Freud called the primal scene. It is both a fantasy of parental coitus, and a fear that one parent will kill the other; it has another form, a corollary, that one or both parents can kill the child. Lacan understood this fantasy as the way the young child constructs the jouissance of the Other. Tyge's construction bundles together raw fragments: his inability to kill the mother, who is left "there"; his growing smaller and smaller (sm-all-er/all her), and finally, a scene of devouration, from which there is no return. These fragments, torn from the Real, do not signify a meaning so much as they embody a terrible jouissance. This fantasmatic construction of the primal scene is the vehicle, in Lacan's expression, of an "extimate *jouissance*"—one *in* the child but not *of* the child (Clemens & Grigg, 2006, p. 307). This jouissance has been transmitted from the family without entering the Symbolic and lives, unnamed in the child's unconscious and his body.

Tyge says, "See what happened?" What is he asking me to witness? What precisely was transmitted to him that he shaped in this particular way?

* * *

When Tyge returns he has red eyes and blinks a lot. His father explains he's picked up "pink-eye" at school. Tyge rubs his eye; his father tells him to stop; this will make it worse. Inside my office, Tyge plays with a little motorcycle. He runs it over the rug and flies it up in the air, moving freely in the office but making no sound. He drops the toy and says, "wipe out". He picks it up and turns to me. "When he wipes out, that's the game I was playing, when he wipes out, there's no sound." "Do you like it that there's no sound?" I ask. "No," he says. "What is the sound of the wipe out?" I ask. He kneels on the rug, straddles the motorcycle with his first two fingers, and moves it back and forth. His hand topples and he makes a sound like a moan, "ooooooh". He goes on: "My Granddad, he is getting some kind of award, um, at a ceremony, but he doesn't want it." "He doesn't want it?" I ask. "But my Dad and Grandma want him to go, so he'll do it." "What is the award for?" I ask. "What he did in the war," Tyge says, "He was a big hero." And he smiles, but his eyes do not smile. They weep, reddened.

I wonder what Tyge is trying to say and play that can find no place, but instead takes hold in the form of the Real of the body. Because the Real comes into the analysis, I consider it in the context of the analytic work, this particular juncture. The formal diagnosis is "conjunctivitis". It comes from Latin, *coninctva, connective* (membrane), feminine of *coninctvus, connective,* and from *coninctus,* past participle of *coniungere, to join together*. The Real of the body has erupted to say something about "join together". I think of his pink locomotive, its cars joined together. How were his mother and father joined—in what unspoken pact that produced a symptom in each of their two children? What is it that Tyge can't see? In what way is his symptom also his inheritance? I remember that his father once told me that Tyge wore an eye patch at age three, that one eye turned inwards, so that he was seeing two versions of the world at once.

* * *

I have delayed meeting Tyge's entire family, since it has been very difficult to arrange for his mother to be present. I insist on a family session, without quite knowing what I am searching for. I have found that in work with children, it is crucial to not to speculate about what I do not know, but to search for the unknowns. It occurs to me that what is unsayable, whatever it is that Tyge cannot see, say, play or imagine, may come from his parents, but may also cross generations in his family. His maternal grandparents are dead some ten years, lost in a car accident. Mark, and his parents, the Grandfather and Grandmother that Tyge lives with, all agree to come in and meet with me. They will bring his little brother, Mark. After some work on my part, his mother, Michelle, agrees to come to the meeting.

It occurs to me that I might be able to discover the silence in Tyge's family in a way that he can witness it. I will ask each member who speaks most often to leave the room, one by one, until I have the most silent member alone with the child. We meet one evening, when they have the waiting room to themselves. I explain that one by one I will ask them to leave the session, so that Tyge can hear each one of them say things that perhaps they have not been able to speak. While this amuses them, since they can't imagine anything they've not said, they agree to this arrangement.

I am not surprised that the grandmother, Maria, speaks most often. She tells little Mark what he can and can't do constantly, and gives Michelle withering glances. I ask her to leave first. She looks surprised as she goes. Tyge's father talks about the award his father has won, a war medal, and how proud he is. I ask him to leave. Without his father or grandmother, little Mark becomes very anxious and begins to speak rapidly in a high-pitched voice, as if he's literally a transmitter for the anxiety in the room. "High and dry?" he asks, over and over. I wonder if this is a commentary on the family, but Mark only flutters his hands when I ask. I usher him out to his father and grandmother.

Then, no one speaks. Tyge's mother plays with her scarf, looks across to Tyge, assures him that she loves him, and says she knows he loves her. Tyge glances at her, but turns his torso away. Michelle talks to me about her troubles of the past two years, how she is the outcast of this family, and of her own family, too. Michelle says, "I love Mark, but Mark is weak; he won't stand up to his mother. And they excluded me since the day we were married. I didn't have a chance." Tyge has turned, listening. I ask Michelle to leave, since the Grandfather has said not one word. I do not speak, but wait to see what will unfold.

Tyge takes the kangaroo, puts him on the toy motorcycle, and zooms him around the room. "Vrooom! He will get them, all of them down there," he says. "There is a fire, and bombs are falling, but he is going to win," Tyge declares. Suddenly, the Grandfather speaks: "It's not like that. In a war, no one wins." Tyge stops and turns. "But you are a hero," he says. The older man shakes his head. "Yes, you are," Tyge insists. "No. In a war, there is no hero. You kill, not to be killed. And those you kill are just boys, like yourself. I fought on the American side. My half-brother was German; he fought on that side. Can you imagine?" The old man stops, as if he can go no further. He gathers himself and looks at Tyge: "War is ugly, and it's cruel. You never forget it. I don't talk about it, but it is always there in my nightmares. No one who is sane wants an *award* for that." Tyge goes to him, stands beside him. The old man has bent his head, but he looks at his grandson, and smiles a small, sad smile, "Don't be fooled about it," he advises.

During this two-hour session, each person in the family spoke, and Tyge was present throughout. Each person is a subject, each one arriving in good faith. When the elder Tyge speaks he does so only when all his family has left the room, save his grandson. He knows, because I have told them all, the purpose of this time is for Tyge to hear from each of them. He speaks his truth against what the others believe. He has been to war and war is cruel; there are no heroes. His half-brother fought on the other side, he tells Tyge. Both their names mean "hit the mark". I wonder if the elder Tyge could *not* hit the mark. What if the mark, the target, was his brother in a field or city, unseen? Then, it might be better to crash, even at the risk of injury and death. The grandfather says nothing of this; it's only my conjecture. But he tells his grandson that it is terrible to kill "other boys" in order not to be killed, and his voice is saturated with his terrible experience. It transmits. Then he advises Tyge, "Don't be fooled about it."

* * *

When Tyge returns he sits back on his heels on the rug and looks at me (Tyge rarely makes eye contact). "We are going to visit my Mom so she can watch us open our Christmas gifts," he begins. "She lives in a new motel now. She wanted a bigger room, but somebody else moved in and she didn't get it." "She didn't get the room she wanted," I say. He nods and says, "There is not enough room, and we can't go live with her." "Not enough room for you, too?" I ask. Changing the topic, he says: "When you get a present, you don't want to know what it is. You want it to be a mystery." "A mystery. Something you don't know. And you have missed her," I say. "Yes," he says, "I have." He zooms the little motorcycle around the room. He puts the kangaroo on the seat. "He could fall off," Tyge says, "But he doesn't fall off. He's having fun."

I see that his eyes are clear. I see that he is free now to acknowledge that he misses his mother, and to accept that he's not able to live with her. There is no play of killing, for the first time.

Tyge's play and speech change after this session. The work of our fourth and last year builds a new space, new possibilities, new trajectories that reconfigure his legacy and his future. To end this chapter I offer three sessions.

* * *

Tyge brings a small action figure. He puts the man on the little motorcycle. "He's a joker," Tyge explains, "But he's no fool!' Tyge drives him around on the rug. "His name is William, like my friend, William Justin the Third." He pauses, "Doesn't that sound important?" "It does," I agree. Tyge moves the motorcycle faster. "The mafia might catch him. He's going to the city hospital. He's been wounded." "He has?" "He fell and he's hurt, but he's not going to die. He has to go through three tunnels. He has to go into the dark three times." Tyge adds: "He needs a shield to get through the dark. Remember Blinky?" I smile. "Yes, the shield from your Dad?" Tyge nods, "This shield, it is William's now. I gave it to him. It protects you; it sees what you can't see by yourself." "What a wonderful shield, what a gift," I say. "Yes," he agrees, "It really is!"

Here Tyge claims a new friend (in his real life) and speaks about his friend as he plays out this scene. The friend, William Justin the Third, is vulnerable; he's been wounded and the Mafia is after him. Tyge is engaged in myth-making, using fragments of his family legacy reconfigured after the family session. "Blinky", the shield connected to his father, is a true gift. Tyge is a child who has had problems with his eyes and wore an eye patch to correct his vision. He gives something precious that works as an eye to his friend. The shield is a way to see dangers "that lie ahead". It will accompany his friend, three times through the dark. Tyge also connects William and the advice of his grandfather: "He's a joker, but he's no fool."

* * *

Tyge turns the bag of rune stones (an old alphabet that works as an oracle) upside down and spills out the stones. He picks up a "T" and an

"M". "I can read these now," he declares. "What do they have to say to you?" I ask. "So many things! Like this M, if you turn it upside down it becomes W, for William, but first it was M, Mark." "Mark?" I ask. "Yeah, my Dad, but also 'lock on'—to a mark, a target." "What is the target?" Tyge zooms the motorcycle around and turns, "M, for moving, a moving target!" and he laughs. "And the T?" I query, expecting him to connect it to the target but he says, "T, is for Tyge the Second." "Tyge the Second," I repeat. He sits very still on the floor, lifts and drops the rune stones on the rug. "T is a T-Bird, too; he wears a big iron mask, he has a big beak, too, but when he takes it off, he is just a man."

Tyge plays with letters, a new reading of names, to discover what a man is, reconfiguring his father's name by turning it upside down for "William". Tyge also claims his own name now as "Tyge the Second", in line with his grandfather. As Tyge creates transformations in words he is making a new language. The birds that once flew to "lock on", to kill or wipe out, are reduced to a letter, "T". Tyge says a "T-Bird" wears an iron mask and has a big beak, very like the phallus, which can be removed. He can take it off, and then "he is just a man". Once Tyge removes the iron mask and the big beak, the phallus becomes symbolic; it points to a lack, from which desire arises (Lacan, 1956–1957). As a man, Tyge will not be impervious, able to do anything, to use force, or impose his will. He will be animated by a desire founded on lack. These are the themes Tyge develops further as he plays in this last year. In this session there is such a sense of discovery, wonder, a new confidence, and relief in "just a man".

* * *

Tyge is subdued at the start of the session today. He takes up the kangaroo and one of the two big trees and just looks at them. He builds a space on the rug with blocks, pillows, and four books, "cornerstones". He places the kangaroo inside, looking out of an opening. "I'm going to summer camp, sleep-away camp," he says, "And did you know, my Dad's getting married?" "Yes, I know that. He told me the last time I saw him." Tyge makes a circle around his enclosure with rune stones. "Someday I will go to Germany, like my granddad, but in a boat, not in a plane," he says. "Why a boat?" I ask. "Because you can see the sea that way! You can see across to where you are going." "You can't see from a plane?" I ask. "No. And Granddad was shot down from the sky." "So, every plane will be shot down?" I ask. "No, but *I* would rather go in a boat!"

He rolls over to his back, picks up the rune stones and lets them fall at his sides. "What is falling?" I ask. "Parts of the universe," is his surprising reply. I wait. "It falls from where the dead go after they die, from up there, parts of their crypts fall back to earth, so we remember them." He sits up and turns toward me. "I have been reading Harry Potter. Do you know Harry Potter?" I smile: "Not personally, but I know about him." "His mother left a scar on his forehead when she died. She was trying to save him, and that's what she gave him. She is gone and he misses her" (he slips into present tense). "He has a scar as a proof of her love." He pauses. "And I have one, too." "Yes," I agree, "What is yours?" "She left a little ring on my ankle. My brother has a rash on his ankle, but I just have this scar" (perhaps the symbolic form of a real mark his brother bears with the name "Mark"). Tyge rolls his sock down and I see nothing. "Only I can see it, Annie," he explains.

This is the first time that Tyge creates an enclosed space with the kangaroo looking out, the animal he was most identified with in all his hours of flying and fighting. He has created a threshold, and he leaves the kangaroo there, with all he has experienced. Then Tyge imagines himself going to Germany, perhaps to put to rest what his grandfather feared. But Tyge tells me he will go in a boat, not a plane, as himself, not as his grandfather. Again, he claims this lineage, but with his own twist, his own desire, which is to "see the sea", "see across to where you are going", which connects back to the shield his father gave him and with his eye problems, his double vision at three years old that was corrected by a patch, and the pink-eye, which developed during the analysis.

Tyge links going to summer camp, "sleep-away camp", and his father's new marriage in the same sentence. I wonder if his father's marriage (which puts his father in a new relation with Tyge's grandmother and mother), frees Tyge to "sleep away" in a new space. For all his play about killing and death, in this session Tyge symbolises death rather than enacting a scene of death. He uses the rune stones to name something that unfolds in this space: "parts of the universe" falling, pieces of "crypts" of the dead falling, so that "we remember". Death is connected here with the universe, the cosmos, what we don't know, and also it is real, and therefore must be remembered. Tyge speaks about Harry Potter and the idea of a scar from his mother. His mother "saves him" at the point when Harry could be killed. Tyge puts his own spin on the scar, remarking that his little brother has a rash on his ankle, something visible (in fact, his brother does have a rash, I learn later). But Tyge's scar is invisible, and only he can see it. The proof of his mother's love is now symbolic, it's invisible, and it also is connected to seeing, that is to Tyge's capacity to see.

Conclusion

I have presented a child case and its trajectory from fighting (which functioned as a phobia against losing) to the eruption of the Real of the body in conjunctivitis (pink eye) at a point when Tyge could go no further in his speech and play. As I look back, the turning point in his analysis came just after the articulation in play of Tyge's worst fear, the fantasy of devouration. He came back with conjunctivitis. The Real comes in to disrupt what has been "joined together" in a family lie. The family intervention functioned to uncover a lie about heroism, and the horror that one might kill one's own brother, and this opened a new space in Tyge's play. Tyge transformed the detritus of words that came to him across generations, making his own myths, his own metaphors. His play articulated a new future, both hopeful and creative, with names coming made of the Real. He was free to create new paths and possibilities in his life.

In the position of an analyst, one does what is *possible,* just that, guided by an *impossible* to name object, the Real at work that runs the show at every crucial juncture, and puts the child to work with the "Father of the Name", a saying that joins language to the Real. This is something mysterious this process from the position of the analyst, and especially so with a child, where we must act quickly and without knowing the consequences. The Real cannot be known, named, imagined, but it guides the act of the analyst. We come to know something of the Real in its effects. The effect of an intervention is clear in retrospect, but wide open and unknown in practice. As an analyst one moves from unknown to unknown, with little theory and many questions, across hundreds of sessions, working in the dark. It is the child who makes a hole in the Real that spits out the Names of the Father, that which has never been named, finding a space to reconfigure his legacy.

References

Clemens, J., & Grigg, R. (2006). *Jacques Lacan and the Other Side of Psychoanalysis: Reflections on Seminar XVII*. Durham: Duke University Press.

Lacan, J. (1956–1957). *Le Séminaire Livre IV: La Relation d'Objet*. 1956–1957. L. V. A. Roche (Trans.). Unpublished.

Lacan, J. (1969). Note on the Child. N. Wulfing (Trans.). In: Object *a* & the Semblant. *Psychoanalytical Notebooks 20*, 2010.

Lacan, J. (1975–1976). *Joyce and the Sinthome, The Seminar of Jacques Lacan, Book XXIII*. C. Gallagher (Trans.). Unpublished.

Lacan, J. (1989). Geneva Lecture on the Symptom. *Analysis, 1*: 7–26.

Rogers, A. (2006). *The Unsayable*. New York: Random House.

Soler, C. (2014). *Lacan—The Unconscious Reinvented*. London: Karnac Books.

Note

1. All the names and identifying details have been changed to project the child's and the family's confidentiality in this paper. The fictive names I have chosen mirror the original inter-generational pattern in the family.

PART V

NEW KIDS: (POST-) MODERN SUBJECTS OF TECHNOLOGIES, GLOBAL CAPITALISM, NEO-LIBERALISM, AND BIO-MEDICINE

CHAPTER FIFTEEN

Psychoanalysis and neonatology

Catherine Vanier

How do we think about the place of psychoanalysis in a high-tech medical service?

In this chapter I will draw on my work with the neo-natal resuscitation unit at the Hôpital Delafontaine in Saint-Denis, Paris, in order to think about and address this question (see also, Vanier, 2015).

The analyst and the hospital setting

Initially I was asked by the resuscitating team to deal with parents who were causing problems for them and preventing them from doing their work. At first I agreed to listen to the parents, but very soon afterwards I also proposed another way of working to the team. Because of the difficulties they faced, they accepted. I suggested that they form working groups, in which they could speak about themselves, about their practice, and the effects it had on them. Gradually they started asking questions about the impact each birth might have on the baby and his family, but also about what the encounter meant for the caretakers. These meetings, which we then decided to extend to the entire unit, led us to think beyond the categories of developmental care and the already established protocols regarding the baby's wellbeing or the mother–child bond.

Together with the doctors, we decided that parents would no longer be seen only "on medical demand" since giving birth to a premature baby is a potential trauma for any parent. Based on his or her history, each parent will react differently. Some deal with the trauma more easily, others less so, but in all cases the event will be an extremely painful one. Currently, we therefore routinely offer an appointment to all parents, as soon as the baby enters the unit and with two consultants, who will remain their key reference throughout the period of hospitalisation: a medical doctor and an analyst, who is introduced to the parents as the psychoanalyst responsible for the baby's psychological care during the hospitalisation. While the baby remains in the unit, the parents can then ask for more sessions, if they wish to do so. The reason why I meet with the parents is not because the team are worried about them, but in order to speak with them about their baby and his development.

The analytic intervention

From the first session, the analyst offers a different type of listening. The parents are not subject to medical or even medico-psychological questioning. It is because the analyst does not respond to their demand with scientific knowledge or even with a psychologising discourse about the baby's psycho-affective development that they can speak to her. Also, it is because she does not explain to them the "correct attitude" or the best kind of behaviour to adopt with the baby, or even the reasons for their distress, that speaking becomes possible and we can trace some of the family drama brought to the fore by the birth, unveiling the web of fantasy, in which the prematurity is inscribed. The distance between the position of the analyst, who has everything to learn from the parents, and that of the resuscitating doctor, allows the former to hear the articulation between the parental projections on their child's body, this "real" fragment of their own bodies, and the baby treated by the doctors.

In these moments of great anxiety, the family's entire fantasmatic structure is mobilised because life and death are at stake. The difference between the "resuscitator"—the one who resuscitates—and the psychoanalyst is of the same order as the difference between knowledge and truth. The doctor's medical knowledge, which applies to all children, is not the same as the truth of a history, which is different for each patient. This distance is what makes the whole difference in the analyst's position. Based on the effects of the transference, the fantasy and family history can be worked through, by deciphering a particular discourse and its effects. The process of deciphering is of interest to doctors as well, so that they, too, may work in a different way. It is important that they recognise that patients have their own view of the illness, different from the doctor's scientific view. For the doctor, a premature birth does not mean the same thing as for the parents of a 500-gram baby. For the parents, the child reveals the entire family drama concentrated around the event of "prematurity". The parents are often at a loss, trying to make sense of the premature birth, trying to find the cause behind this irruption of the Real into their lives.

The analyst looks for neither the effect nor the cause; instead, she tries to see the points of articulation between the malady of premature birth and the parental history, so that the birth can be experienced a little differently and the parents can bond with the baby. In order to identify the signifiers that have an effect on the baby's body, we must be able to listen to the violence and the effects of the death drive. The transference to the team's analyst and their unique way of listening makes it possible for other things to be said, things that would never be told to a resuscitating doctor. It is not a question of taking the parents into analysis, but simply of defusing the fantasmatic traps they are caught in and which prevent them from giving the baby a place in their lives.

Supposing a subject

The problems encountered by the resuscitating teams can sometimes complicate their relationship with the parents, especially with the mother. These days, everything happens as if the precious link between the mother and the baby could never be put in question, as if the pious image of motherhood concealed the last bastion of repression in our society. Today, more than ever before we would like to think that a mother has "only love" for her child. But of course this is not always the case and the questions mothers ask them, as well as their ambivalence, sometimes resonate with the doctors' own difficulties. Doctors expect mothers to show an unambiguous gratitude to them for having saved their child's life. But, a baby trapped between life and death reveals the violence at the heart of motherhood itself. When reality and fantasy come together, traumatic effects cannot be avoided. Seeing her child suffer further accentuates a mother's guilt. But most importantly, what is suspended is the possibility of libidinal investment in/with the child. How could this tiny baby, such a painful sight, possibly create a mother? The premature baby does not resemble "*His Majesty the Baby*"—the term Freud used referring to the new-born infant (1914c, p. 90). The current statistics on very premature babies without neurological sequelae show a high incidence of psychosis, autism, and hyperactivity. In order to comprehend the psychological complications of these resuscitations, which are often long and difficult, we began to theorise the constitution of the baby's psyche.

In thinking about these babies, I have relied on the hypothesis proposed by Alain Vanier in 1989, of "supposing a subject" (Vanier, 2002, p. 12). As we know from Winnicott, "there is no such thing as a baby" (Winnicott, 1952, p. 99). In order for the little human being to become a subject, we must first, as Alain Vanier argues, suppose that there is a subject in the baby. The caring gestures and words that accompany this supposition of the subject will give the baby a sense of existence. At birth, the baby only exists in and through the mother, or another person who speaks to him, names him, tells him who he is (a boy or a girl), what he is feeling and thinking. The subject is in the Other. If at the time of birth, the mother does not speak to the baby, he cannot make himself her object. If the baby does not encounter the mother's desire and has no idea what could possibly satisfy her, he will never offer himself to her as an object because the mother does not show any lack. The baby will have nothing to give to her; he will not immediately assume the position of the imaginary phallus, which would precisely open up the possibility of separation. However, when babies are born prematurely and hospitalised immediately after the delivery, separation cancels itself out. It cannot be symbolised. And yet it is this cut that would otherwise enable a place to be created in the Other, a place that would call the subject into being.

For a baby attached to a machine, everything happens as if the separation of birth has not taken place. In a resuscitation unit, the machine responds to the child's vital needs in an omnipotent manner. It becomes a part of his body. All babies identify with the world around them. For the premature baby, the extremely present world of machines is a kind of pure Real, of which he cannot make any sense. There is a great risk that during the period of resuscitation the baby has no choice but to identify with the machine as an absolute Other, unless another person takes over and puts herself between the baby and the machine.

Once babies are hooked up to machines, it is difficult for them not to stay alive, yet they do manage to "do some silly things", as the doctors say. They may become desaturated; there may be bradycardia. But it is difficult to escape the machine's vigilance and it will restart again immediately. In our service it is rare for babies to die against medical advice. A machine is never not there. And if the drive is activated as an echo of speech in the body, how can its circuit be set in motion? In this environment, the body's structuring by the drive is indeed problematic.

What happens to the child's body of jouissance inside an incubator? The baby is attached to and completely dependent on the machine for his survival. The body's orifices are diverted from their function. The umbilicus remains perforated by the catheter. The nose is used for feeding rather than breathing. The mouth is intubated, so that it can no longer be used for feeding and the baby cannot make sounds. The body is perforated and ventilated. The baby can often be subject to a tracheotomy. Oral satisfaction is disrupted. The babies never feel hungry because they are continually fed. The bodily envelope no longer guarantees the separation between inside and outside. Liquids and gases are collected, measured, analysed. The babies' entire bodies are made transparent by radiograms and echograms, and their only integrity is through the inscriptions of graphs and luminous numbers on a machine that collects together everything that is known about them. During resuscitation, it is the machine that administers the correct dosage of oxygen and feeds the babies without interruption, continuously, without making them wait, without fail. During resuscitation, babies are never hungry and do not encounter any lack; their crying is not transformed into a call by the Other, who could bring help from the outside.

We have often observed that if the baby was not spoken to during the first days of his life, he will withdraw and cease looking for contact and communication; he will become absent. However, the function of the voice, mixed with the sounds of the machine, can change this situation, unless the person speaking to the baby is actually identified with the machine. It is indeed not easy to work with mothers in a resuscitation unit and in the beginning their presence can often be difficult. The baby needs the Other immediately and this Other is often constituted by the caretakers in the unit. The register of the drive cannot be activated without the Other's demand. Yet with the declining gestation age, smaller and smaller babies are resuscitated; resuscitations becoming increasingly more difficult and the risks greater. Just like the parents, the caregivers are therefore also at risk of failure: they are frightened to emotionally invest in a baby because of the possibility of having to make a decision to withdraw all but palliative care a few months later. These days, we are often faced with resuscitating while maintaining some distance to assess the situation as it develops over the course of the following weeks, or resuscitating and not resuscitating at the same time: resuscitating while protecting ourselves from having too much hope. If the team withdraws, expecting the situation to be uncertain, and if the mothers' role is undermined, albeit for different reasons, the babies are left in a void, as evidenced by the difficulties they often face a few years down the line. If the Other's words are not there, the baby cannot inscribe himself in the signifying chain, that is, as Lacan explains, in the symbolic world specific to human beings.

The passage through the Other's signifier means encountering the loss—a real loss and a symbolic lack (Vanier, 1995). Unless he is confronted with the Other, the trauma of the premature baby, left alone with the machine, could indeed be the trauma of the impossibility of being traumatised by the encounter. The encounter with the Other's desire, in other words with the lack in the Other, is a trauma indispensable to the subject's constitution.

From the perspective of the doctors, the resuscitation must go on, it must be attempted again and again; more heart massage, increasing the oxygen, changing the dosage of the treatment. Around them, the team is waiting, fascinated by the jouissance of the spectacle of resuscitation. This also represents a jouissance for the physician, who too is fascinated by the power he now has over the child's body, fascinated by an illusion that is nevertheless very often dispelled by the babies who are "lost" or "slip away". But during these nights, these crucial moments of resuscitation, nothing counts for more than the extreme tension of the moment. How could the doctor not be terrified by this jouissance? During these hours of resuscitation, time ceases to exist and only resumes its course once the readouts on the machine have stabilised and the child is breathing again. The fear of not achieving this, of committing an error, of making the wrong move or evaluation, of not having been vigilant enough and thus being responsible for the baby's death is constantly present. But the fear of failure is no doubt combined with a fear of succeeding because when the baby has finally stabilised and the doctors take off their masks, some questions remain paradoxically unanswered: "Does our society, at the same time as it maximises its prevention measures, therapeutic abortions, and all kinds of screenings, itself produce impaired children through the intervention of neonatologists?" At the same time, how do we refuse to resuscitate a baby when we know how to do it and at last might be able to give the mother a child that could satisfy her? We can hear an echo of this in what most resuscitators tell us and it is not without an effect on, nor unrelated to, the fantasy of each individual doctor. However, what they speak about especially is the possibility—bestowed on them so as to avoid the risk of therapeutic overzealousness, or "unreasonable obstinacy"—of transgressing the murder prohibition by simply pushing a button and stopping the machine that keeps the baby alive. The more this transgression becomes possible, the harder doctors fight to resuscitate, surrounded by their teams, who support them and help them in ways that go far beyond mere medical intervention.

Reanimation vs. *resuscitation*

The complexity of the current issues, which have to do with scientific progress, has led me to believe that if analysts were willing to listen, doctors would call upon them much more often. But many analysts would rather not enter the dangerous territory of medical services. It is often true that in the beginning, their presence is not easily accepted by the teams. But unless the analysts try to lecture them or impose their "psychoanalytical dogma" (which is ultimately always just another resistance to psychoanalysis), all doctors are really asking for is to be able to speak about their practice and the difficulties with which they are dealing. It is not a question of imposing a different knowledge on them or trying to treat the patient instead of them, but simply to allow for speech to circulate differently in the service. The transference established with the analyst running the groups allows the doctors to understand their own experience. In our unit, the doctors have now accepted the risks inherent in the encounter with the baby, as well as with the parents. These types of meetings and working groups have given us much to think about (beyond developmental care, beyond the protocols already in place, which have to do with the baby's well-being and the mother–child relationship) and have helped identify the impact that each individual member of the resuscitation team can have on the development of the babies in our care. In this configuration, the psychoanalyst is no longer an expert called upon to resolve a specific problem, but becomes part of a common project, of a particular orientation, supporting the desire to work differently.

In our unit, we have gradually implemented a different understanding of resuscitation. What we have added is the idea that the "breath of life"—the etymological root of *réanimation* [French for "resuscitation"]—perhaps refers not only to the oxygen provided by the machines, but also to the breath of air of the demand that brings the baby back to life. It seems to me that we have now accepted that the process of resuscitation cannot be reduced to the work of machines. The baby cannot live without oxygen, but neither can he do without the presence and voice of the caretakers, which today covers over the sounds of the machine. This new orientation of the unit has led the doctors and the entire team to change their position and engage with the babies in a different way. The care provided by the resuscitation unit requires a real personal involvement of the team who have to work with struggling mothers and babies who cannot be further traumatised. This involvement goes beyond a mere concern for restoring the mother–child bond, for ensuring the baby's wellbeing and providing developmental care. Implementing protocols is not enough. These protocols, much beloved by medicine, ultimately often enable the caretakers to shy away from the risks inherent in an authentic encounter. Such a way of working prevents doctors from truly seeking contact with infants and their mothers. Putting the "supposition of the subject" at the centre of the entire team's work and making it possible to speak about anxiety, including the anxiety of the team, is necessarily subversive. But if it becomes possible, we see a kind of chain reaction, which has analytical effects on the mothers, their babies and obviously also their doctors.

References

Freud, S. (1914c). On Narcissism: An Introduction. *S.E., 14*: 67–102. London: Hogarth.

Vanier, A. (1995). Contribution à la métapsychologie du temps des processus psychiques. Questions posées par l'observation et la clinique infanto-juvénile. Doctoral thesis (Dir. P. Fédida), Université Paris Diderot—Paris 7. Unpublished.

Vanier, A. (2002). D'une dyade à plusieurs. Quelques remarques à propos d'un travail avec les mères psychotiques et leur nourrisson. *Psychologie clinique, 12*: 39–50.

Vanier, A., & Pelletier, N. (1989). *Évaluation, soutien, orientation pour les enfants de mères marginales à la période périnatale.* In collaboration with Dr N. Pelletier, paper given at the fourth World Congress of the World Association for Infant Psychiatry and Allied Disciplines WAIPAD in Lugano, 20th–24th September 1989.

Vanier, C. (2015). *Premature Birth, the Baby, the Doctor, and the Psychoanalyst.* London: Karnac.

Winnicott, D. W. (1952). Anxiety Associated with Insecurity. In: *Collected Papers: Through Paediatrics to Psychoanalysis* (1958). London: Tavistock.

CHAPTER SIXTEEN

The "iMirror stage": not-so-smartphones and the pre-schooler—some clinical observations

Joanna Fortune

In this chapter I want to examine the idea that the prevalence of new technologies is not only changing the form of the family but is interfering with how the psyche becomes structured. I will argue that the smartphone has become a substitute for the desire of the Other and the child cannot integrate the desire of the Other through the lens of the smartphone. It will be my assertion that the lens of the smartphone does not operate in the same way as Lacan had conceptualised the function of the "Mirror" and that therefore, the Mirror stage is interrupted with effects for the formation of the ego and the structuring of the psyche (Lacan, 1949).

A Californian mother decided to monitor the amount of times her young infants sought out her gaze during their playtime. Instead of passing the time on her smartphone/smart device while her children played, she sat and watched them at play. Of this experience, she wrote: "As I sat quietly in the corner of the room I tallied how many times they looked at me for various reasons: to see if I saw their cool tricks, to seek approval or disapproval for what they were doing, and to watch my reactions." She goes on to wonder what kind of message she would have been sending her children had she missed all of their attempts to seek out her gaze during their playtime, and how might they have interpreted her inattentiveness. During her experiment on this particular afternoon she counted twenty-eight separate instances at which her two-year-old children looked up at her during their play to seek out her gaze.

A 2013 study conducted by mobile technology company, Nokia, found that, on average, mobile phone users check their phones every six minutes or up to 150 times in a day. At the Paediatric Academic Societies (PAS) annual meeting in San Diego (April 2015), researchers cited that more than one third of babies start using smartphones and tablets before they learn how to walk or talk. Furthermore, they cited that more than fifty per cent of those children in their study who were under the age of one year had watched a full TV show, thirty-six per cent had touched or scrolled a screen and twenty-five per cent had made a phone call themselves. This is all before the age of one year and before they had acquired the ability to walk or talk.

In the last decade I have seen a sharp rise in very young children (under five years old) presented by their parents for treatment. These children are described by their parents as displaying overt symptoms ranging from anxious withdrawal to aggressive acting out. This decade has also been a time during which the presence and dominance of the smartphone has steadily increased. Because of these occurrences, I want to examine the idea that life lived from the beginning with the presence of the smartphone lens has a significant impact on the developing child subject.

Not-so-smartphones and the Mirror stage

It is my assertion that life as mediated through a lens short-circuits the structure of infantile jealousy, as detailed in Lacan's writings on the family complexes (Lacan, 1938). Because of this, we are witnessing an increase in pre-school aged children acting out aggressively on their peers, unable to contain the jealousy that suddenly overwhelms them.

According to Lacan, the structure of infantile jealousy plays a key role in the child subject's sociability and capacity to know themselves as human. Lacan's Mirror stage theory regards the ego as a form of misrecognition in that the subject must identify with an image that is actually other (Lacan, 1949, p. 76). Therefore, the ego is always and already alienated and at dialectical odds with the subject. Further, the structuration of the psyche is intruded upon here by connecting the split/alienated subject to their social reality. If the subject is linked with the substituting lens of the smartphone rather than the desire of the other, then their ego cannot be mediated by the desire of the other and this causes a block to the emergence of the necessary rivalrous, jealous, competitive social bond that ought to precipitate the subject's intrusion complex (Lacan, 1938, p. 24).

The ego is constituted via the Mirror stage functions of identification and alienation, which map out a trajectory of "an alienating identity that will mark his entire mental development with its rigid structure" (Lacan, 1949, p. 78). The substitution of the smartphone lens for the gaze and desire of the other significantly impacts upon this process leading to the child subject becoming entrapped in a kind of "hall of Mirrors" whereby the substituting lens of the smartphone amplifies and proliferates what are the already alienating aspects of the Mirror stage.

In stressing the narcissistic structure of the ego, Lacan emphasises the fact that this sort of position is unliveable and brings death in its wake and is based on an illusory image (Lacan, 1949, p. 76). The narcissistic world has no place for others. Lacan will later name this image the "specular image" and it holds an effective value for the child who views it as important and will later become more delighted to discover that this image is in fact an image of themselves (Lacan, 1949, p. 79). This specular image is both real, in so far as it reflects the child's human form, but is also imaginary since the child is not actually *in* the Mirror.

Narcissism and the trouble with selfies

Because the structuration of the psyche has been earlier interfered with by technology, we see this narcissistic structure of ego overtly played out and symptomatic in adolescence through the "selfie culture" that permeates the adolescent's identity and identifications. This selfie culture, as it relates to a re-defining of what is masculine and what is feminine, is being studied by Mary McGill, who is conducting her research on young women, narcissism and the selfie phenomenon. She has spoken recently about her emerging findings at a TEDx Talk delivered in Galway, Ireland.

She explores her hypothesis through a gendered prism and specifically around how femaleness and femininity are understood today. She poses the question "why is femininity so aligned with narcissism?" and uses an exploration of the selfie phenomenon and particularly the social commentary that surrounds this phenomenon to answer this question. She cites Simone de Beauvoir's *The Second Sex*, and especially de Beauvoir's assertion in this text that one is not born but becomes a woman. McGill takes this to mean that women, in this instance young women and their engagement with the selfie phenomenon, are socialised to act in what is perceived as a sexualised manner, rather than this behaviour occurring innately because of their gender.

De Beauvoir's assertions about becoming a woman may be read with the Lacanian notion of becoming a subject; one is not born so, but becomes a subject through the mechanisms of identification, alienation, and separation. One is not born separate but becomes separate and that it is through the Mirror stage that the young child achieves an identification with the specular image and assumes an alienating identity, i.e., that they are an other. Thus the child subject realises that they are a person who exists and the other is a separate person to them who also exists and there is a world outside of them. This realisation also serves as an organising principle of human development in general as opposed to just a passing phase of early childhood development, because if the subject has identified with an image outside of himself or herself, this also means that they have understood that they can *do* things that they could not do before. This enables the subject to enter a phase of growing independence that will continue to grow and develop throughout their lives and be influenced by all others they come into contact with along that journey.

At this point, the ego takes on the structure of both object and subject in so far as the infant realises that they are something to be looked at (object) and to look outward from (subject) upon others/things. They have achieved an identification with the image of the other/counterpart and through this identification the subject moves towards alienation, which brings the subject to accept that they are an other (Lacan, 1949, p. 80). It is also why we look at the Mirror stage in the complex of intrusion because it, quite literally, marks the primary intrusion in the formation of the self because the ego is being constructed precisely while the child's conception of their being the other is developing. Interestingly, this is also where we see jealousy play a role because if the child has accepted that they are an other, and that their mother is an other, then it stands to reason that there may well be other others who could potentially be rivals for them. This is evident when the child makes the choice of accepting the existence of others. However, if the child was to refuse the Real and thereby the existence of others, i.e., not register the other at all, then their conception of reality would be seriously impaired. This would lead to a life of isolation, poor socialisation, and diminished capacity for emotional regulation, anxiety, and aggression to the self and/or Other. A number of pre-school aged children I see have been referred via their Montessori schools who may have taken the decision to exclude/expel these toddlers from school due to aggressive behaviour towards other children, their same/similar aged peers. The young child who has not adequately registered the other, becomes overwhelmed by raw, unintegrated rivalrous feelings when surrounded by other similar aged children competing for the gaze of the other as is the case in group care settings such as Montessori.

Now if we take the selfie phenomenon that McGill speaks of and that permeates so much of today's socio-cultural identity and read Lacan's Mirror stage theory alongside it, we may see that the child whose desire has not been met with the desire of the other, whose gaze has not been met with the gaze of the other but who has, moreover, been met with the substituting lens of the smartphone, we see that the child subject has not assumed an image that is always other (as is the case of the ego in its function as misrecognition) but has assumed an image of themselves. The child subject then becomes fixated on their own image/reflection (as was the case for Narcissus in the myth) and is consumed with their own image overtly enacted in today's society with obsessive posting of one's own image on social media via the selfie.

Why jealousy is good for you

As a result of the substitution of the lens of the smartphone for the gaze of the other the Mirror stage has been impeded upon. This inability to know themselves as other denies the child subject access to the function and structure of infantile jealousy detailed in the complex of intrusion. This impacts greatly upon the child subject's sociability and capacity to know themselves as human. I have come to believe further that this is why we see a rise in anxiety and hysteria based pathologies in the child and adolescent subject and that self-harm and cutting incidents have increased as the subject struggles to know himself or herself as human and real. To cut, to hurt, and to bleed is to know that you exist.

In the intrusion complex, Lacan asserts that jealousy is the basis for all other social sentiments and, as such, is the original model for all social feelings (Lacan, 1938, p. 24). Freud saw the intrusion complex as being underpinned by sibling rivalry, occurring when the child realises that he is to share maternal affection with another (Lacan, 1938, p. 13). Lacan stipulated that there must be proximity of age for infant rivalry. There can be no jealous rivalry without identification.

Jealousy, being quite different from envy, is in fact an identification because in order to feel jealous the child subject must accept, at the level of the unconscious at least, that there is an other who is just like them. Lacan saw this identification being dependent upon a sense of the other that is imaginary, i.e., he theorised that there was an imago, an unconscious representation so to speak, which is linked to the idea that one has of one's own body. For Lacan, the Imaginary is the level where a child can formulate ideas about things (Lacan, 1938, p. 21).

The aggression of rivalry is sadomasochistic in its libidinal qualities and it presents as both active and passive. So the young child identifies with both the aggressor and victim role thereby reproducing the suffering of weaning and attempting to gain mastery over the desire for death that is the result of the weaning process (Lacan, 1938, p. 28).

So the question arises, how can therapeutic interventions help the child subject resolve their intrusion complex?

A child's psychical "development" may be interrupted if they become locked into a closed identification with the other. Therapy drawing upon the concepts and theories of Lacanian psychoanalysis in the clinic of the child can facilitate the child subject to learn how to use their symptoms because in our work the point is not to eliminate the symptom but rather to develop it for utilisation.

Given the Mirror stage has its roots in early infant development, before the acquisition of language, one way to work towards a consolidation of the Mirror stage in the child clinic is in a "doing" rather than solely a "speaking", which will allow the child subject to work through their intrusion complex symptoms. In the clinic of the child, play is how the child communicates and acquires their desire.

In my child clinic, I use both "games" and playing. Here I am interpreting a "game" as being the organised part of playing that can make what is sometimes experienced as terrifying tolerable for the child, especially the anxious child. If the child can use the "rules of the game", which is not "playing", they are on their way to acquiring metaphorisation and thereby fantasy. This is why "games" as well as "playing" can be so useful in the clinic of the child.

I take typical childhood games and attempt to modify them in keeping with Lacanian informed concepts so that the child subject may draw therapeutic benefit from them in the clinic. It is worth stating here that I would not play these games with all children regardless of their structure because with psychotic or autistic children, the rules of each game may be experienced in such a way as to trigger serious episodes for them.

One game that I employ in working with the child subject is that of *Mirroring*. I invite the child to sit opposite me and serve as my Mirror and direct that they must follow my cue and do everything they see me do. I then perform various gestures, expressions and physical movements from either a seated or standing position and the child, synchronously, Mirrors me in doing the same actions. Then we switch and I follow their cues reflecting their every move back to them as they do it.

Another game I engage the child subject in involves us sitting in parallel position, usually on the floor, in front of glass/Mirrored panels I have attached to the clinic wall. These are arranged in such a way that the child, regardless of age/size (from infancy to adolescence) can take in their entire being in the reflected image. We sit in parallel and gaze upon ourselves in the Mirror. I model movement and reflect (verbally) how my Mirror image is making the same movement, how this Mirror image is both me and yet not me. I invite the child to make their Mirror image also move and reflect (verbally) the same of them.

Yet another is a game called "eye signals". In silence, I keep my head straight and allow my eyes to move to the left (child must then jump to that side), to the right (child must jump to that side), upwards (child must jump forward) or downwards (child must jump backwards). The point here is that the child must fix their gaze on mine to follow the direction in an otherwise non-verbal game. This is a game that I find very helpful with these children in facilitating their gaze to be met with the gaze of an other.

In the Mirror stage, Lacan proposes that human infants pass through a stage in which an external image of the body (reflected in a Mirror, or represented to the infant through the mother or primary caregiver) produces a psychic response within the infant that gives rise to the mental representation of an "I" (Lacan, 1949, p. 78). Where this hasn't happened, due to the interfering of the lens of the smartphone for the gaze, I find the use of therapeutic games such as these very helpful in supporting the child subject to work through their unresolved intrusion complex symptoms. Further, I have found such therapeutic games to serve as a means of re-experiencing the Mirror stage in a way that allows the child subject to conceptualise their ego, and by doing so, decrease the prevalence of the overt symptom that prompted their referral to the clinic.

In this chapter I have been reflecting on the impact the smartphone has on the constitution of the ego in the child subject in replacing the gaze of the Other, but in addition to this, I would argue that the Smartphone and similar technological gadgets (including tablets) have also greatly impacted upon what were once normal play patterns and experiences for the child subject. As a result of early exposure to smartphones and such devices, children play differently nowadays. Often their play involves smart technology with much use of a variety of screens and lenses. There is a cost for society in this change.

In the clinic of the child, how we work, the techniques we employ, how the theory underpins our practice, involves helping the child subject to separate from the unconscious history of the family. The work is dedicated to giving the child subject the responsibility of his or her own existence. We must illuminate the unconscious history of the child subject but not confirm it. It is our role to facilitate the child subject in separating from it. This is all vital in working towards a resolution of the child subject's symptom in cases where the Mirror stage has been impeded.

Conclusion

In conclusion, it has been my hypothesis here that modern technology, most specifically the use of smart devices in parenting young children, both in its impact on the changing structure of the family as we understand it and on ego formation, interferes with how the psyche becomes structured in the child subject. The impact of the interference of the smartphone in subjugating the gaze of the other is clinically significant for the child subject and is an area in which Lacanian psychoanalysis will make an important contribution in the clinic of the child.

A key consideration in working in the clinic of the child is that children very rarely present themselves for treatment. They are brought and/or presented by a parent as being, or having, a problem that requires resolution. Lacan, in his paper "Note on the Child" (Lacan, 1969), found that what is presented in the clinic by the parent as being a symptom of the child is indicative of what is actually symptomatic in the family structure. "Family" as a concept is changing as our society evolves and while this fact has and will have an impact on the transmission of ideals and values to the child subject, one point remains unchanged: the "family" always has the responsibility of transmitting desire and represents the desire the child is born from. Ideals are not the problem for Lacanian psychoanalysis—they are the responsibility of society. In the child clinic of Lacanian psychoanalysis, our function is to enable the transmission of desire.

I developed this hypothesis having reflected on the high numbers of very young children who are presented at my clinic with overt symptoms associated with anxiety and/or aggression. What I have found amongst many of these cases are patterns of high smart device usage and minimal evidence of a completed Mirror stage. The constitution of the ego in many of these young children is very weak and of course we know that there has to be an ego in order for life to be managed. We know from Lacan's writings on the family complexes (Lacan, 1938) that the constitution of the ego is based on an alienating identification with the image of the other, which is initially experienced by the subject as joyous and celebratory but will later become rivalrous, envious, and aggressive, and is dependent upon the intervention of the paternal metaphor in order to introduce symbolic castration leading to an identification with the ego ideal. It is my assertion that something within all of this is interrupted and impacted upon because of the use and dominance of smart devices in the modern parent-child relationship. My use of games, such as those detailed above, facilitate the work with the child subject in strengthening the ego so that they might recover the process of alienating identification.

References

Californian Mother's Social Experiment as Detailed in Huffington Post. Available at: http://www.huffingtonpost.com/entry/moms-viral-experiment-urges-parents-to-rethink-screen-time_us_563b7247e4b0307f2cac4020.

Lacan, J. (1938). *Family Complexes in the Formation of the Individual.* C. Gallagher (Trans.). Unpublished.

Lacan, J. (1949). The Mirror Stage as Formative of the *I* Function as Revealed in Psychoanalytic Experience. In: *Écrits: The First Complete Edition in English* (pp. 75–81). B. Fink (Trans.). London & New York: Norton & Co, 2006.

Lacan, J. (1969). Note on the Child. R. Grigg (Trans.). *Analysis, 1990, 2*: 7–8.

McGill, M. (2016). *Young Women, Narcissism and the Selfie Phenomenon.* TEDx Talk Galway February 18th 2016. Available at: https://www.youtube.com/watch?v=Fb2J5eDoFko.

CHAPTER SEVENTEEN

Making a difference: on the non-rapport of psychoanalysis and the discourse of "trans"

Ona Nierenberg and Eve Watson

In 2007, six-year-old Jazz Jennings and the Jennings family appeared on the popular American news show 20/20 with the famous journalist Barbara Walters. The show was called "Understanding Transgender Children" and its subject, Jazz, was identified as "one of the earliest known cases of an early transition from male to female" (Goldberg & Adriano, 2007).[1] Jazz's mother recalled that when Jazz was two, he asked her: "Mommy, when is the good fairy going to come with her magic wand and change ... my genitalia?" Bewildered by Jazz's insistent "No, Mamma, I'm a girl!" she sought professional consultation. When Jazz was four years old, a psychiatric diagnosis of gender identity disorder in childhood was pronounced by Jazz's paediatrician and a therapist specialising in sex and gender issues. The Jennings family told Barbara Walters—and the world—that this marked a turning point; following this diagnosis (and assurances that the "condition" was "born in"), they decided to accept Jazz as a "she", finally allowing her to appear publicly at her fifth birthday party in a one-piece bathing suit which "announced to the world that she is a girl" (Goldberg & Adriano, 2007).

Since then, Jazz has not ceased (along with her parents) to announce her transgender girlhood to the world in a series of *YouTube* videos, as a guest on The Rosie Show, co-authoring a book for children entitled *I am Jazz*, in a documentary on the Oprah Winfrey Network, as the spokesperson for the Clean and Clear skin care line (featuring the tag line "See the real me"), and as the star of a reality-television show on The Learning Channel network also titled *I Am Jazz*, which was recently renewed for its second season. Jazz was also named one of the "25 Most Influential Teens of 2014" by *Time Magazine*, currently has 286,000 followers on her *Instagram* account and nearly 208,000 subscribers on her *YouTube* channel. She is also the co-founder of the *TransKids Purple Rainbow Foundation*, an advocacy group for transgender youth, and regularly speaks worldwide on behalf of transgender rights. While proclaiming identification with the sex other than one's birth anatomy has a long and storied history (let us not forget Tiresias!), Jazz's superstardom partakes of a seismic shift in the public relationship in the age of the internet and mass media to issues transgender. This rapid ascension and overwhelming embrace of matters *trans-* in media, fashion, movies, and television declares itself to be both agent and outcome of ending discrimination (although it is not without a backlash). While certainly changes in public opinion on the side of eliminating prejudice and stigma are to be applauded, we suspect this transformation reveals far more than the transition from a less permissive society to a more enlightened one.

We find in the current proliferation of transgender matters in the mass media a unique opportunity to examine what we call "the discourse of trans", by which we mean the set of explicit statements, underlying beliefs, contradictions, and excluded terms that establish what can be said—and not said—about transgender issues and sexual difference. We hear in the discourse of trans an implicit theory regarding what it means to be human and therefore subject to sexual difference and mortality. It is our desire to bring to the fore what this discourse must "disappear" in order to make its appearance as a supposed knowledge informing us that how we live the question of sexual difference is a settled matter (which we admit to finding most unsettling). Thus we introduce Jazz Jennings not as a case study (we have never met her) but rather as a participant in the production—as well as an example—of the discourse of trans.

Jazz's story, reiterated countless times on television, the internet and print media, is exemplary in that it is grounded in the belief that sexual difference is essential. As the cover of her children's book *I Am Jazz* proclaims:

> [F]rom the time she was two years old, Jazz knew that she had a girl's brain in a boy's body. She loved pink and dressing up as a mermaid and didn't feel herself in boy's clothing. This confused her family, until they took her to a doctor who diagnosed Jazz as transgender and explained that she was born this way. (Herthel & Jennings, 2014, jacket copy)

Jazz thus defines herself as transgender based on having been born with "a girl's brain in a boy's body", a certainty based on her attraction to the colour pink, "girl toys", dresses, and mermaids. While we intend to elaborate this point further, for now, we would simply like to call attention to the contradiction in this narrative between the supposed biological basis of "gender" and its confirmation by way of social stereotypes and conventions. This bedrock paradox is, in fact, the hallmark of the discourse of trans. We hope to question here how this discourse simultaneously insists upon the supposed immovable constraint of biological determinism *and* the purportedly limitless freedom to choose without appearing to contradict itself.

It is our aim here to show how the theorisation of *children* is absolutely crucial to supporting the apparent coherence of a discourse that is fraught with inconsistencies and incongruities. To this end, we will highlight the specificity of the discourse of trans as it pertains to children, part of a broader research project we are working on, listening to the very public discourse of trans in order to hear the "what-cannot-be-spoken" in what is being said. The trans discourse operates as a form of universal knowledge in contemporary civilisation that appears to "know" about gender identity, engendering the notion that one can choose one's sexual identity and align a body with an identification. Our analysis of this discourse is informed by our clinical work as psychoanalysts where we are attuned to the unsayable that drives human thought, action, and pleasure and that speaks through unconscious derivations and other illusive pathways. We are oriented by an approach to human sexuality based not on instinctual development or social norms but solely upon the singularity for each subject of the symbolically-driven field of "[…] what's superimposed upon anatomy, upon the real existence of individuals" (Lacan, 1957–58, session XI, p. 3). We will be guided here, as we are in our practices, by Lacan's reminder: "[T]he fact that one says remains forgotten behind what is said in what is heard" (1972–1973, p. 15).

New diagnosis, new paradigms

The highly contested and perpetually debated *Diagnostic and Statistical Manual of Psychiatric Diagnosis* (DSM) introduced its newest revision in 2013. No less disputed than its previous incarnations, the DSM-V was notable (among other things) for its eradication of the gender identity disorder diagnosis and the introduction of its replacement, gender dysphoria. Surpassing a mere shift in nomenclature, this change represents a radical alteration in perspective regarding the conceptualisation of "gender identity", including an implicit theory of how human beings come to situate themselves with respect to sexual difference.

The American Psychiatric Association declared that the manifest purpose of this substitution was to emphasise that "gender nonconformity is not in itself a mental disorder" with the concomitant belief that "the critical element is the significant distress associated with the condition" (APA Gender Dysphoria Factsheet, 2015). Furthermore, they stated that they wished to avoid stigma for those "whose gender at birth is contrary to the one they identify with" (APA Gender Dysphoria Factsheet, 2015) while sustaining a diagnostic category to allow transgender men and women to obtain insurance coverage and access to care (hormone treatment, surgery, psychotherapy) without supporting discrimination. Here is how they put it, "[P]art of removing stigma is choosing the right words. Replacing 'disorder' with 'dysphoria' in the diagnostic label is not only more appropriate [...] [but] also removes the connotation that the patient is disordered" (APA Gender Dysphoria Factsheet, 2015). By eliminating the word "disorder", the intention was to shift emphasis to the experience of distress related to one's *body*, including "a persistent and strong desire to be the other sex or insistence [...] [on] belong[ing] to the other sex" (APA, 2013, p. 452). Gender dysphoria as a diagnosis was patently designed to eradicate the notion that cross-sex identification is *de facto* problematic: rather, any psychical distress is believed to be "a reaction to the situation, not the underlying condition" (Spack, 2005, p. 1).

The novelty of this new terminology is the weight it gives to *soma* over psyche: The diagnosis is now viewed as a temporary condition of bodily distress which has the potential to be remedied by way of hormonal and surgical interventions. This perspective reconceives cross-sex identification as a "correctable" situation of the "wrong" brain in the "wrong" body. Reformulated as a *physical* rather than a *psychiatric* diagnosis (Spack, Edwards-Leeper et al., 2012), insurance reimbursement for body modification practices such as hormone administration, hormone suppression, and top and bottom surgeries is far more likely. In fact, the standard of care ("best practice") now recommended by the American Professional Association of Endocrinologists is the administration of hormone blockers to children diagnosed with gender dysphoria before they enter puberty, with the American Academy of Child and Adolescent Psychiatrists also endorsing these recommendations.

While gender identity disorder in childhood as a diagnosis undeniably had its own problems, a review of some of the past literature actually does not support the particular claims that motivated the change of nomenclature. In fact, contrary to the statements made by the APA quoted above, in our (admittedly limited) research review, we did not find that cross-gender identity was previously considered to be a disorder *in itself*. Rather, we found that the prior clinical approaches to the diagnosis supported the belief that cross-sex identification was a *symptom* of psychical distress, that a psychical or mental source of suffering was supposed as underlying the wish to change sex, and it was believed that this wish required deciphering in order to relieve the child's suffering. Previously, when children met the criteria for gender identity disorder in childhood, the clinicians whose work we read (Coates & Wolfe, 1995; Zucker, Wood, Singh, & Bradley, 2012) is aimed at discovering how children might be using "gender" as an unconscious solution to either a lived trauma or the transmission of a cross-generational trauma in the context of other bio-psycho-social and psychodynamic factors. Prior approaches emphasised the *symptomatic* nature of the cross-gender identification and working through the psychical and familial issues at stake (Zucker, Wood, Singh, & Bradley, 2012). Any simple, direct biological path to gender identity in any of its forms was explicitly eschewed by these writers.

Thus, it becomes clear that the difference between the former gender identity disorder diagnosis and its replacement, gender dysphoria, is the change of causal attribution. The current discourse of trans promotes the shift to an exclusively biological basis as a progressive step towards greater acceptance and the elimination of discrimination against trans men and women. However, we would like to point out the fundamental flaw in this argument. If gender identity is held to have a biological basis how can cross-gender identification be anything but a disorder? Whereas biological causality may *appear* as a way to evade stigma, it is based on the belief that the alignment of body and mind when it comes to sexuality is the fruit of Nature (see Nierenberg, 1998), According to such a theory, gender dysphoria is *by definition*, Nature gone awry and therefore, "disordered".

What should not be forgotten is that over a century ago, Freud shattered the dream of human sexuality as natural, revealing that human subjects are irretrievably out of sync with "nature", with sexuality and the unconscious insisting as the scars of this rupture. It is the radical, perpetually shocking announcement of psychoanalysis that no aspect of human sexuality—sexual desire, sexual object choice, or even sexual identification as a man or women—is innate or biologically determined. This torturous, traumatic, uncertain process of taking up a position as man or woman is, for psychoanalysis, decidedly un-natural for all human subjects regardless of how "normal" they may appear (with "normality" to be absolutely distinguished from "natural"). We would like to emphasise that while the apparent "solution" of gender dysphoria has as its consequence the silencing of any questions related to how cross-sex identification operates for a particular subject, psychoanalysis has as its foundation the ceaseless questioning of all aspects of human sexuality for each and every subject, whether s/he manifestly conforms to norms or transgresses them. In this way, the gift of psychoanalysis is to de-stabilise the categories of the "normal" and the "pathological" while creating and sustaining an opening for wonder.

"True gender self" psychotherapy: language, children, and sexuality

We would now like to turn to the work of Diane Ehrensaft, an American developmental and clinical psychologist who has become a prominent media and professional spokesperson about issues pertaining to transgender children. Ehrensaft is the Director of Mental Health at the University of California San Francisco Benioff Children's Hospital

Child and Adolescent Gender Center Clinic and has written several books and numerous articles about transgender children. She is a fierce and formidable advocate of what she calls "Gender affirmative" or "true gender self" therapy, believing this to be in the best interests of the child. According to Dr Ehrensaft, "[…] the kernel of gender identity […] is there from birth, residing most importantly in our brain, mind, and body" (2015, p. 36). It is the aim of "true gender self" therapy to ascertain this innate, transcendent kernel of truth, so as "to provide the space for children to explore and establish their *authentic* gender self" (2014, p. 572, emphasis added). Despite abundant research showing that childhood gender dysphoria more frequently than not desists by puberty and that there is no predictable way of discriminating the "desisters" from the "persisters" (Zucker, 2012, p. 375; Drummond et al, 2008; Waller & Cohen-Kettenis, 2008; Steensma et al, 2013), Ehrensaft insists that even the youngest children (two and a half to three years old) can be confirmed as transgender through "true gender self" therapy (2014, p. 573, 578). Most interestingly and without a hint of recognising any fundamental contradiction, she describes transgender children as "[…] the ultimate anti-essentialists […]" (2015, p. 37) while describing the basis of her treatment approach as the search for the "authentic" "true" inborn gender. Ehrensaft takes great pains to describe herself as neither an essentialist nor a social constructivist (2014, p. 574), a protestation that has certainly perplexed her commentators (see Schwartz, 2012; Weinstein & Wallerstein, 2014).

The *sine qua non* of true gender self therapy is the belief the child is telling the transparent truth that he or she truly "belongs" in the body of the opposite sex: "If you want to know a child's gender, ask the child; it is not ours to tell but the child's to say […]" (Ehrensaft, 2016, p. 164). In nearly every one of her numerous articles, Ehrensaft makes some version of this statement: "If you want to know what a child's gender is, listen: The child will tell you. It is not for us to say, but for the child to affirm" (2014, p. 580). She unequivocally recommends that clinicians take children literally and without ambiguity or symbolism. If we listen carefully to Ehresnsaft, we hear a theory that presumes gender as real, able to be unequivocally spoken, and most importantly, that children can speak it. What is curious is that this is so readily accepted by so many despite the preponderance of evidence to the contrary. We would like to examine why such questionable suppositions about children's sexuality might be so important to the adults who are insisting upon it. The discussion below is indebted to *The Case of Peter Pan or The Impossibility of Children's Fiction* (1993) by Jacqueline Rose which we found most inspiring in its analysis of how the theorisation of children serves the unconscious needs of the theorisers, rather than reflecting their supposed object, children "themselves".

The essential role of the trans-child

We found it very interesting to discover in our literature review of gender identity disorder, as contrasted with gender dysphoria, a consistent emphasis on the *differences* between children and adults. To make this point, we believe it is worth quoting Coates and Wolfe at length here (in an article specifically focused on boyhood gender identity disorder):

> In some respects, symptoms of the disorder seems analogous to those associated with the adult condition of transsexualism [...]. In fact, research into childhood gender identity disorder was initially spurred by the search for childhood analogues to the adult condition on the basis that adult transsexuals typically report severe anatomical and gender dysphoria for as long as they can remember. But it has since emerged clearly that the childhood condition is neither the exact analogue, nor, except in vary rare cases, a precursor to the adult one ... Nor is its phenomenology truly equivalent [...] the boy does not truly behave like girls his age; rather he acts like his stereotyped idea of what being a girl is like. (Coates & Wolfe, 1995, pp. 8–9)

This perspective identifies and supports the gap between child and adult, a division that has been effaced by the biological causality attributed to gender dysphoria. It is only by virtue of the fundamental belief that the child possesses the ability to speak the truth of an immutable innate core gender identity that "true gender self therapy" can exist. This core principle ignores what may seem obvious: "[W]e cannot listen to children in the same way that we listen to adults" (Schwartz, 2012, p. 471). The fact that there is a "confusion of tongues" separating child from adult seems undeniable; thus we find it quite remarkable that the discourse of trans attempts to efface this chasm. We believe it is important to question why such an apparently dubious claim would be made at all, and furthermore, made to seem credible.

We hear in the attempt to suture the incommensurability between child and adult an inextricable link to the position that language is transparent, that it offers unmediated access to objects, the world and ourselves. As Rose points out in her study of children's literature:

> [...] the child can be used to hold off a panic, a threat to our assumption that language is something which can simply be organized and cohered, and that sexuality, while it cannot be removed, will eventually take on the forms in which we prefer to recognize and acknowledge each other. (Rose, 1993, p. 65)

It is certainly no accident that the psychoanalytic conception of sexuality goes hand-in-hand with an appreciation for the complexity of language, including its limits, it detours, and its ability to deceive. For psychoanalysis, both sexuality and language are shifting, unstable, and far from self-evident. To assert that a child can unequivocally "know" his/her sexual identity and proclaim it, is a denial "that the adult abstraction gender [...] likely refers to something very different from the child's idea, of which the child has a yet little knowledge" (Schwartz, 2012, p. 473). One of Freud's most radical discoveries is the perverse, polymorphous, diffuse sexuality of the child that is never completely organised or totally repressed by the wrenching traumas that produce subjectivity. Its traces are found in those eruptions that we call formations of the unconscious, the dreams, slips of the tongue, bungled acts, and creations that constitute human psychic life. They require interpretation precisely because they are the fruit of censorship and utilise language's poetic properties including equivocation, homology, alliteration, metaphor, and metonymy to pass to consciousness in a ciphered disguise.

From the first, childhood sexuality is marked by its status as scandalous; it constitutes the repressed by definition and is that which we do not want to know anything about in order to stabilise the illusion of a secure identity. Unseemly to, and repudiated by, each and every subject, it is not surprising that childhood sexuality is also disavowed by the culture at large through the "cult of innocence" that can be traced to the Greeks, the New Testament, the Romantic poets, philosophers

Locke and Rousseau, and the Victorians. We all forget, ignore, and deny that sexuality owes its origins and outlines to infancy and childhood, but as Freud reminded us: "[N]o one who has seen a baby sinking back satiated from the breast and falling asleep with flushed cheeks and a blissful smile can escape the reflection that this picture persists as a prototype of the expression of sexual satisfaction in later life" (1905, p. 182). While infantile life constitutes our pre-history, Freud demonstrated that human sexuality emerges not out of biology but out of curiosity, that is, the child's fundamentally unanswerable questions about sex and desire, such as "where do I come from?" The tumultuous insult, for example, of a new child in the family is the provocation for sexual theorisation, which Freud identifies as the birth of theory itself, akin to the philosopher's attempts to solve "the problems of the universe which are too hard for human comprehension" (Freud, 1908c, p. 212). That Freud uses the story of Oedipus to describe the process of ordering childhood sexuality alerts us to the mythical dimensions of this process that is at best precarious and never complete (Rose, 1993, p. 14). According to psychoanalysis, there is no stable sexual identity in the unconscious; our vulnerability rests on the fact that we can only rely on the alienating, fragile positions regulated by the symbolic order.

It is our thesis that the discourse of trans endeavours to transform the child into a guarantee of the impossible, attempting to secure adult sexuality by securing the child as an object of self-transparency and self-knowledge about sexual identification. Thus, it is by way of the figure of the trans child that "[…] the [supposed] translucent clarity of childhood [is used] to deny the anxieties we have about our psychic, sexual, and social being in the world" (Rose, 1993, p. xviii). In fact, the discourse of trans *requires* the trans child to anchor the purported inborn, biological status of sexual identification. What better proof that Nature dictates "authentic" "true" inborn gender than to ground it in the self-knowledge of the child? The perfect alignment of knowledge, body, and identity would offer proof of the fantasy of "the sexual rapport"—the notion that man and woman can be perfectly cohered and complementary which also implies a world where unity, totality, and completeness are possible (Lacan, 1971–1972, p. 32). When Lacan asserts that the "sexual relationship does not exist" (1971–1972, pp. 32–33), he is referring to an entire universe of impossibilities, including the fact that we are not transparent to ourselves and that words do not correspond to "things".

While the discourse of trans that we have examined here purports to be about the sexual identity of the trans child, it is our contention that it is "more crucially [...] [about] how our subjectivity is divided in relation to itself" by sexuality (Rose, 1993, p. 15). As Rose points out,

> [...] positing children as a pure point of origin allows adults to indulge in the fantasy that we can create a simplified form of language that transparently reflects reality or gain access to a primitive past or experience selfhood and sexual identify as completely stable and secure. (1993, p. 8)

As a result, the child who experiences cross-sex identification is now presumed to "know" by the discourse of trans, and thus forbidden the conflicts, confusions, uncertainties, and internal strife that is inimical to subjectivity in all its forms.

The impact of the paradigm of "choice"

Being presumed to "know" about their sexuality, current psychiatric and psychotherapeutic approaches are, as Lament puts it, "designed to facilitate the psychological wellness of the transgender child" (2015, p. 16) and this wellness invariably means facilitating the wish to transition. Clinicians do not question a child's wish to transition or seek to locate it on a spectrum that includes psychical factors and instead anxiously warn of the dangers of suicidality of gender non-conforming children if they are not treated according to their wish to transition. There are however no studies showing with any degree of certainty that suicidality is reduced by transitioning and against this, an important long-term thirty-year study in Sweden indicates higher rates of suicidality in transsexuals who transition (Dhejne et al., 2011). While this apparently liberal approach of psychiatry can be set against its troubled past of normativising approaches in the treatment of gender non-conformity, the seemingly limitless freedom to choose is full of contradiction and illusion.

First, the idea that the body can be perfectly aligned with a sexual identification is a myth of the seamless rapport of body and mind, man and woman. Second, in eliding the role of psychical causality in transgender issues while seeming to offer "choice", clinicians are de facto pathologising the psychical while upholding a biologically essentialist discourse of sex and gender. This relegates individual autonomy and uniqueness to a series of simple diagnoses treatable with pharmacological and surgical intervention, a list of menu items that can be collectively consumed, with no role for unconscious desire. A third illusion rests on the very notion of "choice" itself. The forms of choice available are not free and are linked to dominating trends and discourses that are pervasive and persuasive and follow the seamless model of capitalism with its unlimited, unending, and expansive reach into the world in real, virtual, and communicational ways (Fisher, 2009, p. 25). The role of market forces, precipitating for example, the movement of sex-change interventions from the public to the private domain is notable. In this light, today's easily available remedies fit in with what Salecl describes as dominant trends of treating bodies like self-improvement projects that can be manipulated and ultimately mastered (2010, p. 54). How often have we heard from children and adolescents, for example, that they first "discovered" the idea of changing their bodies to the other gender via the internet? We find at the heart of these illusions of "choice" further indications of the essential of children in trans-related matters. This leads to a troubling conclusion: given the necessity of children to the essentialist aims of the trans discourse, children cannot be seen to change their minds.

Conclusion

We hope that we have brought to light some of the many elements that must be excluded in order for the discourse of trans to sustain its coherence, consistency, and congruity. Most importantly for both culture and clinic, biological determinism as essentialist discourse requires the elimination of the psychical and the role of speech and language—that messy disordered aspect of human subjectivity riven with unconscious desire, conflicts and forgotten dramas. As Lacan observed, "the *natural* is the field of science in which no one uses the signifier to signify" (1955–1956, p. 187).

We believe that the discourse of trans owes its power and ubiquity to its attempt to deny the complexity of sexuality as defined by psychoanalysis and thus to repudiate the division constitutive of subjectivity. Partaking of the all too human twin illusions of the transparency of knowledge and the adequacy of language, it appears to realise our fantasy that the word and the thing are perfectly commensurate to one another. While "true gender self" therapy relies on the child's speech as indisputable evidence of a pre-existing truth, psychoanalysis reveals that knowledge and truth do not coincide in any direct manner. The belief in an "authentic gender self" is founded upon a-historicism and faith in the transcendent: paradoxically, it is a discourse which does not leave room for change. While portending to be progressive, it endorses the belief that what is has always been and will always be. It is our assessment that this discourse deprives children of their specificity as children and their right not to know because it requires the category of trans-children to elide its own contradictions.

It is our aim to bring the ethics of psychoanalysis to bear on what we believe to be one of the paramount ethical issues of our time. We hope that by calling attention to the use of children by the discourse of trans, we can support a clinic that can be *of use* to children. This would be a clinic that upholds a space for listening to each and every child in all his or her vulnerability, particularity, and specificity; a place to sustain the unknown as well as the unknowable; and to provide room for the dignity of finding without seeking when it comes to gender as one of the infinite questions a child may pose on the path of finding his/her way in our bewildering world.

References

American Psychiatric Association. *Diagnostic and Statistical Manual of Mental Disorders.* (4th edn). Washington, DC: American Psychiatric Publishing, 2000.

American Psychiatric Association. *Diagnostic and Statistical Manual of Mental Disorders.* (5th edn). Washington, DC: American Psychiatric Publishing, 2013.

American Psychiatric Association. Gender Dysphoria. Factsheet. Available at: http://www.dsm5.org/documents/gender%20dysphoria%20fact%20 sheet.pdf. 2015.

Brinich, P. (2015). Discussion of Diane Ehrensaft's "Listening and Learning from Gender-Nonconforming Children". *The Psychoanalytic Study of the Child, 68*: 71–78.

Coates, S. & Wolfe, S. (1995). Gender Identity Disorder in Boys: the Interface of Constitution and Early Experience, *Psychoanalytic Inquiry, 15*: 6–38.

Dhejne, C., Lichtenstein, P., Boman, M., Johansson, A. L. V., Långström, N. & Landén, M. (2011). Long-Term Follow-Up of Transsexual Persons

Undergoing Sex Reassignment Surgery: Cohort Study in Sweden. *PLoS ONE 6(2)*: e16885. doi:10.1371/journal.pone.0016885.
Drummond, K. D., Bradely, S. J., Peterson-Bradali, M. & Zucker, K. J. (2008). A Follow up of Girls with Gender Identity Disorder. *Developmental Psychology 44(1)*: 34–45.
Ehrensaft, D. (2015). Listening and Learning from Gender-Nonconforming Children. *The Psychoanalytic Study of the Child, 68*: 28–56.
Ehrensaft, D. (2016). *The Gender Creative Child: Pathways for Nurturing and Supporting Children*. New York: Workman.
Fisher, M. (2009). *Capitalist Realism: Is There No Alternative?* Winchester: O Books.
Freud, S. (1908c). On the Sexual Theories of Children. *S.E., 9*: 209–226. London: Hogarth.
Goldberg, A. & Adriano, J. (April 27th, 2007). I'm a Girl—Understanding Transgender Children. Available at: www.abcnews.go.com/2020/story?id=3088298&page=.
Herthel, J. & Jennings, J. (2014). *I am Jazz*. New York: Dial Books.
Lacan, J. (1955–1956). *Book III: The Psychoses*. London: W. W. Norton and Co. 1993.
Lacan, J. (1957–1958). *Book V: Formations of the Unconscious*. P. Young (Trans.). Unpublished.
Lacan, J. (1972–1973). *Book XX: Encore: On Feminine Sexuality, The Limits of Love and Knowledge*, London: W. W. Norton and Co., 1999.
Lament, C. (2015). Transgender Children: Conundrums and Controversies—an Introduction to the Section. *The Psychoanalytic Study of the Child, 68*: 13–27.
Menvielle, E. J., Tuerk, C., & Perrin, E. (2005). To the Beat of a Different Drummer: The Gender Variant child, *Contemporary Pediatrics, 22(2)*: 38–45.
Nierenberg, O. (1998). A Hunger for Science: Psychoanalysis and the Gay Gene. *differences, 10(1)*: 209–242.
Rose, J. (1993). *The Case of Peter Pan, or the Impossibility of Children's Fiction*. Philadelphia: University of Pennsylvania.
Salecl, R. (2010). *Choice*. London: Profile Books.
Schwartz, D. (2012). Listening to Children Imagining Gender: Observing the Inflation of an Idea. *Journal of Homosexuality, 59*: 460–479.
Spack, N. P. (2005). Trangenderism. Available at: www.imatyfa.org/wp-content/uploads/2012/06/spack-article.pdf.
Spack, N. P., Edwards-Leeper, L., Feldman, H. A., Leibowitz, S., Mandel, F., Diamond, D. A. & Vance, S. R. (2012). Children and Adolescents with Gender Identity Disorder Referred to a Pediatric Medical Centre. *Pediatrics, 129(3)*: 418–425.

Steensma, T. D., McGuire, J. K., Kreukels, B. P. C., Beekman, A. & Cohen-Kettenis, P. (2013). Factors Associated with Desistence and Persistence of Childhood Gender Dysphoria: A Quantitative Follow-up Study. *Journal of the American Academy of Child and Adolescent Psychiatry, 52(6)*: 582–590.

Wallen, M. S. & Cohen-Kettenis, P. T. (2008). Psychosexual Outcome of Gender- Dysphoric Children. *Journal of the American Academy of Child & Adolescent Psychiatry. 47*: 1413–1423.

Weinstein, L. & Wallerstein, H. (2014). If we Listen: Discussion of Diane Ehrensaft's "Listening and Learning from Gender-Nonconforming Children". *The Psychoanalytic Study of the Child, 68*: 79–88.

Zucker, K. J., Wood, H., Singh, D. & Bradley, S. (2012). A Developmental, Biopsychosocial Model for the Treatment of Children with Gender Identity Disorder. *Journal of Homosexuality, 59*: 369–397.

Note

1. All quotes are taken from the 20/20 show of April 27th, 2007 as narrated by Goldberg and Adriano and available at: www.abcnews.go.com/2020/story?id=3088298&page=.

CHAPTER EIGHTEEN

Left to their own devices? Child psychoanalysis and the psycho-technologies of consumer capitalism

Kaye Cederman

We know that during the last decade the technological revolution has "opened up" the world and impacted on our lives in ways that are often exciting, enabling, humane, and creative. But isn't there also something deeply unsettling about how this global phenomenon has happened so fast, powerfully, and irrevocably? We might even feel the sensation is like Freud's "[...] buried spring or a dried up pond. One cannot walk over it without always having the feeling that the water might come up again" (Freud, 1919h, p. 223). We can almost hear the water lapping at the portals of child psychoanalysis, as children's experiences of unhappiness, loneliness, and anxiety, within familial and other social dynamics, now seem to be compounded by adverse encounters with the new technology, for example, social media and cyberbullying. Recent clinical psychoanalytical literature, e.g., Benvenuto, (2014), Bredt, (2014), reminds us that our work with children includes engaging with symptoms with a distinctive contemporary bias. Verhaeghe's, (2012) insight is that these very symptoms are now being reclassified as diseases.

The most ubiquitous reflect disorders of Depression and Post-Traumatic Stress, and Neurological "Information Processing" Difficulties/ Disorders.

We might say that children's symptoms today seem to be related to the latest configurations of western societies, most obvious in the power and persistence of the marketing technologies, or psycho-technologies of consumer capitalism. The individual infant or child encounters this drive-oriented phenomenon through various devices, such as the material on TV, smartphones, tablets, video games, and computers. We can think of these devices as drive-oriented because their allure is not based on satisfying any bodily need, but solely on sustaining the jouissance generated by a repetitive, mechanical, and excessive circuit of behaviours. Small, swiping, and flickering finger movements immediately titillate, inform, intrigue, and often horrify, at the same time as they make a point of connecting to what each child identifies as being uniquely theirs. The marketing process individualises each connection through appealing to the child's favourite cartoon character, pet, colour, or music. It also sets a child up to be part of the market, with their own specific purchasing power, wielded through their own, and their parents' desire for consumer items linked each child's individual choice. The question is, what are children's symptoms and suffering telling us about their experiences within the milieu of the marketplace?

Do the symptoms reflect the ubiquity of, what Baudrillard (1994), or Žižek (2003), might call the injunction for each child and their parents and/or caregivers to *Buy Now*! and *Enjoy?* Or does this very injunction echo something else altogether? What is the role of psychoanalysis in this environment? Is there anything we *can* do when hyper-consumerism is so entrenched, so fascinating, and so all-consuming? Clearly, we cannot change this global trend, but this chapter explores how psychoanalysis might perhaps reinvigorate the desire for knowledge so that, as Colette Soler suggests, we might "reinvent or renew the practice in circumstances that were always adverse" (2014, p. 200).

The baseline of Lacan's "Note on the Child" (1969), broadens out to include contributions from a range of authors whose work lends insights into today's child clinic, where, despite, and in the face of new technologies, we might reflect upon how to continue to renew our work with children.

Note on the child

Lacan's "Note on the Child" (hereafter referred to as "Note"), gets right to the heart of child psychoanalysis in modernity; "the child's symptom is found to be in the position of answering to what is symptomatic in the family structure" (1969, pp. 7–8). For Lacan, the symptom represents the truth of "the sexual couple" and is linked to the mother's subjectivity when the child corresponds to a fantasy of hers. This "fantasmic" capture means that there is no mediation by the father when the child identifies with the ego ideal and part of the mother's desire; "[h]e becomes his mother's object and has the sole function of revealing the truth of this object" (p. 7).

The child then appears at the centre of the text; he first becomes the *objet a*, substitutes himself for the object, and saturates the lack by which the mother's desire is constituted (in whatever structure). He embodies, animates, and demands protection, and stops his mother from ever accessing her own truth. The "somatic symptom" means that this *méconnaissance* (or misrecognition) endlessly sustains the mode of the mother's desire. This mother/child relationship gives the mother "what the masculine subject lacks—the very object of his existence, appearing in the Real. As a consequence, it is offered to greater subornation in the fantasy in proportion to what is real in what it presents" (p. 8).

Lacan stresses that the non-intervention of the Law in the form of the Name-of-the-Father is more serious than it might appear. Such intervention is crucial because it allows the child to proceed from the imaginary to the symbolic realm, and facilitates the subject's sexual positioning, and subjectivity. The oedipal process therefore engages with the truth of the familial couple, of the object of castration, the function of the father, the imperative that the child should not satisfy the lack constituting their mother's desire; and how problematic it is for the child to constitute *objet a*. "Note" provides markers for psychoanalytic work with children, so that the truth of the family kept hidden through the generations comes to light through the transference, to determine the construction of the child's subjectivity.

The place of desire in the young child's psyche ultimately promotes human life, despite each family's social or economic milieu. This means that "Note" can be read as a radical diagnosis of the capitalist conditions of modernity, in which Lacan found himself. My claim is that almost fifty years later, "Note" also sheds unique insight into what is problematic in late-modernity, in the realm of consumer capitalism. Lacan stresses that the whole social fabric of western culture depends upon each family unit transmitting the law that is fundamental to how attributes of social capital, sexuality, and subjectivity, are transferred between generations. This leads us to ask what has happened today to the human qualities so crucial to this transmission?

Hyper-consumerist times

Freud's first clinics in 1920s, post-war Vienna also reflected the ideology of the times in which he lived; his clinics upheld social democracy to challenge the unfair distribution of wealth and social privilege under prior Viennese administrations. Elizabeth Danto (2005) describes how Freud's early clinics were accessible to all social classes including poor children, adolescents, and their parents, and those with a wide range of psychosomatic illnesses. His clinical practice promoted insights into how the most desirable form of human life is based on attributes of interdependence, attachment, and collectivity.

Conditions in which:

> [...] psychoanalysis would release the reasoning abilities in oppressed individuals and that personal insight (combined with critical thinking) naturally led to personal independence ... human survival does not lie solely in individual strength or free will ... The replacement of the power of the individual by the power of a community constitutes the decisive step of civilisation. (2005, p. 302)

Freud's ideal of civilisation, "of interdependence, attachment, and collectivity", might now be read ironically, as children are indeed interdependent and attached—but to machines—in a completely integrated circuit. They are also being trained collectively to be well-organised and competent consumers. Notice the chatter about the evolution of *AI* (Artificial Intelligence), to augment cognition in a "deep way" so that we never forget *anything*, the virtual reality machines such as "sensory goggles" flooding this season's holiday markets, while, for those deemed autistic, the computerised learning platform, Gemllni, (DVM or Discrete Video Modelling method) sells web-based therapy programmes.

As psychoanalysts, we are also hyper-connected to the market-place generating information via social media, text, email, blog, twitter, and so on. These display "our services", conferences, solutions for anxiety and depression, psychoanalytic websites, information, and opinions *ad infinitum*. As part of the globalised discourses of "psy", is the child psychoanalyst just another expert marketing therapy and advice? Or might our role be to notice what the symptoms of childhood are telling us about the current experiences of infancy and childhood? For example, what are the psychic implications when a child's first words are "Dada" *and* "I-Pad"?

Furthermore, what does it mean for the panoply of family complexes when each family structure is now distracted by machines that light up when touched, problem-solve, boost memory, make connections, simulate sex, keep babies alive, find "mates", and comfort the dying elderly? What about the gaze? The fantasmic capture? Is the infant stupefied or hyper-stimulated when she sees the car dashboard flash with talk, hears Mama on the iPhone, slides the iPad screen to make the puppy bark, and dances towards the "Skype-machine". Is this fascination any different from being excited by the shadows moving past the door of the cave, or distinct from following the hoof prints of deer through the snow? Well yes—I argue that it is! Exponentially different!

As we witness in our analytic work, children are now at the interface of machines that take no account of their humanity. It might be said that the young of previous eras, working in cotton mills or labouring in fields, were in the same position. What is different is that previously there was a social dimension to life, of language, intimacy, and familiarity; a realm of social capital, which enhanced humanity and the socio-cultural, but excluded machinery. Nowadays, machines are on intimate terms with us, or on terms denoting, what Rob Weatherill more accurately calls "*electronic* intimacy and transparency" (2004, p. 103). Machines now nudge, comfort, delight, frighten, arouse, measure, and speak, and will one day perhaps be embedded into our very being. Will we one day be posthuman and evolve the delusory ideals of transhumanism—transcending death itself?

The posthuman perspective, according to Katherine Hayles, includes a blend of embodiment, technology and culture, with an emphasis on valuing information more than the "natural" aspects of our human embodiment, and where liberal humanist subjectivity is understood as a mere evolutionary blip. By reading Hayles with an eye on the child, the posthuman child's body would be seen as the first of many prostheses that a girl or boy would handle and control. The child is therefore seen as being assembled in such a way as to be "seamlessly articulated with intelligent machines" (1999, p. 5).

Hayles raises important insights about how humans and intelligent machines are connected. She stresses that the scarce commodity in this realm is *human attention*, and argues that technology will counteract this by freeing up attention for only the most important tasks (p. 287). The posthuman view is that lives are enhanced by sharing our thinking with intelligent machines. Yes, they do provide instant information, but at what social and psychical cost? How can the processes of subject formation, of father's mediation, mother's attachment and desire, and a child's identifications within family dynamics compete with the hand-held, or wrist-carried, flickering signification generated by TVs, smartphones, tablets, and computers? What Lacan intimates in his "Note" is that the process of subject formation demands moments of intense human attention: loving, watching, listening, waiting, and responding—between parents/caregivers, and their child. The process demands an immersion in the myriad of socio-cultural experiences of sound, speech, gaze, language, human interaction, and movement related to desires, demands, and needs. But can the subtlety, nuance and complexity of familial interactions and experiences compete with psycho-technology; the highly enticing visual messages of technology?

Soler's claim is that the symptoms of childhood suffering come from the socio-cultural sphere where today's families strive for "some sham surplus jouissance, without any transcendence, and the ineptitude of scraping a living within the balance of producer-consumer" (2014, p. 191). The only social bonds are between the consumer and the product. This milieu leads to "an increasing fragmentation and an instability of social bonds, and leaves individuals always more exposed to insecurity and loneliness" (p. 191). Place this idea alongside "Note on the Child", and we can hear Lacan explaining the basis of symbolic capital, the knowledge that adults are responsible for their child's social bonding, psychical development, and sexuation, in other words, the values that support humanity. As Soler puts it, such knowledge "offer[s] the support in organising [their] innermost defences" (p. 192). The human values that do exist are not part of the globalised marketplace but are fragmented, local and individual, in a milieu where, "the prescribed purpose of psychoanalysis goes in the direction of restoring a social bond beyond the resolution of the alienation of the Other that analysis strives to bring about" (pp. 97–98). Citing Lacan in *Encore*, she reiterates:

> Governed by their drives, yes, doubtless, but what the effect of language leaves them with regard to satisfaction-which is nothing

> if not limited, fragmented, and certainly unable to create the fusion of which Eros dreams-makes them dream of something else … The famous death drive, if one wishes to use the term for anything which threatens the homeostasis of discourse, is not only on the side of cynical jouissance, but takes sustenance from expectations of despair that when subjects are left to themselves, they sublimate with a vengeance. (pp. 194–195)

This infers that the death drive is tensional with current marketing technologies, and that such sublimation can threaten the subject's ability to focus on what is important in forming crucial family and societal relationships. In short, the psyche itself is jeopardised by the transmission of normative and pathologising symbolic material. Bernard Stiegler's claim is that the "super-egoic and sublimatory apparatuses" constituting "a transindividuation process that ties generations together" is "short-circuited by the psychotechnologies submitted to the hegemony of psychopower, and which results in short circuits in transindividuation" (2011, p. 156).

> The premier question that the capitalist industrial economy poses for the theory of the unconscious, and for the theory that desire is founded upon repression, is the question of the technicity of this desire, that is, of its historicity such that, given the fact of its existential exteriority, an exteriority that we must relate to what Winnicott called the transitional object and transitional space, the libidinal economy can be destroyed by its industrial exploitation through the use of the psychotechnologies of psychopower. (2011, p. 156)

Each child's encounter with the form and function of technology generates "a drive-based regression founded on the destruction of libidinal energy insofar as it binds the drives through the intermediary of pharmaka that weave the symbolic, from Winnicott's transitional and preverbal object to the signifier that founds the thought of Lacan" (2011, p. 160).

According to Stiegler, marketing technologies have also distorted adult and child relationships, so that adults have become less responsible for their children. Parents and grandparents are infantilised in a reversion of values "that confuses all normal references, dynamites traditional hierarchies, destroys culture and education […] this becoming adult, develops from infancy through a relationship of identification with parents who educate the child" (2010, p. 4). He characterises Freud's concept of primary identification as being

> [...] practically indelible and that it is in operation throughout the first five years of life. It is a condition of access to the superego through which the adult transmits to the child being educated the ability to internalise, the familiar name of which is "the law": in identifying with the adult, the child identifies with what the adult identified with while being educated, and this is repeated from generation to generation: this repeated identification is thus what both distinguishes and links the generations. (2010, p. 4)

When a young child's attention is constantly diverted by technology the process of identification is undermined. There are also changes in the synaptic organisation of young brains to the detriment of "deep attention" so that children are more susceptible to attention problems and hyperactivity (2010, p. 18). Reflecting Lacan's observations in "Note", the key issue is that identification and deep attention underpin the adult transmission of knowledge, which is crucial to each child's subject formation.

> In this sense, adults' primary responsibility is the transmission of the reality principle as a formalised and encoded accumulation of intergenerational experience. And as the internalisation of these inherited symbolic representations, bequeathed by ancestors and transmitted by parents and other adults, this intergenerational relationship constitutes the formation of attention, constructed of retentions, which then create protensions, that is, the expectations without which attention is impossible. (2010, p. 8)

As the psycho-technologies assume control of the child's developing attention, they problematise transitional spaces and the transitional objects. These spaces are pivotal to all systems of care and nurturing; a transitional space is primarily about caring. According to Stiegler, "[t]o play with a child is to take care of the child, opening the paths by which transitional spaces are created, paths that stimulate [...]

everything that forms the symbolic order and the 'dream language of myths'" (2010, p. 4). He cites Winnicott:

> [t]ransitional objects and transitional phenomena belong to the realm of illusion which is at the basis of initiation of experience. This early stage in development is made possible by the mother's special capacity for adapting to the needs of her infant, thus allowing the infant the illusion that what he or she creates really exists [...]. This intermediate area of experience, unchallenged in respect of its belonging to inner or external (shared) reality, constitutes the greater part of the infant's experience, and throughout life is retained in the intense experiencing that belongs to the arts and to religion and to imaginative living, and to creative scientific work. (2010, p. 14)

Stiegler argues that such care is destroyed in the current milieu, because a child's undivided attention is crucial to transmission of the symbolic realm from adult to child. "This lost care is also the reciprocal recognition of ancestors by their descendants, which is also vital to the formation of proper attention" (2010, p. 15).

Psychoanalysis in circumstances that were always adverse

Does psychoanalysis have a specific role to play in light of such problems with processes of identification, attention control, and subject formation? We certainly have insight into the falsehoods promulgated by the psycho-technologies, ideologies of parenting, and things that mothers, fathers, and/or carers tell themselves, that attach them to their child. Today, this includes symbolic material coming from TV and the internet. Such material is both a force that stimulates change by spreading the discourses of "psy", science, new medico-psychological information, resources and therapies etc. It also reveals something it is vital for capitalism to repress in order to, for example, maintain the persuasive force of consumer capitalism, normative childhoods, reproductive sexuality, child-rearing norms, and an eternal supply of fresh brains for the workforce, and buyers for the marketplace.

This echoes Eve Watson's analysis of the scientific "ideal" of mental health, critique applying equally well to the child of psycho-medical and technological discourse, and the marketplace, as all focus on generating increasingly differentiated norms of development, gender, size, sexuality, behaviour, etc. Her claim is that psychoanalysis "give[s] a dignity to human suffering as an expression of profound social and personal discontent, as well as hope for extraction out of overwhelming conflict and life-crises" (2012, p. 28).

Consequently, our role in the child clinic can be understood as deconstructing "uniformity, invariance and reductionism"; the structures of regulation, which have consequences for the symptoms, and the mental health, of children and their families (p. 28).

Renewing the practice

It is all very well to grasp how children are enmeshed in consumer capitalism, but what does this mean for our work as analysts? Our role in deconstructing prevailing discourses is through what Michael Plastow calls "the inscription of modes of enjoyment or jouissance, that can be effectively discerned only through speech, speech being the medium through which psychoanalysis operates" (2015, p. 197). The discursive formula remains a structure whereby the family myth is changed into the individual fantasm, the subject's anxiety and fear of the Real underpinning speech and the imaginary form. Parents deny the perversity of their daughter or son through a negation of sex and death. This reflects the process of repression whereby specific memories and thoughts are voided from consciousness into the unconscious.

As Plastow highlights Lacan's discussion of little Hans, we can hear the flickering finger movements engaging technology. Plastow explains that each child discovers their own perversion through masturbatory pleasure, pacification, and "the anguish in the *tuché* that is experienced, an anguish that exceeds the *automaton* of *self-soothing*" (pp. 197–198). Girls and boys must each discover and take ownership of their own perversion in order to "de-form" the surplus the child has "inherited through the original sin of the parents" (2015, p. 198). To become a subject, the child must put an end to the regimented and controlled patterns of their lives as ordered by their parents. Then, by doing things in a markedly different way they might generate their own discourse *vis-à-vis* their connection to jouissance. According to Plastow, our transference with each of the parents places them in a position of mourning the loss of a fantasm, "the ideal of themselves as they imagine they were as children" (p. 199). The subject may be formed through a type of destruction as the child is, what Plastow calls, "razed"; following Lacan's claim that "through the function of the *objet a*, the subject separates himself off, ceases to be linked to the vacillation of being, in the sense that it forms the essence of alienation" (p. 258). This is the alienation of the image constituted through language in which the child is frozen and from which they must break free. Most significantly for Plastow, the subject is one who assumes responsibility for his or her own suffering and symptom.

Rather than understanding the child as an idealised and forever unobtainable object from the past, the child analyst can contest, and put the idealised fantasies parents have about their child into stark relief, in spite of the distractions of intelligent machines. The idealised child does not exist but merely reflects fetishised, transplanted fantasms from parents' own idealised childhoods.

Think of how Françoise Dolto managed her work with children. Following Lacan, Dolto argued, "the treatment acts through helping the child happily resolve his castration complex and his Oedipus complex" (2013, p. 111). This is not achieved through "personal influence or suggestion" but, because young children are not able to use free association, she uses a method "of play, of spontaneous drawing, of 'conversation', which is understood as having been triggered by various remarks made by the child" (pp. 111–112). A child's questions are not replied to directly but are referred back with "what do you think?" using as few words as possible; such "conversation" includes the adult looking, listening, and carefully observing the child's gestures, expressions, mimicry, sayings, lapses, mistakes, as well as spontaneous drawings (p. 112).

Mine-craft

I began by asking what the symptoms of childhood have to tell us about the state of the times in which we live. As recent literature suggests, a key aspect of childhood symptoms now signals the juxtaposition of psychic, familial, and societal processes with the new psycho-technologies of consumer capitalism. Hours spent on drive-oriented devices, within the web of hyper-consumerism, reduce human engagement with the techniques so crucial to the transmission of life-enhancing, symbolic capital. It is no wonder that children's symptoms mirror problems with identification, attention control, and subject formation. These simply reflect how children experience:

- intergenerational relations (limiting the quality and quantity of human attention);
- psychic identification, (exacerbating problems with deep attention);
- transitional spaces and objects basic to education and care, (replacing intricate long-term mechanisms—with drives based on need and satisfaction, and,
- adult responsibility regarding their role with children.

Child analysts also engage with the unconscious in this milieu, and Lacan's words are a touchstone of this work, privileging the singularities generated by the knotting of the real, symbolic, and imaginary realms, and the *sinthome* of the Borromean knot of jouissance and desire. To complement Lacan's work, recent theories remind us that child clinics are now juxtaposed with advanced technology. This means considering:

- how we can prioritise clinical opportunities to utilise the scarce commodity of *human attention* in the interests of "speaking well";
- how families can also privilege *human attention* as they "raze" their daughter or son, and mourn the loss of their ideal child.
- how we can continue to design neutral spaces outside of parental regulation, that also allow for a child's engagement with technology;
- how, despite digital paraphernalia, we can stay committed to seeing that every child's analysis, reflects the singularity of the subject.

In a snippet from my case notes, twelve-year-old Sarah (highly articulate, and with a psychological report saying she is mildly autistic) is speaking about the intergenerational links between characters in her new box set of "Dr Who". She interrupts her flow to say she has been playing Minecraft at home and that; "the Minecraft store sends you skins for your gender. They allocate gender on the basis of what your gender was when you set up your account. I was originally set up on my mother's account". I repeat, "[y]ou were originally set up on your mother's account?"

Here is a direct encounter between a repetitive, market-based, computer video-game, and a clinical moment in the analysis of a girl, when a formation of the unconscious emerges through the transference. The snippet shows that it is through the discourse of Minecraft, with all of its robotic structures and contraptions, that Sarah has an opportunity to sense how the analyst identifies her as being an object separate from her mother. While we see that the world of commodification is a place where gender is bought and sold, we can also hear a child entangled in the maternal fantasy. There, in the whisper alighting on the knowledge of the object she "was originally set up" to be for the Other, Sarah has a glimpse of the possibility of moving to the place of a subject. As Miller explains from Lacan's "Note on the Child"; "[l]et's not forget that the analyst doesn't realise the presence of object *a*. When we identify it in the analytic discourse, we don't consider that we take upon ourselves the truth of the patient's symptom. That is why Lacan says that the analyst merely constitutes a semblance of the object a" (2010, p. 15).

This is only the beginning of the technological revolution. The psychoanalytic understanding of children and childhood symptoms now confronts complex new technologies and the global marketplace. Children's symptoms shout out that a child should never be reduced to being a consumer with purchasing power; and that our role must continue to uphold their dignity and singularity. This demands a renewal of our clinical work. Alongside a thoughtful process of engagement with, and deconstruction of, the new discourses and materials constituted by "the marketplace" and "devices", we should also be staunch in our analytic practice. As the Real of child psychoanalysis encounters the Real of hyper-consumerism, and children are increasingly left to their own devices, we must continue to examine what it means to practise "my craft" in the context of Minecraft.

References

Baudrillard, J. (1994). *The Illusion of the End*. C. Turner (Trans.). Stanford: Stanford University Press.

Benvenuto, B. (2014). Childhood and Today's Discontent, *Child Analysis, Journal of the Centre for Freudian Analysis and Research, Issue 25*: 62–77.

Bredt, L. (2014). From Cotton Reel to Virtual Reel, *Child Analysis, Journal of the Centre for Freudian Analysis and Research, Issue 25*: 78–91.

Danto, E. A. (2005). *Freud's Free Clinics: Psychoanalysis and Social Justice, 1918–1938*. New York: Columbo University Press.

Dolto, F. (2013). *Psychoanalysis and Paediatrics*. F. Hivernel & F. Sinclair (Trans.). London: Karnac.

Freud, S. (1919h). The Uncanny. *S.E., 17*: 217–256. London: Hogarth.

Hayles, N. K. (1999). *How we Became Posthuman*. Chicago: The University of Chicago Press.

Lacan, J. (1969). Note on the Child. N. Wulfing (Trans.). In: Objet *a* and the Semblant, *Psychoanalytical Notebooks, 20*, 2010.

Miller, J. -A. (2010). The Child, a Response from the Real. In: Objet a and the Semblant, *Psychoanalytical Notebooks, 20*, 2010.

Soler, C. (2014). *Lacan—The Unconscious Reinvented*. London: Karnac.

Stiegler, B. (2010). *Taking Care of Youth and the Generations*. S. Barker (Trans.). Stanford: Stanford University Press.

Stiegler, B. (2011). Pharmacology of Desire: Drive-based Capitalism and Libidinal Dis-Economy. In: *New Foundations Number 72*. D. Ross (Trans.). London: Lawrence & Wishart.

Verhaeghe, P. (2012). *What About Me? The Struggle for Identity in a Market-Based Society*. J. Hedley-Prole (Trans.). London: Scribe Publications Pty. Ltd.

Watson, E. (2012). Science and the "Ideal" of Mental Health. In: *The Review. APPI Newsletter*, Summer, *2012, Issue 20*.

Weatherill, R. (2004). *Our Last Great Illusion*. Exeter: Imprint Academic.

Žižek, S. (2003). *The Puppet and the Dwarf*. London: The MIT Press.

INDEX

For Product Safety Concerns and Information please contact our EU
representative GPSR@taylorandfrancis.com
Taylor & Francis Verlag GmbH, Kaufingerstraße 24, 80331 München, Germany

www.ingramcontent.com/pod-product-compliance
Ingram Content Group UK Ltd.
Pitfield, Milton Keynes, MK11 3LW, UK
UKHW021502240926
475702UK00035B/217
* 9 7 8 0 3 6 7 1 0 4 0 5 4 *